For Stanley,
a new friend —
thanks for everything!
Gerry Sorin

the
prophetic
minority

THE MODERN JEWISH EXPERIENCE

Paula Hyman and Deborah Dash Moore, editors

the prophetic minority

american Jewish immigrant radicals, 1880–1920

Gerald Sorin

INDIANA UNIVERSITY PRESS

BLOOMINGTON

Library of Congress Cataloging in Publication Data
Sorin, Gerald, 1940–
The prophetic minority.

(The Modern Jewish experience)
Bibliography: p.
Includes index.
1. Jewish radicals—United States.   2. Jews—United
States—Politics and government.   3. United States—
Emigration and immigration.   4. United States—Ethnic
relations.   I. Title.   II. Series: Modern Jewish experience
(Bloomington, Ind.)
E184.J5S66   1985   973'.04924   83-49287
ISBN 0-253-34618-5

1 2 3 4 5   89 88 87 86 85

פֿאר מײן עלטער־זײדע ברטשע

1862–1958

And for Myra and Anna,
who would have loved him

*With special thanks to Faye R. Cohen
for indispensable aid in the work of
translating*

CONTENTS

Preface

This study begins with the assumption that in the modern era Jews demonstrated a disproportionate affinity for radicalism. Through the medium of collective biography, it goes on to explore the *roots* of Jewish radicalism in the American working-class immigrant community from 1880 to 1920. Collective biography, with its special combination of the particular and the universal, made it easier to probe some generalizations about working-class history. It was especially useful in looking at the interplay between class and culture. Using mainly interviews, memoirs, autobiographies, and the letters and diaries of 170 Jewish socialists,* it was possible to see, in more intimate ways, the impact of proletarianization—the selling of one's manual labor and the increasing loss of control over work—and to compare that impact with the continuing influence of community viability and religious and cultural traditions.

The biographical evidence for the American Jewish immigrants suggests that "class" was not the only, or even the single most important, determinant of Jewish radicalism. Proletarianization was necessary but it was not sufficient to bring the Jews to socialism. New groups of workers responded to industrial labor in strikingly different ways, and few other proletarianized groups joined radical political movements in proportions comparable to the Jews. Jewish culture, including religious values, was critical to the formation of radical consciousness. Socialist Jews, as we shall see, were vitally in touch with their traditional culture and very much rooted in a transplanted Jewish community.

My debt to others who have dealt with this subject previously will become clear in the body of the book. I do want to mention directly, however, Irving Howe, Moses Rischin, Arthur Goren, Elias Tcherikower, Ezra Mendelsohn, and Alice Kessler-Harris, whose work made mine easier. Special thanks are due to those men and women who not

*See Appendix.

only allowed me to interview them but made me feel welcome by their generous hospitality, and who, by their warmth and openness allowed me to share, if only vicariously, in a variety of intense experiences. Their names are used throughout, and a list is available in the bibliography.

Archivists and librarians were particularly helpful at the Columbia University Library, and the Columbia University Oral History Collection, the New York Public Library, Manuscript Division. Harold L. Miller, Archivist at the State Historical Society of Wisconsin, went beyond the call of duty. Jon Bloom at Tamiment Institute Library at New York University put into my hands materials I would not have found otherwise, and at YIVO, Institute for Jewish Research (New York City) Marek Web proved indispensable. James Goodrich and his able staff at the library of the State University of New York, College at New Paltz, were always accommodating. And Haig Shekerjian graciously allowed me to make use of his fine photographic talents.

I want to thank Herbert Gutman, CUNY Graduate Center, Deborah Dash Moore, Vassar/YIVO, and Joseph Dorinson, International Psychohistorical Association, for giving me the opportunity to "air" parts of this work in different scholarly audiences, and Paul Buhle for his help with the Oral History of the American Left Collection at Tamiment Institute Library, and for his encouragement. Professor Moore is to be thanked, additionally, for her careful reading of the manuscript and for her perceptive suggestions.

Dr. Stanley Coen, Dr. Ruth Imber, and Mr. Stuart Pellman generously allowed me some New York City space and thereby saved me countless trips. My research was also facilitated by a generous grant from the Joint Awards Council, University Awards Committee of the State of New York Research Foundation.

Richard Fein, former Director of Jewish Studies, SUNY, New Paltz, was a wonderfully effective Yiddish "troubleshooter," helping often with particularly difficult idiomatic constructions. There is no way I can adequately thank Faye R. Cohen for her tireless, loving commitment to the work of assisting in the translation of many hundreds of pages of Yiddish language materials that constitute an important part of the sources of this study. Finally, my wife, Myra, not only typed and edited but put up with me and this project for six years, and even, while teaching full-time herself, willingly listened to and commented upon my fretting and thinking out loud about it.

the
prophetic
minority

1

INTRODUCTION

Exploring the Radical Connection

More than two million East European Jews came to the United States between 1881 and 1924. These immigrants transplanted themselves, and important parts of their rich and long-evolving culture, by concentrating in neighborhoods in a number of large cities, particularly the lower East Side of New York. They had, from the beginning, an impact on American life and—at least for a time—on American politics way out of proportion to their numbers.

In 1908, while this process was well under way, over 100,000 Jewish emigrants arrived at Ellis Island. One of these was Pearl Halpern. She brought with her an eighteen-month-old child, much older cultural baggage, and some recent political experience. In little more than a year here she would be involved in the great shirtwaist makers strike that led to the success of the International Ladies Garment Workers Union (ILGWU). Soon thereafter Pearl Halpern was deeply involved in militant union and socialist activism, and for well over fifty years she would remain in the movement.

Pearl Halpern was hardly a rarity on the densely Jewish East Side. Jews, there and elsewhere, played an extraordinarily disproportionate role in socialism and other radical movements. Most socialists were not Jews, and, even more important, most Jews were not socialists. Socialism, however, was significant in all Jewish immigrant concentrations in the late nineteenth and early twentieth centuries. In New York and Chicago, and to a lesser extent in Philadelphia and Boston, socialist Jews constituted a visible and felt presence, a "vital minority" in the community of their fellow immigrants.

As early as 1886, Jews gave significantly more support than the general New York electorate to a socialist-endorsed left-wing mayoral candidate. In the 1890s, Socialist Labor Party candidates managed to get 2 to 3 percent of the votes in New York City but nearly 10 percent on the Jewish lower East Side. The Socialist Party, formed in 1900–1901, could make no significant inroads in any section of New York City not dominated by Jewish Americans. Indeed, by the turn of the century, working-class Jews and German-Americans were the twin pillars of American socialism. And after 1908, the Jews in New York City alone would constitute the largest, most powerful single element in New York State socialism. And New York State socialism was the largest single element in the national party.[1]

Even this does not begin to measure the place of socialist commitment and values in Jewish immigrant life. Jews also affiliated with socialism through unions, cooperative enterprises, mutual aid societies, and journalism; and the numbers involved here far outstripped those in the political movements. By 1907, for example, the Yiddish socialist daily *Forward* surpassed the respective circulations of its bourgeois and religious rivals; and by 1917 it had a circulation of 200,000, becoming the largest pro-socialist newspaper in the United States.[2]

The garment industry's leading trade unions were socialist for a considerable part of their history. The largest and most famous was the International Ladies Garment Workers Union, which, along with the Fur and Leather Workers Union, the Cap, Hat, and Millinery Workers, and other Jewish unions, "became the financial backbone and chief organizational props of the Socialist Party," until as late as 1932.[3]

This study does not attempt to make the case for the Jewish-radical connection. That has been done, persuasively, elsewhere.[4] It does, however, attempt to develop a credible explanation for that connection by exploring the lives of 170 Jewish immigrants who were radicals, here meaning activists in socialist unions or in socialist politics in the broadest sense. Wherever possible their own words will serve to foster the exploration.

Pearl Halpern explained that in the old country her father was a bristlemaker,

and was in the first bristlemakers' strike. He was very active and was also
a very religious person. . . .[5]

When the strike was lost, my father was not taken back . . . and he
had to seek work in small towns. He would be gone a whole week and
come only for *shabos*.

We were a family of eight. . . . My father earned very little. There
were times when we actually had no money. . . .

He got pneumonia and died when I was sixteen. . . . When I got up
from sitting *shiva*, I was taken into the movement—the Polish Socialist
Party. . . .

[Soon] My mother started to work at cigarette making, and from
that time on we had it comfortable. . . .

[Nevertheless] . . . from then, and for the rest of my life . . . I was
active in the movement.[6]

Pearl Halpern's story, and so many of the others that we will
observe throughout, contain important pieces of the puzzle of Jewish
radicalism: increasing proletarianization, exploitation, and Jewish
culture. This last is especially important to this study, which attempts
to demonstrate that without the cultural dimension, without Jewish
religious values, proletarianization and exploitation by themselves will
not explain Jewish socialism.[7]

The evidence strongly suggests that the Jewish socialists were a
prophetic minority, responding to biblical norms of social justice, interpreted in a modern context. They were men and women who had
been deeply immersed in the moral commandments of Torah and
Talmud, in messianic belief-systems, traditions of *tsedaka* (not mere
charity, but righteousness and justice toward others), mutual aid, and
communal responsibility.

Louis Waldman, labor lawyer and Socialist assemblyman, came to
America "up to his ears in Talmud" and filled with a deep sense of
obligation to his fellowman; activist A. L. Goldman came "knowing
Torah [and] understanding everything"; and Rose Cohen, militant
union organizer, left the old country saturated in the religious literature her mother encouraged her to read. They and the vast majority
of other socialist Jews did not become radicals irrespective of their
intense exposure to traditional religious ethics and injunctions. Most
were not quite as explicit as Morris Winchevsky, who said:

. . . for almost everything I write I have to thank [Isaiah] that poet-
preacher who entered my heart and mind with love for . . . oppressed
people.[8]

But all, in their actions, their language, and their allusions, clearly demonstrated again and again that their radicalism had an important foundation in their deeply internalized religious culture.

The Jewish immigrants brought their culture with them to America and with it transplanted a community here. Despite hardships, that community and its institutions and affiliations allowed large numbers of Jews, including socialists, to feel relatively rooted, or at least rerooted. This is an important point because the historical literature on American Jewish radicalism is pervaded by a different general interpretation: "The sudden transplantation of the Jewish immigrants" was at least temporarily demoralizing, and left them "in a state of confusion and bewilderment." Early immigrant life, "torn away from the old moorings and not yet anchored in the new realities," was marked by "anxiety" and a "dreadful anomie" which promoted receptivity to radical unionism and socialism.[9]

The social-scientific basis for this interpretation is the concept of marginality. Marginality is generally defined as a condition in which a person has some connections with and participates to some degree in at least two distinct and partially incompatible cultures.[10]

In Pearl Halpern's case, this would presumably mean that by standing on the edges of the older *shtetl* culture, with its emphasis on stability and tradition, and the more modern culture, with its demands for mobility and change, she was a marginal person. This condition, with a variety of negative psychological symptoms—anxiety, confusion, inconsistency, and irrationality—would become, theoretically, even more critical with emigration, as Pearl Halpern would now find herself stretched between the relatively familiar though rapidly changing Eastern European Jewish culture and the raw newness of America.

In America, Pearl Halpern "had to learn a trade"

because until then I didn't do any kind of work. . . . I entered a shop to learn shirtwaists. And I received five dollars a week; from that I had to pay . . . for a room, three dollars a week to a woman . . . to take care of my baby, and from the other dollar and a half we had to eat and to dress, and [buy] everything a person needs. . . .

In 1909 the shirtwaist makers strike broke out. . . . I worked in a shop of several hundred workers—only forty went out on strike, and the rest remained working. And so naturally we lost that shop. But I got into the union as soon as we went on strike. And from that time on I remained active. . . .[11]

Within the general framework of the theory which employs marginality as an explanation of radicalism, Pearl Halpern would be seen as an uprooted Jew, bewildered and anxious, desperately and irrationally seeking surrogate community and support in radical unionism. All of this is a far cry from an older, more positive notion about marginality which contended that the marginal person, on the borderline of various cultures, was in a particularly advantageous position to formulate innovative, progressive ideas about social development.[12] We need not accept this older view to see some of the flaws in the newer "negative" one: it seriously underestimates the resiliency of human beings and their ability to be creative, even consciously rational in their redefinition of identity.

My work with the Jewish radicals among the immigrant population of America strongly suggests that we need to make at least some distinctions between a marginal *person,* who has one unsteady foot in each of two partially antipathetic social settings, and a marginal *culture,* one which is uprooted but at least partially transplanted in a new setting. By making this distinction, we are more likely to see two important things. First: the *substance* of the marginal culture, not simply the *condition* of marginality, can contribute, under particular historical conditions, to the formation of radical consciousness. Second: men and women, like Pearl Halpern, depending on the nature and intensity of their connections with the marginal culture and community, could and did deal with their marginality in widely varying, often creatively synthetic ways.

That there was a marginal *culture* on the lower East Side, partially transplanted, partially rewoven with new threads, and highly girded by social formations, has been demonstrated elsewhere and will become clearer here in chapters 3 and 4. The great majority of immigrant Jews, including the important minority of socialists, were significantly caught up in a "web of overlapping group affiliations."[13] Residential concentration, the family, the synagogues, *landsmanshaftn,* educational alliances, theater groups, mutual aid societies, reading clubs, the workplace, the union were all important social formations— places wherein one could sustain status and identity by being part of something larger than the atomized self. This was true too for the informal social networks: the neighborhood, the block, the rooftop, the *landsleit* cohort, the candy store, and the tavern. Adolph Held, Yiddish journalist and socialist member of the New York City Board of Aldermen (1917–1919), recognized the importance of both forms of associations:

> Our people are social minded, [we] immediately formed clubs . . . societies, landsmanshaftn.
> The sidewalk was one of the great islands of Jewish youth. . . . and of course there was the roof. Sleeping [there] in the summer; it was a terrific agency of communication.[14]

The quintessential association, though already seriously challenged in the old country, was the family. Jewish emigration was preeminently a family emigration, and the great majority of socialists and those who were to become socialists were no exception. They emigrated with members of their families or came to relatives already in the United States.[15] Jewish families continued to function cooperatively once they reconstituted themselves here. Pearl Halpern's husband joined her in 1909;

> then we took in my grandmother, who had already been here. And she took care of my baby when I went out to work.[16]

Families also influenced the nature of the workplace itself. Garment workers brought their relatives into the factory, instructed them in work routines, and sustained them during slack seasons. Sam Rubin, militant union activist who came to America in 1908, remembered:

> My brother-in-law was an operator and he took me into his shop and he taught me how to be an operator. . . . My brother-in-law tried to give me a few dollars more than I was able to earn. . . . My sister gave me food and drink. And when it got slack, she even gave me a few dollars in my pocket.[17]

Julius Gershin, who left Russia in 1904 to avoid the draft and in less than a year in America was on strike for sixteen weeks, recalled other sources of association and sustenance.

> Jacob Schiff had a kitchen at that time on East Broadway. There we could get food for three cents a day. And there we lived. During the time of the strike we would also go into a saloon and for five cents we would get a glass of beer and potatoes and herring. That was the way it was until I brought my wife here in 1905.[18]

Unquestionably, some people who were extremely marginal or "atomized" could not cope. And the strain of the transitional moment took its toll in increased social pathologies, including depression, suicide, desertion, and prostitution.[19] Even those deeply rooted in the rich marginal culture of Jewish concentrations in New York or Chicago experienced significant tension. The sensitive Gentile journalist Hutchins Hapgood in 1902 wrote of the struggle in the life of the Jewish "ghetto boy."

> The struggle is strong because the boy's nature, at once religious and susceptible, is strongly appealed to by both the old and the new. At the same time that he is keenly sensitive to the charm of the American environment, with its practical and national opportunities, he has still a deep love for his race and the old things. He is aware and rather ashamed of the limitations of his parents. He feels that the trend and weight of things are against them, that they are in a minority; but yet in a real way the old people remain his conscience, the visible representatives of a moral and religious tradition by which the boy may regulate his inner life.[20]

The Jewish immigrants were men and women undergoing the complex processes of proletarianization and urbanization. Yet, with Hapgood's "ghetto boy," most hung on and did not become undone. They still had at least one foot firmly planted, not only in the rich world of Jewish social formations and group affiliations, but in the world of Jewish ethics, religious values, and the prophetic tradition. This was true, in varying degree, as we shall see, for the great majority of the radicals in this study, including even those who came close to denial of, or outright hostility to, Judaism.[21]

When the twenty-year-old Emma Goldman arrived in New York in 1889, the year Pearl Halpern was born not far from Vilna, she believed that all that happened in her life

> . . . was now left behind me, cast off like a worn-out garment. A new world was before me, strange and terrifying. But I had youth, good health and a *passionate ideal*. Whatever the new held in store for me I was determined to meet unflinchingly.[22]

Despite Emma Goldman's belief that her entire past was "cast off," and despite her remark to a reporter years later—"I am an anarchist of the Topsy variety—I was just born so"—her "passionate ideal" was surely the result of a complex of experiences.[23] She had read, along with so many other Russian youths, Nikolai Chernyshev-sky's *What Is To Be Done?* and consciously patterned part of her later life after Vera Pavlovna, the heroine who had adopted nihilism. More important perhaps, she was in her politics a product of the rapid economic dislocations in late nineteenth-century Russia, virulent Russian antisemitism, and her own proletarianization—having done some factory work in her teens near St. Petersburg and then again in Rochester, New York. Emma Goldman, as her biographer tells us, was also significantly a daughter of the rich ethical demands of the prophetic strain of Judaism.[24]

She herself might reject this particular interpretation, but the pages of the magazine *Mother Earth* that Emma Goldman edited from 1906 to 1917 are filled with Yiddish stories, tales from the Talmud, and translations of Morris Rosenfeld's poetry. Moreover, her commitment to anarchism did not divert her from speaking and writing, openly and frequently, about the *particular* burdens Jews faced in a world in which antisemitism was a living enemy. Apparently, Emma Goldman's faith in anarchism, with its emphasis on *universalism,* did not result from and was not dependent on a casting off of Jewish identity.[25]

Fannia Cohn, activist and long-time Secretary of the Education Department of the ILGWU, understood this possibility of synthesizing the particular and the universal. After nearly twenty years in the labor movement in the United States, Cohn, "the daughter of a proud Jewish family," wrote, "Yes, we are not only what we are, but also what we were."[26]

The biographical materials on Jewish radicalism in America suggest that the roots of Jewish radical collective action lay not in irrational responses by uprooted, atomized individuals to the strain and hardship brought by extensive social change. In their radicalism these Jews were making claims on society as a cohesive group. They were organized around articulated interests that were shaped by social change, hardship, class-consciousness, and *cultural background.*[27] A rich mixture of modernization, including significant proletarianization, secularized Judaism, and continued connection with and participation in mainly Jewish social institutions, transplanted or rewoven, helps explain the Jewish-radical connection.

As a counterhypothesis to the theory of marginality, then, which emphasizes its negative psychological implications as an "explanation" of radicalism, we should consider a theory of qualified marginality, one that emphasizes the creative dimensions, one that sees groups that are damaged yet still alive, viable, and rich in social institution as those most ready to mobilize, under the appropriate historical conditions, for collective action. Rather than breakdown, fragmentation, alienation, anxiety, and confusion at the center of the drama of collective action, the American Jewish radical experience proposes that we place there in their stead continued viability, reconstituted association and community, and a healthy commitment rooted in coherent values.[28]

2

ROOTS OF RADICALISM

Life, Work, and Politics in the Old Country

I n 1880 close to 6 million of the world's 7.7 million Jews lived in Eastern Europe, more than 4 million confined to the Pale of Settlement in the northern and western provinces of the Russian Empire. Before the onset of the First World War in 1914, one-third of the East European Jews, mainly from the Pale, would leave their homelands. This is a rather extraordinary "event," not simply in modern Jewish history, where it is comparable only to the flight from the Spanish Inquisition, but in modern history generally; one "must go back to the great Irish emigration in the middle of the nineteenth century to find an exodus of equal magnitude."[1]

Yet not everyone left. Even after the widespread, murderous pogroms of 1881–1882, and the massacre at Kishinev in 1903 in southwest Russia, most Jews apparently thought they could still "make a life" in the Russian Empire—though some of them believed this possible only if Russia were to undergo revolution.

Disproportionate numbers of Jews in Russia affiliated with and participated in radical movements, beginning slowly in the 1870s and building rapidly through the October Revolution of 1917.[2] One of these Jews was Morris Shatan, born in 1887 in Kutno near Warsaw. Shatan was a yeshiva student from 1900 to 1901. Soon thereafter he joined the Bund, the major Jewish socialist movement in Eastern Europe, and in 1905 he participated in the massive demonstrations and uprisings against the czarist regime. But, despite his earlier optimism, Shatan would also emigrate. The Revolution of 1905 was defeated. Moreover, because many Russian radicals continued to see antisemitism as a tool to mobilize the masses, they were disturbingly equivocal toward the anti-Jewish pogroms of the 1880s and early 1900s. Jews like Morris Shatan were led to wonder what place they could have even in a revolutionized Russia. This spiritual struggle of individual youngsters would become the hallmark of Jewish socialism.

What kind of world produced Morris Shatan and the many others so like him—teenagers, really—who struggled with the need to harmonize the ideals and values of their familiar Jewish milieu and the demands and enticements of modernity?

THE *SHTETL* CULTURE

For several centuries large numbers of Jews had settled in the small towns *(shtetlekh)* of Eastern Europe or established new ones. The *shtetl* was usually of a size permitting everyone to know everyone, though even the smallest had several hundred people, not all of them Jewish. Most often the *shtetl* serviced the surrounding villages. Jews, generally prohibited from ownership of land, lived mainly by trading and craftsmanship, and their *shtetlekh* provided an important economic function in an underdeveloped agricultural economy. At the center was

> the marketplace, with its shops, booths, tables, stands, butchers' blocks. Hither come daily, except during the winter, the peasants and peasant women from many miles around, bringing their live-stock and vegetables, their fish and hides, their wagonloads of grain, melons, parsley, radishes, and garlic. They buy, in exchange, the city produce which the Jews import, dry goods, hats, shoes, boots, lamps, oil, spades, . . . and shirts.[3]

The tumult of this marketplace has been described as "one of the wonders of the world"; poverty was nonetheless a general condition in the *shtetl* from at least as far back as the middle of the seventeenth century, and the situation worsened in the eighteenth and nineteenth centuries.

The *shtetl,* however, was not first or foremost an economic entity; it was a religious community, though religion is much too narrow a term to describe the all-encompassing spiritual culture that existed

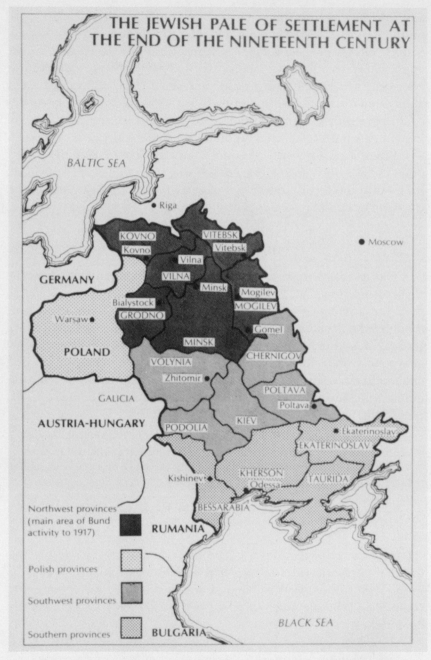

THE JEWISH PALE OF SETTLEMENT AT THE END OF THE NINETEENTH CENTURY

Reprinted by permission of Schocken Books, Inc. from *While Messiah Tarried*, by Nora Levin, Copyright © 1977 by Schocken Books, Inc.

there. The linchpin holding the community together was an orientation toward God and otherworldly values. The ideal, so manifest in Jewish behavior, literature, and folklore, however, was for the two "worlds" to come together eventually. Much of Jewish biblical eschatology was restorative, looking forward to a return to good, *old* times when the two "worlds" *had* been together (e.g., idealized views of the reigns of David and Solomon), but it also included the more radical, universalist style of the prophets (e.g., Isaiah 2), who expected the future not merely to be good but to be significantly different and better than ever. This was the messianic dimension that was a permanent feature, in varying degrees of intensity, of Jewish history. And it was already important by the time the Jews began their long history in exile, dispersed, despised, and often physically persecuted.[4]

In *some* forms of messianism the expected future was not an event in history but something outside history, something mythological, sometimes focused on a personal messiah. The king, or "inspired man," however, was rarely, if ever, seen as a god or as the son of god. Inspired by the prophets, and always with the people, he was to bring about "Utopia." And he was to do this through good government on this earth. As historian Gershom Scholem maintains, "Judaism, in all its forms . . . has always maintained a concept of redemption as an event which takes place publicly, on the stage of history and within the community." Spiritual elements were added over time but they never replaced this concrete historical messianism.[5]

The " 'thirst for the future,' the orientation of the whole being to that which is to come, is the very essence of messianism," writes sociologist/theologian Will Herberg: "and messianism is the very essence of the historical existence of the Jew." As we shall see, for many of the Jewish socialists in this study, messianism "permeated the thinking and feeling of believer and unbeliever alike, even those who have felt compelled to reject it as a doctrine along with the faith in which it is grounded."[6]

Scholarship was the pathway to God and the future, and every *shtetl* had a *heder* (Hebrew school) and societies for the purpose of providing poor boys with an education to the end of their thirteenth year. Often there was a yeshiva, a school of higher instruction in Jewish learning, chiefly for students preparing to enter the rabbinate. Religious education was formally the domain of men, most boys attending *heder* till thirteen; girls generally received only a few years of

A man teaching his grandson the alphabet while child's grandmother looks on.

Jewish Daily Forward

tutoring. But by their own piety women set an example and helped transmit Jewish values to their sons and daughters. Future radical Rose Pastor Stokes grew up "learning about Torah, poverty and emigration." Rose Cohen "became very devout," she said, because at home "besides the Bible we had a few religious books." "I read these," she wrote, "again and again."[7] And Social Revolutionary Fannia Cohn "was brought up by [her] mother on books."[8]

Transmission of values is often elusive and difficult to specify and to prove; but education, formal and informal, though it sometimes degenerated into obscurantism, meant saturation in Jewish ethics and prophetic tradition with its emphasis on justice and *tikn olam* (repair or improvement of the world), messianism, and communal responsibility. Sidney Hillman, yeshiva boy, revolutionary, and later a major

Although girls were "free" from the obligation of studying Torah, these two, like Rose Schneiderman and Fannia Cohn, were being taught to read from a prayer book.

Jewish Daily Forward

figure in the Jewish labor movement in America, sat with his siblings on Saturday afternoons while their mother read to them from the Bible or from Jewish story books.[9] And "on many a Saturday evening," socialist Baruch Charney Vladeck remembered, "before the lights were on Mother would sing of the Messiah and tell me all about it. I knew that Messiah has to come and knew also how." The rabbi of the town (Dukor), who was Vladeck's uncle, also "took care that the golden thread of faith and tradition not be lost" to him.[10]

In addition to the directly educational, there were many other communal institutions that helped transmit values. Each *shtetl* had a ritual bath, a ritual slaughterer, sometimes a cemetery, and always, at the heart of it all, a *shul*. Here the daily prayers were recited, and the

Torah was read and studied every *shabos*. Joe Rapoport, labor radical in the American knit-goods industry, recalled that in his *shtetl* in Stanislavchik, Ukraine,

> Simkhas Torah was my favorite holiday. . . . It celebrates the finishing of the reading of the Torah. It is read in *shul* a chapter a week. . . . This is how [we] . . . knew the Torah so well. . . . And naturally, the day of finishing the Torah was like New Year's Eve. There were whiskeys in *shul*, there were parties, there was singing and dancing in the streets. One of the Yiddish poets described how the people were mixing—
> Hand on shoulder, the beard in the sky
> Let there flame a dance.[11]

Celebrations and holidays brought the five hundred Jews of Stanislavchik closer together and reinforced the sense of community. This sense needed reinforcement from time to time because although, as in almost all the *shtetlekh*, most of the people were poor, there were some "class tensions." It "was not class struggle like you found in the cities," Joe Rapoport recalls, "but there was . . . division in the *shtetl*."[12]

There were in the *shuls*, besides the rigid separation of men and women, the *shayne yidn* (beautiful people) and the *proste yidn* (the simple or common people). And sometimes there were even separate *shuls* for artisans and craftsmen. Though scholarship was a pillar of status, so clearly was wealth and family background.

Community life was organized by the *kehillah* (Jewish community council) and the many voluntary social welfare organizations it helped administer. The *kehillot* were run most often by a coalition of the rabbis and the relatively wealthy. At least as early as the middle of the eighteenth century, serious complaints were voiced by the poor—and sometimes they even rioted—against the authority of the rich and the clergy, particularly in the area of taxation and conscription for the Czar's army.[13] The poor *were* disproportionately drafted, and an ironic folk song of the period went:

> It's a *mitzva* to hand over the simple people,
> Shoemakers, tailors are good-for-nothings.[14]

Rose Schneiderman, militant organizer for the Capmakers Union, remembered with some bitterness that as an only son [my father] was supposed to be exempt from military service but it happened that a wealthy Jewish family had bought their son's way out and my father was drafted to fill the village quota.[15]

The *kehillah* did, however, maintain orphanages and schools for the poor. Some *hevras* (committees) dealt with free loans, dowries, Passover supplies, and clothes for the needy. The rich were "obliged" to participate in their respective *kehillah* sections, and ideally "recipients of aid were in no way beholden to the donors: it was their due. The word for benefice—*tzedaka*—derives from the word for justice. In fact the donor owed thanks to the recipient for the opportunity to do a *mitzva* [one of 613 obligations]."[16] So radical a writer as Moishe Olgin could say about his upbringing in traditional Jewish society that even the poorest always remained a "free man; poverty did not corrode his soul, did not break his spirit."[17]

Time and distance have probably blunted some of the tension and bitterness, but the differences between the classes were in any case hardly extreme. All Jews in the towns of Eastern Europe could be classified in relative terms as *kleine menschen* (little people), rather than be divided into fully formed rival classes; few owned significant means of production, and fewer still made their livings by selling their labor. Even just beyond the *shtetl* in concentrations approaching the size of a *stot* (or city), Jewish "class conflict" could still look very much like "pauper against pauper." Flora Weiss, whose town boasted an agricultural school and several libraries, "stormed with revolutionary impetus." In 1916 she joined the Young Bund and was sent to organize a bakery:

> I had an inkling regarding workers in a bakery, or for that matter in any institution, like I know astronomy. . . . But I did it. I went into the bakery, which was a cellar room that employed two craftsmen. I couldn't distinguish who were the employers, and who were the employees. A shriveled little Jew had noticed a small young girl near him so he thought that I came to buy a bread. He asked what I wanted. I walked up to him bold and proud. "I came to organize the workers." He started to plead with me with tears in his eyes, that he has to finish his pastries and I should hold off for awhile. I do not remember the results, whether I took the two workers from that awful bakery factory or not. But into that work I plunged. . . .[18]

Up to the last third of the nineteenth century, and outside the more industrialized areas of the Russian Empire, that sharp gulf which divided the classes in the non-Jewish world was absent. Jews were responsible for one another; their conception of human relations, sanctioned by religious philosophy, generally promoted mutual interdependence.

THE IMPACT OF MODERNIZATION

Even the preceding brief sketch of traditional East European Jewish society suggests that the classic *shtetl* was never so stable as it has sometimes been portrayed. Moreover, the future radicals were growing up in the *shtetlekh* at a time when life therein was increasingly challenged by the "modern," from without and from within. The "modern" did not destroy the traditional, however. Instead, it increased efforts, particularly among the young, to find, sometimes unwittingly, new forms of Jewishness and it impelled the traditional segment of the community to close ranks and treat "innovation" as heresies.

The decline of rabbinic authority was already in process by the middle of the eighteenth century. The Polish government squeezed the Jews for money for wars with Russia and Sweden, and to put down Cossack uprisings. The *kehillah* had to drastically raise taxes on their own people. This undermined the legitimacy of community leaders in the eyes of many Jews. The process of delegitimation continued and intensified when Russia gobbled up most of Poland in the late eighteenth century. The czarist regimes forced Jewish community leaders into the unwanted, but in any case unfairly administered, responsibility of conscription for the Czar's army. By the mid-nineteenth century the two main poles of czarist Jewish policy had become conscription and conversion, through the military. At that time, too, and as part of the attempt to coerce the Jews into "Europeanization," the community councils were abolished altogether in Russia except as government fiscal agencies. The wide-ranging network of voluntary associations they had administered, however, continued to operate and to maintain and revitalize the community.[19]

In many areas of Eastern Europe in the nineteenth century, the peasant-based economies were slowly eroding. This process was accelerated by the coming of the railroads in Russia, the freeing of the serfs in 1861, and the concomitant increase in the rate of industrialization. The functional role played by large numbers of Jews in the small market towns changed radically. Many middleman operations were virtually eliminated by the economic changes and by government decree; and peasant cooperatives, the emergence of modern banking, and the factory system seriously undermined all areas of Jewish enterprise and artisanship.

All of this was exacerbated by the May Laws of 1882 which forbade Jewish settlement in villages, and by the expulsion from the rural areas of the Pale in 1882 of 500,000 Jews, who were then forced to live in towns or *shtetlekh* in the Pale; 700,000 additional Jews living east of the Pale were driven into the confined area by 1891. In that year alone 20,000 were expelled from Moscow, and 2,000 from St. Petersburg, many of them in chains.[20]

Between 1894 and 1898 the number of Jewish paupers increased by 30 percent, and in many communities the number of families of *luftmenshn*, persons without marketable skills or capital, approached 40 percent of the entire Jewish population.[21] Sam Davis, born in a Lithuanian *shtetl*, remembered that his father had three trades, "and with the three trades we were starving." His family somehow got permission to move to the city of Riga, outside the Pale of Settlement. The vast majority of Jews of course stayed in the Pale, but the numbers moving from *shtetl* to urban concentrations increased significantly from 1885 to 1915. By 1897, 49 percent of the Jewish population of the Russian Empire lived in cities, and if we count *miesteckos*—settlements that served as commercial and, to a lesser degree, industrial centers for the surrounding countryside—that figure rises to almost 78 percent.[22]

Approximately half of the Jewish socialists in this study had some experience with "uprooting" and spent a brief time in urban concentrations before their emigration to the United States. But the group as a whole was not significantly more urbanized than the general Jewish population of the Russian Empire, and was still vitally in touch with *shtetl* culture. Furthermore, in moving to cities they took good parts of their culture with them. City Jews, like *shtetl* Jews, had economic ties with Gentiles, but the focus of their cultural and social life was almost exclusively Jewish. Indeed it has been argued that by the late 1890s the larger towns were the "real centers of Jewish culture in Eastern Europe" and the so-called "*shtetl* community" was no longer confined to *shtetlekh*. In creative and vibrant forms it had experienced a reawakening and reweaving in town societies.[23]

Jewish workers participated in this transplantation. In the newer

A tailor
Jewish Daily Forward

Three rag peddlers
Jewish Daily Forward

A chairmender

Jewish Daily Forward

A bagel peddler

Jewish Daily Forward

A baker

Jewish Daily Forward

In the 1870s and 1880s increasing factory production drove many Jews into small-shop proletarianization and into keener competition with one another.

urban concentrations there were few well-organized associations for mutual support, and the Jewish artisans tended to look to co-workers rather than the larger community for solidarity. They set up *kases,* or unions, for mutual aid. These were not only expressions of immediate need, however, "but in full accord with the traditions of the Jewish community." As the *kases* began to grow toward becoming *kampf-kases* (unions of struggle), they sometimes used synagogues to present grievances against employers by bringing them to a traditional *din-tora*—a lawsuit conducted before a rabbi who played the role of arbitrator. As the class struggle became even sharper, this mode of operation would become less common, but the internalized cultural and religious norms that had produced it would continue to play an important role in Jewish radicalism.[24]

It was in the cities primarily that a Jewish proletariat developed, as did some hardening of class feeling. These cities, the major urban concentrations of the northwest region, included Vilna, Minsk, Bialystok, Grodno, Vitebsk, and Kovno; and in every one of them the number of Jewish workers was significantly disproportionate to the total population.[25] This was a proletariat, however, of craftsmen and artisans and very few factory workers.

According to Ezra Mendelsohn, the foremost student of class struggle in the Pale,

> Of the approximately 200,000 Jewish workers in the "North-West" at the turn of the century, some ninety per cent were artisans, laboring in small shops at such traditional crafts as tailoring and carpentry. The very low percentage of Jews employed in factories was to a great extent a function of the backward character of the "North-West," one of the least industrialized areas of European Russia [but a relatively highly industrialized area of the Pale of Settlement]. Only Bialystok, a major textile center in Grodno province, stood out as an exception. In that city, however, the larger and more modern factories preferred Christian to Jewish labor, and the sizeable Jewish weaver proletariat of Bialystok remained a proletariat of shops and small shop-like factories.[26]

Part of the reason factory owners preferred Christian workers was prejudice of the malevolent or myopic variety, but other factors were probably more important, especially since Jewish factory owners also tended to prefer Christians. Jewish workers were less experienced, did not want to work on the Sabbath, and were considered "trouble makers." Thus the Jewish proletariat, with the exception of the cigarette and match factory workers, remained a "proletariat of small shops and declining fortunes."

It was difficult for this small shop Jewish proletariat to compete with the factories or with the handcraft enterprises of the masses of emancipated peasants. And the employers, themselves squeezed and less independent now, were inclined to intensify their exploitation and to abuse whatever power they had. The Jewish artisans were generally aware that they fared worse than the Russian factory worker. There were a significant number of strikes reported in the socialist press, and small shop Jewish weavers in Bialystok had more than one pitched battle with Polish workers in their efforts to gain employment in the larger modern plants.[27]

Much new labor history suggests that proletarianized artisans, everywhere in the modernizing world, dominated working-class movements of protest and revolt, while factory proletarians played a clearly secondary role.[28] Perhaps, then, disproportionate proletarianization of Jewish artisans and the deteriorating economic position of that class are, by themselves, enough to explain East European Jewish affinity for radicalism in the modern era.

It is important to look closely at this. Of the 79 Jewish immigrants in this study who were converted to labor radicalism in Eastern Europe, and whose status at the time of radicalization could be determined, 23, or 30 percent, were proletarians—manual workers who sold their labor power and had little control over the conditions of their work. Thirteen, or almost 17 percent, were independent craftsmen, small store owners, youngsters just out of school, or daughters not "gainfully employed." And 41 (53 percent) were students and intellectuals—the intelligentsia—writing and teaching.

The majority of these immigrants were not proletarians, and the percentage of proletarians among them was no higher than the proportion of proletarians among the gainfully employed Jewish population in the Pale or in the Russian Empire as a whole.[29] But, and it is a large but, among their fathers whose occupations could be determined there were even fewer proletarians (25 percent), and the students, and even the teachers, given the economic context described above, were very likely en route to proletarianization. Class, or proletarianization, then, is surely a factor. Before we conclude, however, that it is the only or even the single most important determinant of Jewish radicalism in late nineteenth- and early twentieth-century

Eastern Europe, we need to look at the history of a representative socialist who was one of the proletarians, and then ask what else, beyond class, the Jewish socialists shared.

Morris Shatan was born to poor parents in 1887, and by the time he was eleven years old he was employed making paper bags. "But," he said, "my father and mother wanted me to study. I too wanted this." He did study and became a bar mitzvah and then went on to yeshiva in Vlatzlavek. He missed his parents and did not enjoy the tradition of being fed on different days by different "strangers" (though some were his cousins) who were enjoined to support yeshiva boys in this way.

> I was ashamed; I felt insulted to eat at strangers . . . to sit at a strange table. And I had the impression that's a beggar's way. I couldn't stand it.

A woman guest at one of these "eating days" told the studious Morris, "In these times a young boy like you, not from rich parents, has to think of a different purpose." And she offered him a job in a store in Alexandrov for food, lodging, and 25 rubles for the "season." Tired of "begging" meals, "dirty shirts," and cramped quarters, Morris accepted. He wrote informing his father of this decision.

> In due time I convinced him not to be afraid—that I am with very pious Jews and continuing to study the Talmud. My father was pleased that I studied with a teacher, a Cohan, though it hurt him that I left Yeshiva because he wanted me to be a rabbi. This would have been for him a source of great honor. Jews had no military generals, and other careers and professions for Jews were very few. . . . There were rabbis in my family. My father wanted to be a rabbi himself, but he didn't qualify. Also, as a prospective rabbi, one is able to get a rich bride.

After the season, Morris returned to Kutno to work in an iron warehouse because, as he put it, to stay in Alexandrov or Vlatzlavek was "again to be a stranger." The elder Shatan, despite his earlier disappointment, was glad to have his son home. "A father is above all happy when his child comes home," Morris said, and his father was pleased in any case because Morris used all his free time "for studying."[30]

Morris Shatan did spend much of his time studying, but it was not always Talmud. In late 1901 *Der Freint* (The Friend), a radical Yiddish newspaper, began to appear. Morris and a friend, the son of a rabbi with whom he was studying, took a joint subscription.

The message of the paper, according to Morris, was that "one has to struggle to achieve a better world, and that the big capitalists hold most of the power. But they don't worry about others." Morris's experience at work had already prepared him to be impressed by this message.

> There is riches and there is poverty and the poor get treated very badly by the rich. And if you work for someone else, no matter how good you are treated, eventually you are the loser. No matter how faithful and trustworthy you are he is still your boss. . . . There are many opportunities for the boss to let you know *he* is the boss.

Morris was also sympathetic to the political position of *Der Freint*, because as he tells us, he was "a religious child."

> I was brought up in a religious home, went to pray and study in the house of worship, in the orthodox synagogue. . . . We have respect not only for money, or for pretty hats, but for studying and for persons who study. At work we were in slavery . . . the bosses demanded that the person should be a slave. . . .
>   The idea that people should have enough to eat moved me. Because by us there was seldom enough food. Even though at work . . . *I* ate well, I thought of my brothers and sisters and my father and mother who didn't have enough. . . .

The young Shatan also "heard revolutionary slogans and rhetoric from Jewish soldiers [who came through town], words such as we never heard before." *Der Freint* and the soldiers "made such an impression on me. I thought the Messiah was on the way."[31]

By 1903 Morris Shatan was a leading member of the Bund, active in Vlatzlavek and Kutno. He was not a particularly marginal person. The "uprooting," proletarianization, and exploitation of Morris Shatan were critical to his radicalization, but so apparently was his rootedness in religious principles and cultural background. The new historical literature on *general* artisan radicalism also points away from marginality and toward rootedness, often in things other than class.[32] In the case of Morris Shatan the rootedness was in Jewish religious culture.

Shatan was not alone. In this study, of 17 Jewish artisans who were active on the left in Eastern Europe and about whom I could find this kind of information, 14 were significantly versed in Jewish religious culture and 3 more were virtually saturated in it. For the

TABLE 1
Connection of Radical Jews to Religious Culture (N = 59)

	Proletarians	Students/Intellectuals	Independents*
Little or none	6	0	6	0
Significant	37	14	12	11
Deep	16	3	12	1

*Shopkeepers, independent craftsmen, and non-working youngsters.

students/intellectuals who were radicalized in the Russian Empire, 6 of 30 had little or no "training" in Jewishness, but 24 had strong Jewish upbringing, including 12, deeply immersed in tradition, who were sons and daughters of rabbis, cantors, Hebrew school teachers, Talmudic scholars, or who had had rabbinical or advanced Jewish schooling themselves. Of 59 Jewish radicals in Eastern Europe who eventually emigrated and for whom I could find data, 37 had significant and 16 had very deep immersion in traditional Jewish culture, while only 6 had little or no connection with such religious tradition.

It appears that Jewish culture, along with urbanization and proletarianization, has to be counted as a key ingredient in Jewish radicalism. Some 30 percent of the radicals in this study had been proletarianized (no more and perhaps less than the general Jewish population of the Russian Empire), but 90 percent of the radicals were still vitally in touch with Jewish ethics and moral commandment, prophetic conceptions of justice, and historical messianism. Twenty-seven percent were products of the profoundest socialization in that world. And 15.5 percent had fathers who were rabbis, cantors, and teachers of Hebrew and Talmud, while in 1897 significantly less than 5 percent of the gainfully employed in the Pale held these positions. Paul Novick, the editor of the left-wing Yiddish daily *Freiheit*, who described his extremely orthodox father as a "hasidic, Trisker rabbi," tells us:

> I got my "socialist leanings" . . . even before I became a worker. The youth drifted into the revolutionary movement, and already in 1905—I was only 14 years old—I ran after all the demonstrations and meetings [and] about 1907 I joined the Bund.[33]

But even those who were proletarianized at the time of their radicalization were imbued with Jewish culture and religious tradition. Abraham Lieb Goldman, working at twelve, a "unionman" at fourteen, could read the Talmud and "was able to read the books of Moses, the Bible." He could "do the daily prayers by heart and understand everything."[34]

THE SEARCH FOR NEW JEWISH IDENTITIES

In the formation of radical consciousness, then, Jewish culture was critical. But in the nineteenth century that culture was hardly static. At the same time as the important economic and demographic changes described above were taking place, new social and political thought was impinging on *shtetl* life and Jewish culture generally. The new trends constituted an independent force as well as a symptom of the decline of rabbinic and communal authority, and were as much an indication that Jewish life was undergoing a rebirth as they were signs of fragmentation and deterioration. The "continuities of tradition were as complex as those of change in Russian-Jewish life."[35]

As far back as the late eighteenth and the early nineteenth centuries, Hasidism, an enthusiastic, pietistic movement of religious renewal, temporarily challenged rabbinic traditionalism. In demanding spontaneity and rejecting rote and formal ritual, it appealed to and brightened the spiritual lives of the mainly *proste yidn* (plebeians).

Later, from the West, came the *Haskalah,* or Enlightenment, which strove toward complete emancipation and Jewish citizenship and the virtual elimination of the *kehillah* as intermediary between Jews and the state. In the West, Jews had achieved, at least temporarily, individual liberties in return for the corporate rights that the respective European states had abolished. In Russia, where neither individual nor corporate rights were guaranteed, the process of integrating the Jews, supported by the *maskilim* (enlightened Jews), tended to take on a repressive character. Instead of genuine emancipation there was a "revolutionary dismemberment of the legal integrity of Jewish society," increased poverty, and the erosion of cohesiveness and solidarity.[36] This led in the last thirty years of the nineteenth century, those decades with which we are most concerned, to great turmoil and effervescence. There emerged a plethora of new cultural and political movements—including Zionism and socialism,

and various combinations of the two. Traditional Jewry also united in
Orthodoxy, a new militant defense against dangers from within and
without. All the movements competed for converts.

Socialism won quite often, particularly among students.
Significant numbers of workers would soon be attracted, however,
and even the denizens of *shtetlekh*, as we shall see, were responsive.
Close to half the future immigrants who were converted to socialism
were students at the time of their conversion. During the reign of
Nicholas I (1825–1855) Jews were generally kept out of the gymnasia
and were "recruited" for crown schools and "official" rabbinical
seminaries and teacher institutes. These schools, part of Nicholas's
Jewish policy of "Europeanization through education," were dedicated to the "eradication of the superstitions and harmful prejudices
instilled by the study of the Talmud." But educational policy under
Alexander II (1855–1881) was temporarily liberalized along with
much else. The percentage of Jewish boys among the student population in gymnasia in the Pale increased from 1.25 in 1853 to 13.2 in
1873.[37] Even some young girls successfully pressured their parents
into sending them to gymnasia.[38]

The schools, and the universities, which were also increasing
their enrollment of Jews, became centers of revolutionary ferment.
Between 1884 and 1890, Jews, approximately 4.5 percent of the general population and only little more than that of the university population, provided more than 13 percent of those who stood trial for
subversive activities. By 1901–1903, that figure rose to 29 percent.
The fact that language barriers rendered "Jewish Social Democrats
far less subject to police surveillance than their Russian counterparts"
probably makes these figures conservative, and makes quite credible
Count Witte's remark to Theodor Herzl in 1903 that half the revolutionaries in Russia were Jews.[39]

Morris Winchevsky, the *zeyde* (grandfather) of Jewish socialist literature, was enrolled in the tuition-free training college for state rabbis in Vilna in 1874. The school was a center of student radicalism.
Four years later Abraham Cahan, probably the foremost American
Jewish socialist journalist, went there. And by 1880 the young Cahan,
who had been anxious to train for the rabbinate, had had significant
contact with revolutionary students and was converted to socialism.
Later, in remembering the experience, he implicitly connected his

religious background and his newfound political identity. Cahan had read the radical student political literature, which he described as

> a forbidden object—its publishers are those people . . . who live together like brothers and are ready to go to the gallows for freedom and justice. . . . I took the pamphlet in hand as one touches a holy thing. I will never forget it.
>
> All of this became part of my new religion, and had a great effect on my feelings. After my conversion to Socialism, I withdrew from all foolishness. I was definitely a better, more serious and philosophical man. . . .[40]

Aaron Lieberman, the virtual founder of Jewish socialism, had been graduated from the Vilna Institute several years before, and articulated the connection between Jewishness and radicalism more explicitly than Cahan. By 1875 Lieberman had developed the belief that Jewish history and teaching had prepared the Jews for revolutionary socialism:

> Socialism is not alien to us. The community is our existence; the revolution—our tradition; the commune—the basis of our legislation as quite clearly indicated by the ordinances forbidding the sale of land, by those on the Jubilee and sabbatical years, on equal rights, fraternity, etc. Our ancient Jewish social structure—anarchy; the real link between us across the surface of the globe—internationalism. In the spirit of our people, the great prophets of our time such as Marx and Lassalle were educated and developed. . . .[41]

In some circles this statement had created a furor. Several Russian radicals saw the Jews as an exploiting harmful class which lived "exclusively at the expense of the petty-bourgeois population." Others saw Lieberman's position as "backward nationalism," a dilution of class consciousness. By 1876 Aaron Lieberman, cross-pressured, moderated his stand. Late in that year he exhibited what Jonathan Frankel calls the "dilemmas of Messianic conscience."

> That I have tried to publish a paper [in a Jewish language] . . . is far from being nationalism. You know very well that I hate Juda-*ism* just like any other national or religious *ism*. . . . I am an internationalist . . . but I am not ashamed of my Jewish origins and I love, among all the oppressed, also that section of mankind which the prevailing national and religious principles mark off as Jews. But I say again I do not love all [Jews] but only the suffering masses and those persons capable of joining them. . . .

Abe Cahan soon after his "conversion" to socialism at the Vilna
State Training College.

From the Archives of YIVO Institute for Jewish Research

And I regard myself as a *Russian* socialist not by nationality but by the territory on which I work, by the place in which I was born, the country which I know even better and by the interests of that country which attract me even more. . . . Believe me I do not want *to take pride in my Jewishness,* not from the religious or historical angle (that you must believe) and not even from the racial aspect. I recognize only men and class, no more.[42]

Aaron Lieberman grew more and more distraught, apparently seeking relief in an overwhelming but unrequited love for Morris Winchevsky's cousin, Rachel. He followed her, a married woman with a young daughter, to America. Late in that year, while Abraham Cahan was creating a relatively viable synthesis between his Jewishness and the socialism that had partly grown out of it, Lieberman came to Rachel's home in Syracuse, New York, and shot himself dead. His suicide note asked "that nobody judge me unless he is in my place," a variation of the classical Hebrew saying in *The Ethics of the Fathers,* "Do not judge your neighbor until you are in his place."[43]

Unlike the unfortunate Lieberman, most Jews who became socialists were more able to blend the two dimensions of their personalities and belief systems, or to move between them without breakdown. Numerous Jewish student radicals and intellectuals, at least up to the pogroms of 1881–1882, were convinced assimilationists. Gregory Weinstein was aware that

like zealots of a new religion, we discarded everything—valuable as well as valueless—of the old teachings. In my home we gave a semblance of conforming with the observances and ceremonies of our parents' religion, but outside we joined the young rebels in their defiance of the ruling despotism.[44]

The views of many of these young people contained elements of self-awareness that belied their claims to complete assimilation. And in a great number of instances their negative attitudes were toward the Orthodox and bourgeois leaders of Russian Jewry, not necessarily toward Jews as a people. Even where there was implanted in the students and intellectuals a conception of the Jews as a parasitic class, this often disappeared with personal rebuff within the movement and with the pogroms and the stunningly disappointing response of Russian radicals to the mass murderous violence against the Jews.

Abraham Cahan reported that in the wake of more than two

hundred anti-Jewish uprisings that spread across southern Russia and into Poland from 1881 to 1882, young people went to synagogues to demonstrate their solidarity. In Kiev, one speaker confessed to the assembled worshippers:

> We are your brethren. We are Jews like you. We regret that we have up to now considered ourselves as Russians and not Jews. Events of the last weeks . . . including the pogroms . . . have shown us how grievously mistaken we have been. Yes, we are Jews.[45]

This did not mean that students, intellectuals, and quasi-assimilated young people generally would flock back to religion, nor did it mean, since they believed correctly that the pogroms were government supported if not initiated, that they would give up on the need for revolution.[46] It did mean that some of them would be in varying degrees *Jewish* socialists. And the movement would be even more infused with Jewish spirit, feeling, and knowledge by the participation of the so-called semi-intelligentsia. This group was recruited mainly in the Lithuanian yeshivas, which, in addition to their educational role, were centers of religious ferment (though generally within the limits of Orthodoxy).[47]

Right up to the end of the czarist regime there were some Jewish radicals for whom there was apparently little positive content to their Jewishness. Leon Trotsky and Rosa Luxemburg leaned heavily to univeralist politics, were hostile to *any* form of Jewish separatism, and mocked efforts to build a Jewish nation even in the name of socialist ideals. The numbers involved in these activities, however, were quite small. And in the 170-member subject group of this study they were no more than a handful.

There is little doubt that conflicts with regard to their own Jewishness existed for many Jews attracted to socialism, and some engaged in hostility or studied indifference to Jewish culture. But a commitment to socialism, unlike conversion to Christianity, did not require denial of ethnic origins, and most of the Jewish radicals in this study could not easily be labeled "self-hating," or "marginal persons," exhibiting the negative psychological characteristics of that condition. These were persons struggling, often creatively, to make new identities out of the materials of the "traditional" and the "modern." Most Jewish socialists acted within the Jewish mainstream. The handful who, with Trotsky, were hostile or even indifferent to Jewishness were too few and too far removed in culture and interest from the Jewish masses to influence Jewish behavior.

THE SOCIALISTS FIND THE PROLETARIAT

By staying in, or returning to, the Jewish mainstream, the Jewish intelligentsia would soon have impact on the Jewish proletariat. In the 1870s and 1880s, however, workers acted mainly on their own initiative. After a strike in a Vilna tobacco factory in 1871, the police report indicated that the striking workers were recent arrivals from southern Russia, where similar strikes had taken place earlier. In Bialystock the textile workers staged a series of strikes in 1877 and 1878; and in the 1880s across the northwest, bitter strikes kept breaking out. This early Jewish strike "movement" was spontaneous, sporadic, and generally uninfluenced by Jewish socialists. An organized labor movement developed only when the Jewish socialists, from among the intelligentsia we have dealt with above, established significant contact with the proletariat.

Marxian socialism, as distinct from the philosophy of the *Narodnaya Volya* (People's Will) and other populist groups, was in the ascendancy after 1880, and emphasis shifted from peasant to worker. The late nineteenth century strikes made it more credible to speak of a "Jewish proletariat," and the pogroms made the existence of a "Jewish problem" more difficult to deny. All of this opened up new possibilities for socialist activity among the Jewish working class.

Many of the Jewish socialists believed the future of the revolutionary movement lay in the great concentrations of Russian workers in factories; their initial efforts among the Jewish artisans therefore were generally aimed less at trade union organization and revolutionary activism in the northwest itself, and more at creating *some* class-conscious socialists to work among the Russian working classes in the industrialized cities. This they would do through educational programs in worker "circles."[48]

Printers, jewelers, binders, and tailors were to be the beneficiaries of a working-class version of *Haskalah* (enlightenment). One of these tailors was Julius Gershin, who came to the United States in 1904. In 1895, when Gershin was ten, he was an apprentice tailor in the town of Gomel (Mogilev province). Here, the workers movement . . . took in all the small children—they took them under their wing. . . . The Jewish intelligentsia, the students . . . used to teach us reading and writing . . . also a little Russian.[49]

By the time he was a teenager Julius fled Gomel, pursued by the police. Jacob Levenson, while still a *heder* student and not yet working, was taken into a "circle" in Vitebsk and got "involved in 'revolutionary' activities—mostly reading, singing, and pamphleteering."[50]

The reading and the pamphleteering, and perhaps even the singing, appear to have worked not so much to create revolutionary agitators for Russian industrial centers as to help develop class-conscious socialists among the Jewish artisan proletariat as it grew in numbers through the 1890s and into the new century. In Minsk, Vilna, Kovno, Grodno, Bialystok, and other cities of the northwest region, the Jewish proletariat organized militant trade unions. Beginning in 1893 a successful strike movement swept over several towns in the Jewish Pale. By 1894 Vilna, with twenty-seven *kases,* was the center of what could now be called a Jewish labor movement, and by 1896 in Minsk extraordinarily high percentages of Jewish artisans were formally organized. In all the larger towns in Lithuania, underground revolutionary groups were in place by 1897. In Poland, Jewish labor organizations that were established in Lodz and Warsaw made contact with the Vilna groups.[51] Even in Galicia as early as 1880, seventy Jewish carpenters were involved in a general carpenters' strike. In 1886 the Jewish bakers staged a strike, and in 1892 *Naprzód,* a Polish socialist bulletin, reported the following:

> On July 24, 200 [prayershawl *(tales)* weavers] assembled in the house of the rabbi. Comrade Zetterbaum . . . described the woeful plight of those assembled. . . . Trembling and emaciated old men supported his statement and called out that they . . . will beat up [scabs] . . . even if they have to pay for it with months in jail.
> In order to ensure that workers in smaller factories will not go to work . . . the meeting demanded an oath on the holy Torah.[52]

Eventually four hundred *tales* weavers, "Jews with beards and earlocks went on strike." *Pobudka,* the journal of the Polish emigrant socialists in Paris, carried the following statement:

> The strike attracts general attention and calls for support because every day it takes on an increasingly pronounced socialist character.

Three hundred persons have taken their oath on the Torah and stand firm on their demands.[53]

The great majority of those who participated in radical labor and political activities, while partly motivated by deeply ingrained values from the Jewish tradition, were generally significantly younger, more secular, and more "assimilated" than these *tales* weavers. But that these Orthodox Jews went on strike, a strike apparently taking on an increasingly "socialist character," further suggests that in addition to tension between Jewishness and socialism there was also, for working-class people, under particular historical and economic conditions, considerable complementariness.

A Jewish proletariat, conscious of its class interest and its cultural identity, grew, and with it grew activism and organization. Jewish labor militance from 1895 to 1904, as measured by the number of strikes and lost work time, has been calculated as proportionately three times higher than that of any other working class in Europe.[54] Georgii Plekhanov's statement to the 1896 Congress of the Socialist International in London, that "from a certain point of view the Jewish workers may be considered the vanguard of the labor army in Russia," was ringing increasingly true.

In 1897 many of the local organizations united to form the social democratic party known as the Bund. This was the first and the most important Jewish socialist party. The Bund, or General Jewish Workers' Union in Russia and Poland, was a revolutionary party with a mass base, and the leadership moved slowly toward the idea of an autonomous Jewish socialist party combining loyalty to the Jewish people, indeed to Jewish peoplehood, with class war. Often these goals were blended in individual Bundists; but within the leadership there were some that held that the aim of the movement was the liberation, by the proletariat, of the Jewish "nation," and others who saw the Bund as a "branch" of the *general* revolutionary movement and assumed (with Lenin and Trotsky) that one of the results of the revolution would be the total integration of Jews into Russian society. The spiritual struggle of individuals became the burden of an entire movement.[55]

For no one was the synthesis simple. Abraham Liesen, the gifted writer and poet who fled the czarist police and came to the United States in 1897, had given lectures in Lithuania combining socialist propaganda with Jewish history. In the 1890s he wrote:

I do not know what and how the connections were made, but it just so happened that when I learned I was a convinced Marxist, I also discovered I was what I was: not a Russian, not just a human being (which is merely an abstraction), but a Jew. Marxism intensified my sense of reality, and the reality surrounding me was Jewish. This Jewish reality found no expression in Marxist literature. . . .

At first I tried to fight off these sinful thoughts . . . just as ten years earlier I had tried to struggle with the religious doubts which tormented me. But I saw that the struggle was lost. I had become a nationalist.[56]

Liesen, before he was forced to flee Russia, apparently thought of returning to his earlier studies in order to achieve ordination; then he could use rabbinic authority and Talmudic teaching to propagate socialism among Jews.

This struggle, this attempt at synthesis, was not a monopoly of the leadership. Many of the rank and file workers who were involved in the movement tried to combine the new socialist ideology with the old traditions. Bristle workers in Vilna, like the *tales* weavers earlier, swore on a Torah scroll not to break a strike. A boycott of Janovsky's cigarette factory in Bialystok was announced to congregations in a number of synagogues, and the term *herem,* signifying in its religious context "excommunication," was persistently employed. In Krynki in 1897 there was a general strike and some of the worker-organizers had been fired. Three hundred Jewish tanners held an outdoor meeting. They stood in the rain for two hours discussing strategy, and all swore by a pair of phylacteries, in a solemn religious ceremony, that they would support the fired workers. Then everyone immediately sang the "Oath," the official hymn of the Bund—a revolutionary song.[57]

The rich mix of Jewish religious culture and elements of modernization was also evident in the lives of those who were not workers or members of the intelligentsia, at the time of their radicalization. Rose Pesotta, who at ten was distributing revolutionary leaflets and eventually followed her sister to America in 1913, was raised in a provincial trading town served by a railroad, which brought some element of cosmopolitanism. In contravention of *shtetl* tradition, she was encouraged to pursue formal studies. Among her subjects were the Hebrew language and Jewish history. In addition her father was extremely outspoken in political discussion.[58]

Lucy Sperber, who came to America at fourteen full of "revolutionary ideas, equality and justice and all of that," was also encouraged to study. Her mother, who Lucy describes as "ahead of her time," had her learn Hebrew and sent her to gymnasium for two years. Neither of Lucy Sperber's parents was particularly pious, but each attended synagogue occasionally and "always on high holidays."[59]

And Isidore Nagler, who would make a career as an executive in the socialist unions in America, had lived in a fairly sizable town in southeastern Galicia. Here the Jewish community of 2,000 was a minority, "steeped in fundamental religious orthodoxy" but beginning to be touched by a growing "cosmopolitanism." Isidore's mother was a "buyer" and had often attended fairs at nearby larger cities. Her growing modernism led her, successfully, to refuse to shave her hair and wear a *sheitel* (wig), which was prescribed for Orthodox wives.[60]

Jews in Eastern Europe were experiencing a period of complex transition so pervasive that even beyond the cities, *miesteckos*, and larger towns—in those stuffy *heders* and ritualized *shtetlekh*—there were Jewish boys and girls hungering for fresh air and new space. Florence Levenson, who lived in a *shtetl*, is an example.

> I don't know why I was rebellious. My parents were observant Jews, but I gathered with people who were not satisfied with religion alone. We felt some turmoil inside, knew something was wrong. . . . My cousin who was training to be a rabbi brought me revolutionary literature to read.[61]

FAMILY DYNAMICS AND POLITICS

The illustrations above, which could be multiplied tenfold for the subject group of this study, touch on the question of the nature of the East European Jewish family, and on the relationship of the family constellation and family dynamics to politics. This is a very difficult area of inquiry and the evidence required to deal with it is fragmented, elusive, and mostly missing. That there was significant generational conflict and a challenge to parental authority in these decades of extraordinary and rapid change is unquestionable. That there was some degree of simultaneous challenge to political authority is also clear. Whether this translates simply into the point that Jewish youngsters were more likely to be radicals because of a disproportionate conflict of generations which they acted out in the "safer" arena of politics is very much less clear.

Sidney Hillman, president of the Amalgamated Clothing Work-

A *heder*, where between prayers and learning Torah there was
still time to "talk politics."

Jewish Daily Forward

ers of America, rebelled against both Orthodoxy and his father when
he dropped out of a yeshiva near Kovno where he was studying to be
a rabbi. Benjamin Feigenbaum, for forty years one of the most ubiqui-
tous figures in the radical political and cultural life of the lower East
Side, reacted strongly in Warsaw against the religious restrictions of
his parents. Emma Goldman suffered severe beatings from her father
as a young child in Kovno; and Yossef Bovshover, radical labor poet
and son of a Talmudic scholar, grew restless and tired of his father's
nagging, and often disappeared from his home in Libawitz. A somewhat similar pattern of "serious" generational conflict could be pre-

Yeshiva boys studying the Talmud. Sometimes, as with I. E. Rontch, between these pages were hidden pieces of revolutionary literature.

Jewish Daily Forward

During a break between services men gather outside a *shul,* the center for prayer, Torah study, and sometimes political discussion.

Jewish Daily Forward

sented here for seven more sons and daughters who are subjects of this study.

But for twenty-six other Jewish socialists who eventually emigrated to the United States there is evidence of significant familial *harmony* prior to radicalization. Seven of these could in fact be described as products of familial political socialization. Louis Painkin, who was born in Lomaza, Poland, in 1895 and came to America in 1911, explained that his father

> was active in social movements. . . . [H]e was religious, but not fanatical. My older brothers and sisters were all . . . revolutionaries. Our family were radicals and it came to me naturally. . . . [A]t the age of ten I was already involved.[62]

Meyer London, the socialist congressman from the East Side, had a close and abiding relationship with his father, who, though trained in Talmudic studies, was a "free thinker and social radical." And Rose Pesotta's father

> had the courage of his convictions, a deep sense of responsibility toward his fellow-man, and was always ready to undertake any task for the good of the community. . . . In the market place discussions, dad advocated equality among the people and he practiced it conscientiously.[63]

There are other relationships worth considering too, though they defy precise categorization. David Dubinsky, president of the ILGWU, who arrived in the United States in 1910, was raised in Lodz, the largest industrial city in Poland. At age eleven Dubinsky was working in his father's bakery. By the time he was fourteen he was a member of the militant Lodz Bakers' Union, organized by the Bund. And in 1907, Dubinsky's fifteenth year,

> everything looked so black and the workers were so discouraged that we had to do something to keep up morale. So we decided to call a strike of all the bakers in Lodz.[64]

The shops picketed by Dubinsky included his father's. In response to the question "Was your father against the strike?" Dubinsky responded: "Good Lord, no! The strike was really a demonstration against the system, and my father was certainly with us."[65]

The Czar, of course, was not. David was arrested, imprisoned, and exiled—and then arrested, imprisoned, and exiled again for revolutionary activities. His father worked hard to get him released from prison, and sent him money so that David could bribe his way into an "escape." The pressure of time had made it necessary to violate the Sabbath in order to wire the money. One of Dubinsky's brothers pointed out, "Tatte, it's shabos!" The elder Dubinsky responded, "'According to the Bible, you can do it to save a life.'"[66]

Elie Wiesel includes the following scene in his powerful and moving novel *The Testament*. It is 1920s Hungary; an Orthodox Jewish father is talking to his Communist son, who has outwardly continued his religious duties:

> "You hope to change man," he said, "very good. You want to change society. Magnificent. You expect to eliminate evil and hatred. Extraordinary, I am in full agreement."
> "... in helping the poor, in looking after and listening to those who need us, we are but exercising our privilege of living our life. ... I don't know your Communist friends. ... I only know that their aim is to diminish unhappiness in the world. That is what counts, that is all that counts. They're said to rebel against the Almighty; that's between them and God. Let Him take care of it. What matters is that they are fighting for those who have neither the strength nor the means to fight. ... So long as you persist in fighting injustice, defending victims, even victims of God, you'll feel alive, that is you'll feel God within you, the God of your ancestors, the God of your childhood. You will feel within you man's passion and God's. The real danger, my son, is indifference."[67]

Most of the time the evidence for the connection between Jewishness and radicalism, and for familial harmony, is not so explicit. But a "true" story that poet-writer-historian I. E. Rontch tells echoes Wiesel's "fiction." Rontch's great ambition, which he shared with his family, was to become a rabbi. But as early as age seven or eight he witnessed strikes in Lodz and saw "police beat up workers." At nine years of age he was persuaded by a fourteen-year-old Bundist girl to distribute radical pamphlets, which he hid inside his *Gemara* (Talmudic commentaries). By age eleven he was himself a member of the *kleinem Bund* and was seemingly launched on a political career. Rontch thought the final blow to his "religious career" had come a year earlier at *heder*. "I asked a question about sex. I wanted to know what 'adultery' meant." The rabbi smacked him and Rontch ran home, announcing, "No more *heder* for me—you can kill me!"

A year after Rontch joined the Bund, his father, a Talmudic scholar and fully aware of his son's radical activities, lay dying. He called the twelve-year-old Rontch to his side.

> I want you to promise me to be a Jew and an honest person. I don't care if you will not be very religious. . . . Honesty is more important than religion.[68]

Jewish teenagers were rebelling against their parents and parts of their parents' culture. They were also responding positively to political socialization by their mothers and fathers. At times they appear to have been doing both simultaneously.

Children were affected not only by the relationships they had with respective parents but by the relationships their parents had with each other. The East European Jewish family is alleged by some to have been disproportionately one which, for complex historical reasons, contained an ineffectual, "scholarly" father and a powerful, intrusive, business-oriented mother.[69] The Jewish son views his mother as a devouring figure who has already destroyed the father. The mother is desired and terribly feared, and the son, because of his father's weakness and his mother's "strength," develops strong doubts about his own masculine potency. This ambivalence about power and authority is alleged to be the root of Jewish radicalism under particular historical conditions. Jews, it is contended, put their doubts about power to rest by identifying with certain lower-status but physically powerful groups—for example, with peasants or factory workers in nineteenth-century Russia, or, later, with blacks in the 1960s—and by attacking established authorities, in coalition with these groups.[70] Despite the fact that this characterization makes a host of unprovable assumptions, fails to deal in any way with female radicals, and implies that family dynamics for Jews were unique and the same throughout the Pale (and stayed the same in America in the 1960s!), versions of it are common coin in the literature.

The Jewish radicals, in this study at least, do not fit this mold. First of all, 34 of 170 of them were women. Secondly, the fathers of the radicals were rarely full-time "scholars" without some gainful employment in the old country; only 6 of 95 fit this description. Twenty-five fathers were manual laborers. Fourteen others were carpenters, builders, overseers, millers, cattle dealers, and even farmers and a lumberjack. Surprisingly, I could find "employment" information for

TABLE 2
Work Patterns: Parents of Jewish Socialists (N = 95)

Fathers		Mothers	
Manual laborers	25	No employment information	63
Subsistence merchants	24	Not gainfully employed	11
Professionals	15	Employed earning supplemental	
Moderately prosperous		income	8
merchants	11	Employed earning primary	
Independent artisans	6	income (spouse deceased or ill)	6
"Scholars"	6	Employed earning primary	
Managers	5	income (spouse alive)	7
Farmers	2		
Lumberjacks	1		

only 32 mothers. Twenty-one could be identified as "gainfully employed," if this term was interpreted as broadly as possible, including every activity that contributed to the household economy, except traditional child-rearing and housekeeping. Seven of these mothers were indeed the true breadwinners, but 6 others "did business" only after the death or incapacitating illness of their respective spouses. And 11 of the 32 appear not to have been involved in nontraditional economic roles. Even if we add all mothers for whom we have no other information, and all who were wives of subsistence merchants (8) on the assumption that they at least "minded the store," only a minority (23 of 95) appears to have been "business-oriented." An even smaller minority of families fits the picture of "worldly" wife, "scholarly" husband. This picture may have represented a more widespread pattern for the general Jewish population of Eastern Europe, but for the families of the radical Jews studied here the "classic" constellation is next to impossible to sustain.

EMIGRATION

Many young Jews left Eastern Europe not only to escape, but to fulfill hopes instilled in them in part by parents. The autobiographies, memoirs, and interviews are filled with evidence that Jewish emigres were energetically seeking outlets for deeply felt aspirations. "To become" was always central to Jewish culture. Modernization redirected and intensified that desire, and increasing Russian antisemitism frustrated it. For large numbers, relocation seemed the only answer. Sons

A group of Jewish porters, members of the Porters Union in Kutno, Poland, where Bundist Morris Shatan was raised.

Jewish Daily Forward

Jewish political prisoners awaiting exile to Siberia for their part in the 1905 Revolution.

Jewish Daily Forward

and daughters, radicals and soon-to-be radicals, along with the great mass of declassed petty-bourgeois Jews, began their exodus in the late nineteenth century. Pogroms in 1881–1882 and again in 1903–1906 speeded up a process already germinating, not only for the *folksmasn*, the ordinary Jews, but for a small part of the intelligentsia and for thousands of the artisans who were increasingly proletarianized through the 1890s.

Several of the radicals in this study, drawn from the intelligentsia, were involved in the *Am olam* (Eternal People) movement, which began in 1881 and had important units in Vilna, Odessa, and Kiev. The goals were not always clear, but they seemed to include the spiritual and physical rejuvenation of the Jewish people through collective agricultural enterprise in the American West. Abraham Cahan, who was wanted by the Russian authorities in 1882, radical poet David Edelstadt, who was almost killed in the Kiev pogrom in 1881, Nicholas Aleinikoff, a somewhat older, much admired intellectual, and numerous others were involved. Nothing enduring came of this. But contemporary observers were impressed as early as 1882 with the increasing participation of these and other Russian educated Jews in a movement with clearly Jewish emphasis. It had been assumed that Russification meant alienation from the Jewish world; therefore, the "spectacle of returning sons," some with the Torah in one hand and *Das Kapital* in the other, "aroused widespread wonderment."[71]

Right on through the 1880s and 1890s, small numbers of the radical intelligentsia, usually those without much experience with the Jewish proletariat, continued to emigrate, some to England, some to America, many fleeing from the czarist police. These refugees included Morris Hillquit and Louis Boudin, two of American socialism's most important theoreticians; Saul Yanofsky, the cantor's son who became an anarchist journalist; and Anna Ingerman, who brought with her a medical degree from Switzerland.[72] They were a tiny island in the ocean of nearly 200,000 paupers, petty merchants, wanderers, and dispossessed, "the surplus population of the decomposing *shtetl*" who came to industrializing America between 1881 and 1900.[73]

The 1900s saw a new additional phenomenon: mass artisan emigration from the Russian Empire. The Jewish proletariat of "small shops and declining fortunes" with no chance to enter the large modern factories where meaningful concessions might be gradually won, and with no chance for their evolving socialism to break out of the limits of the Pale, had strong incentive to flight. These people, including Jacob Levenson, "a good socialist, a good union man and striker," were "looking for a new life, a better life," and "opportunities to earn." Jews were obviously fleeing, but the autobiographies, memoirs, and interviews are filled with evidence that they were also energetically seeking outlets for deeply felt aspirations.

After the Kishinev pogrom of 1903 and the repressions following the political failures of 1905, some Bundists emigrated. Several were on the run, others left thinking the possibilities for revolution in the old country exhausted. This gave America the militant union leadership of David Dubinsky and Sidney Hillman, the socialist activism of Baruch Charney Vladeck, and the work-a-day radical commitment of Morris Shatan.

Of 108 immigrants who are the subject of this book and for whom I could find the data, 61 (56.5 percent) had had some kind of radical political involvement in Eastern Europe. For those who arrived through 1900, the figure was 40 percent, and for those who arrived after that date the figure was 68.8 percent: a significant majority, then, brought a developing radicalism with them. But these figures also show that a *significant minority* of the Jewish immigrant socialists disembarked at Castle Garden or Ellis Island *prior* to their radicalization, and often prior to proletarianization.

In this latter group was Minnie Rivkin, who brought "beautiful memories" of her "very religious home" along with her less than beautiful "bundles," and went on to play an important role in organizing needle trades shops in Toronto and in union activities in New York City.[74] There was Benjamin Schlesinger, son of a small-town rabbi, who eventually became president of the ILGWU, and Jack Sperber, who, before he became radicalized by his experience in the garment shops at the age of fifteen, sold bananas, Indian nuts, and pretzels on Hester Street.[75]

Students, youngsters, a handful not so young, some radicals, some political neophytes; men and women, some with work experience, others without—almost all, however, socialists and potential socialists—brought with them the Yiddish-speaking culture of Eastern Europe and the energy and aspiration generated by its revival in the late nineteenth century. All had suffered antisemitism, political oppression, and economic dislocation; and all shared the status of alien newcomer. The variables were in place for the fragmentation *or* the reconstruction of community.

Immigration, Atlantic liner, 1906.
Edwin Levick/Library of Congress

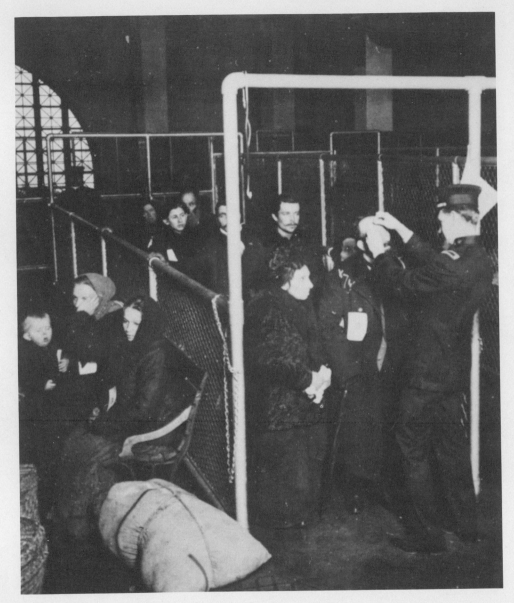

Ellis Island examination

Underwood and Underwood/Library of Congress

3

GOLDEN AMERICA

*Half Dream,
Half Nightmare*

THE DARKER SIDE

Pauline Newman, a remarkably effective garment union activist and Socialist Party organizer, came to America in 1901
at the age of ten.[1] She had lost her father in Russia and was
sent for by her brother, who lived on the lower East Side. By
this time, that area of New York was bustling with Jews. Between 1886
and 1906 over 70 percent of the Jews who landed in New York City
stayed in New York City, and the overwhelming majority of these
lived on the lower East Side (75 percent in 1892).[2] The radicals conformed to this pattern, with some ending up in Chicago, Philadelphia,
and Boston, each of which attracted enough Jews to establish its own
Jewish "quarter."

"From Ellis Island," Pauline Newman tells us, "we went by wagon
to my brother's apartment on Hester Street," at the very center of the
East Side and one of the most densely populated neighborhoods in
the world.

> Here you had people coming and going and shouting. Peddlers, people
> on the streets. Everything was new. . . . Having come from a little bit of a
> village [I was] bewildered by so many people and so much noise.[3]

Inside the apartment where she soon lived with her mother and
two sisters, things were not much better.

Hester Street
Library of Congress

The tenements where we lived [were] dark and cold in winter, hot in summer. . . . no ventilation. . . . Some of the rooms didn't have any windows . . . and the facilities were down in the yard. . . . In the summer the sidewalk, fire escapes, and the roof of the tenements became bedrooms, just to get a bit of fresh air.[4]

In 1888 the *American Magazine* carried this description of the East Side tenements:

They are great prison-like structures of brick, with narrow doors and windows, cramped passages and steep rickety stairs. They are built through from one street to the other with a somewhat narrower building connecting them. . . . The narrow court-yard . . . in the middle is a damp foul-smelling place, supposed to do duty as an airshaft; had the foul fiend designed these great barracks they could not have been more villainously arranged to avoid any chance of ventilation. . . . In case of fire they would be perfect death-traps, for it would be impossible for the occupants of the crowded rooms to escape by the narrow stairways, and the flimsy fire escapes which the owners of the tenements were compelled to put up a few years ago are so laden with broken furniture, bales and boxes that they would be worse than useless. In the hot summer months . . . these fire escape balconies are used as sleeping-rooms by the poor wretches who are fortunate enough to have windows opening upon them. The drainage is horrible, and even the Croton as it flows from the tap in the noisome courtyard, seemed to be contaminated by its surroundings and have a fetid smell.[5]

Few families could afford to live by themselves even in such places as these. Many took in lodgers and boarders, which led to further overcrowding. Abraham Sherer, the activist coatmaker whose older brother, like Pauline Newman's, sent him a ship ticket to come to America in 1902,

lived with a family on Willis Street. There were four rooms. The family was . . . a man, a woman, two sons and four daughters. And in that four room apartment they still had two boarders![6]

Charles Zimmerman, vice-president of the ILGWU for thirty-eight years, was provided a ship ticket by a sister already here, and lived for a while with an uncle in a Ridge Street tenement.

I slept in the kitchen on two chairs . . . with boards laid across. You had to dismantle it right away [in the morning]; otherwise [no other boarder] could walk from the front room to the kitchen or . . . to the hall where the facilities were.[7]

25 Public School 63
26 Music School Settlement
27 Asch Building
28 Astor Library
29 Cooper Union
30 Hebrew Technical School for Boys
31 Labor Temple
32 Rand School
33 Hebrew Charities Building
34 Metropolitan Life Building
35 Madison Square Garden
36 City College

Boundaries of sub-ethnic districts
······ Hungarian
—+— Galician
—o— Rumanian
⋀⋀⋀ Levantine
— — — Russian

Shaded blocks indicate Tenth Ward

0   ¼ MILE

THE LOWER EAST SIDE

1 Newspaper Row
2 World Building
3 Chatham Sq. Library
4 Beth Israel Hospital
5 Israel Elchanan Yeshiva
6 Seward Park Library
7 Forward Building on Yiddish Newspaper Row
8 Educational Alliance
9 Henry St. Settlement and Clinton Hall
10 Machzike Talmud Torah
11 Hebrew Sheltering House
12 Hebrew Technical School for Girls
13 Home for Aged
14 Jewish Maternity Hospital
15 Young Men's Benevolent Association
16 Camp Huddleston Hospital Ship School
17 Beth Hamedrash Hagadol
18 Pro-Cathedral Mission
19 University Settlement
20 Grand Theater
21 Yiddish Rialto
22 Thalia Theater
23 People's Bath
24 Police Headquarters

Reprinted by permission of Harvard University Press from *The Promised City*, by Moses Rischin, Copyright © 1962 by the President and Fellows of Harvard College

Coal cellar tenement. Making ready for Sabbath.
Jacob A. Riis/Jacob A. Riis Collection, Museum of the City of New York

This situation was not limited to New York City. Bella Dvorin followed her oldest brother to Chicago: "He took me to a friend's house—3 girls were sleeping on the floor, and I became the fourth on the floor."[8]

By the time Pauline Newman was eleven years old, she left the tenement every day to go to work for the Triangle Waist Company. She was not alone.

> There was a section in that factory which could have been regarded as a kindergarten, we were all kids, all youngsters. . . . We worked during the season from 7:30 in the morning to 9 in the evening.[9]
>
> When the operators were through with sewing shirtwaists there was a little thread left and we youngsters would get a little scissors and trim the threads off.
>
> And when the inspectors came around . . . [t]he supervisors made all the children climb into one of the crates that they ship material in and they covered us over with finished shirtwaists until the inspectors had left, because of course we were too young to be working in the factory legally.[10]

Louis Nelson, a left-wing socialist and an activist with the Amalgamated Clothing Workers Association (ACWA), related that his father "was not a big provider," and even though the Nelsons took in three boarders to increase income, Louis had to go to work when he was thirteen.

> [T]here were more, even younger, children than me working in the shop at the machines. . . . I worked 62 hours a week. . . . When an inspector came in they pushed me in the back; as soon as he left I came out and started over again.[11]

The Jewish immigrant socialists were young, even when compared with the general Jewish immigrant population, which was overwhelmingly a movement of young people. Over 64 percent of the radicals arrived in the United States before they were nineteen years old. And as the illustrations above imply, they went to work early—42 percent of them before they were fourteen.

With Pauline Newman and Louis Nelson, and the majority of other Jewish immigrants, the socialists worked in the garment industry. Nearly 70 percent of the socialist immigrants had some experience there, whatever else they ultimately went on to do. And nearly 60 percent of them spent their working lives with garments.

TABLE 3
Age of Immigrants

At Arrival (N = 123)		At First Work Experience (N = 76)	
Age	Percent	Age	Percent
6–12	10.5	under 14	42.1
13–19	53.6	10–15	77.7
20–25	24.4	10–16	84.2
26–32	8.1		

Immigrants Arriving Under 14 Years of Age	
This study (N = 123)	17.0 percent*
General Jewish (1899–1910)	24.8 percent
General Immigration	12.3 percent

*This figure is "deflated" because no one under 6 years of age qualified by my definition as an immigrant.

There are several reasons the garment industry saw such a concentration of Jews. The industry was undergoing a period of rapid expansion precisely at the time of the East European arrivals, and by 1910 New York City was producing 70 percent of the women's clothes and 40 percent of the men's clothes made in the United States. In 1888, when Jewish immigration was beginning to mushroom, German Jews owned more than 95 percent of the clothing shops in the city, and their East European cousins believed they would find familiarity in those shops and the possibility of *shabos* off. Tailoring, moreover, was not unknown to many of the Jewish immigrants, including the socialists and socialists-to-be. Then, of course, as Jews were attracted to concentrations of other Jews, ethnic homogeneity fed itself.[12]

The immigrant socialists did engage in many other fields; in fact, over 30 percent were professionals, concentrated mainly in journalism, and there were some in the tobacco industry and in the painting and building trades. However, the vast majority of socialist proletarians, indeed 87 percent, were garment workers—a higher proportion than in the Jewish proletariat generally.[13] Their experiences in that industry no doubt contributed to their radicalization. Exploitation was rampant. Pauline Newman's pay in the garment factory, for example, was quite low:

$1.50 [per week] no matter how many hours I worked. . . . The employers were bent on getting all they could get out of you and paying as little as possible.[14]

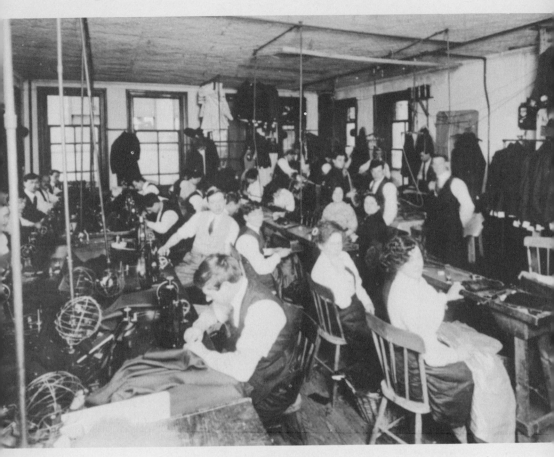

Garment shop, 1912.

Lewis W. Hine/George Eastman House

TABLE 4
Occupation of Socialists

	This study (N = 162)	percent	General Jewish (1890–1914)
Permanent garment workers	92	56.8	
Short-term garment workers	15	9.2	
Total	107	66.0	58–61 percent
Merchants	0	0	15–20 percent
Journalists, writers	36		
Doctors, lawyers, teachers	14	33.3	1–3 percent
Other professionals	5		
Total	55		

As an eleven-year-old and a female, Pauline was significantly more exploited than the general run of garment workers, but contemporary observers and researchers tend to agree that garment industry employees were generally paid less than other industrial workers in the late nineteenth century and early twentieth century.[15] This was due in part to 1) the seasonal character of the enterprise—the slack season could be three to four months annually; 2) the greater percentage of lower-paid women workers—as late as 1913 the dress and waist industry, for example, was more than 70 percent women, and 54 percent of all employed Jewish women were in the garment field; and 3) the highly competitive and relatively small-shop character of the industry, which was further fragmented by contracting, subcontracting, and home work.[16]

All of this made great exploitation possible. An extraordinary proportion of the Jewish socialists who worked in shops paid for their first jobs and worked several weeks for the "learning" and no wages, even though the teaching was done more often by a cousin or a *landsman* than by an employer. Louis Waldman, socialist labor lawyer, through the efforts of his sisters was made an apprentice to a cutter of ladies' garments. "I worked six weeks without pay, but this was considered a privilege."[17] Charles Zimmerman, who paid a foreman ten dollars for a job in a knee-pants shop, "was supposed to work two weeks for nothing, but they squeezed out a third week from me."[18] Garment workers also often paid for needles and electricity to run their machines, were overcharged for mistakes, and were fined for lateness. In the early years, victims rarely complained, mostly because they were fearful of losing their jobs. Pauline Newman believed that the "employers didn't recognize anyone working for them as a human being." And Isidore Schoenholtz, a vice-president of the ILGWU, said it "was really like Egypt. . . . The industry was slavery."[19]

And the workers, even some of the radicals-to-be, at least sometimes, behaved slavishly. Abe Hershkowitz came to the United States in 1907 and got his first job

> as a helper making pockets. I worked 62 hours a week and I earned 6 dollars. . . . A *landsman* of mine that worked there took me into that place.

Fearful of being fined for lateness, and desperate to keep a job at which he earned about ten cents an hour, Abe had his wife wake him every morning.

> I didn't have 65 cents to buy an alarm clock and I had to wake up at 5 a.m. . . . to go to work. . . . One time my wife woke me and says it's very light outside. I went into the front room and saw it was really light. I was afraid I was late. . . . When I got into the street I didn't see a living soul. . . . It was [only] 3 a.m. . . . A snow had fallen, the moon was very bright and . . . had given the impression it was morning. I was afraid to go back to bed for fear I would oversleep. So I walked to the factory and when I arrived there at 4 a.m. there were already people at work! . . . The workers were paid by the week and didn't get anything for overtime. Yet they came early because they were afraid of the Boss . . . to show that they are loyal to the Bosses.[20]

Perhaps the economic exploitation was not even the worst of it. The pace and general conditions of work were dreadful. Morris Raphael Cohen, the American philosopher who early on had flirted with socialism, had had occasion to visit his father's "shop,"

> and I was impressed with the tremendous drive which infiltrated and animated the whole establishment—nothing like the leisurely air of the tailor shop in Minsk where my Uncle Abraham had worked and where the men would sing occasionally.[21]

Morris Sigman, for a while an IWW organizer among the garment workers and at one point in his career indicted for the murder of a strikebreaker, described his first visit to a reefer (children's coat) shop:

The shop was very busy. The workers were at the machines behind barricades of "bundles." Though the shop had several windows, it was dark because of the dust which filled the air. The floor was littered with rags . . . which cluttered the spaces between the machines. Every time a worker crossed the shop, he would wade through the rags and raise clouds of dust. The two foremen walked about with sullen faces and drove the workers on.[22]

Workers like those described above knew that the materials they worked with were flammable. And fires were not rare in the shops in those days when there were few, and seldom enforced, fire regulations. Pauline Newman left the Triangle Waist Company in 1909, two years before the holocaust there took the lives of over 150 young workers, mostly women. Louis Nelson's family was not so lucky:

My older sister worked in that factory. . . . [After the] fire broke out . . . we hadn't heard from her for a few days because they had taken her to a hospital. She was very badly burned.[23]

The tragedy was compounded by the knowledge that there had been little regard for the safety of the employees. Indeed, because most workers were assumed by the bosses to be untrustworthy, many exits from the factory had been closed off.[24]

The risk of injury was even greater than the risk of fire. Mollie Linker, whose father taught her Talmud at the kitchen table and who at fifteen took almost three hundred people on strike, did piece work in Chicago at Hart, Schaffner, and Marx:

It was so hot . . . and you had these big heavy winter coats on your lap and you worked and you sweated. . . . flies too. . . . The machines were roaring. . . . You had to be careful not to stitch your fingers in.[25]

Unfortunately, fingers did get stitched in, and conditions, according to Isidore Schoenholtz, were such that "when a woman had stabbed herself in the hand with a needle, the girl that sat next to her machine was not allowed to pick herself up and help her."[26]

As bad as the factories were, the sweatshops—lofts and tenement rooms converted to garment shops—were in several ways worse. Working for a subcontractor generally meant lower pay. The subcontractor's margin of profit was quite low, for he had to get bundles of cut garments to be sewn from contractors who had picked them up

Sweatshop, 1908.

Lewis W. Hine/National Committee on the Employment of Youth

Carrying work home, ca. 1910.

Lewis W. Hine/National Committee on the Employment of Youth

Homework, garters, ca. 1910.
Lewis W. Hine/George Eastman House

from "inside shops." Exploitation, including exploitation of the self (as the subcontractor usually worked along with his employees), was more intense. There were extremely long hours, often in the subcontractor's home, in terribly close quarters. The sweatshop combined the worst of the factory and the worst of the tenement.

Exploitation and poor working conditions existed outside of the garment field as well, and several of the Jewish immigrant socialists were victims. Louis Waldman, before he became a cutter's apprentice, was employed in a chandelier factory—really a hot, noisy loft—at a press which bent a strip of metal into a ring, from 7 a.m. to 6 p.m. in an unvarying routine. One afternoon there was, however, an unfortunate bit of excitement. The machine tore two fingers off a woman co-worker, and Waldman

tore a strip from [his] shirt and made vain efforts to staunch the flow of blood. . . .

The foreman pushed his way through the crowd [that had gathered] angrily shouting: "Come on! Back to your machines. Get back to your machines!"

Louis Waldman, who had been saturated in Talmudic ethics in the old country, refused to sign a report indicating the accident was the fault of his female co-worker. He was discharged and as he put it, "I had my first lesson in labor relations."[27]

Philip Zausner, whose father took pride in showing up the cantor in the synagogue in Lvov, and who eventually led several important strikes of painters in New York City, had been doing odd jobs in Brooklyn.

Once a week or so, I used to go to New York to meet my new East Side acquaintances, some of whom were painters. From then on I heard a lot more about miserable conditions, low wages and inhumanly long hours.

Nominally, the eight-hour workday was universal. It had been established in the building industry, in all its branches, decades before, but without benefit to the unorganized painters. These slaves in white labored from dawn to dusk during the longest hours of a summer's day. There were no regular hours. It was the invariable habit of the bosses to blow in on the men just at quitting time and it was too bad for the painter who took his five o'clock quitting time seriously. "What are you, a union man?" the boss would yell irritatedly. "Afraid I'm gonna get rich on you?" It made no difference how much work the man had accomplished for the day. The boss always expected him to either "finish up" or "get things started, to make it easier for the next day."

But long hours were not the only curse in the alteration painter's life. His wages, often as little as $1.50 a day, were not enough to keep body and soul together even in the "good old days" of the big schooner of beer with the bowl of soup and bread and cheese and baloney into the bargain for one nickel.

Those that were married and had children lived "for themselves" in room-bedroom, that is, a kitchen and a black airless windowless hole called a bedroom. The single men were boarders with or without board. Their home often consisted of a corner in the kitchen and a broken down couch or sofa, the springs of which made circular imprints on the boarder's body so distinct that one was ashamed to go to a Turkish Bath. There was no sense in complaining for what could one expect for three or four dollars a month?

The East Side immigrant painter, particularly the Columbus product, knew nothing about the poisonous effects of his trade. When as a result of his hurried lunching with lead-covered hands he conveyed the poison into his bowels and got a sudden attack of lead-colic, he didn't know why he was in pain. Maybe it was the extra large piece of watermelon which he ate with bread for supper last night—maybe that had caused his bellyache.[28]

In addition to proletarianization, exploitation, and the oppressive density and working conditions in the shops, Jewish immigrant radicals, along with their co-religionists, sometimes experienced brutality in the streets. The Irish population was never completely displaced by the Jewish influx, and in Haskel Gittelson's neighborhood as in many others, the Irish apparently "did not like the Jews." Gittelson recalled: "I fought with them and I received a broken nose from them, because I didn't take any insults. . . ."[29] Rose Cohen had seen "from the first" that

Jews were treated roughly on every street. . . . and yet as soon as I was safe in the house I scarcely gave the matter a second thought. Perhaps it was because to see a Jew maltreated was nothing new to me. Here where there were so many new and strange things for me to see and understand, this was the familiar thing.[30]

In Chicago, peddlers and their helpers had to set up a "protective association" to defend against attacks by Gentiles. Police appeared to turn a blind eye on the hooligans, and their own frequent bullying of strikers did not inspire confidence in law enforcement. Nor did what happened to Rivele. A radical boarder at Isadore Wisotsky's home, Rivele was a "watcher" at the polls. When he insisted that the Tammany politicos play by the rules, after observing their manipulation of the vote against the socialist candidate, he was severely beaten. Wisotsky later recalled:

I wanted to console Rivele that better times would come. He answered "It is too late. I spit with blood from my lungs." We extinguished the light and went to bed. I did not sleep that night. I saw another America; not the one I imagined.[31]

HOLDING ON

There were some elements of bewilderment and confusion and even degrees of resignation among the Jewish immigrant socialists. Rarely, however, was there complete disintegration. For the general Jewish immigrant population, particularly in the more difficult early years, before a substantial permanent community had become rooted here, dislocation did create some serious problems. Studies by the United Hebrew Charities done between 1910 and 1923, the fiction produced by the immigrants themselves, the memoir literature, and the substance of letters to the Jewish *Daily Forward* asking for advice all indicate that desertion, prostitution, alcoholism, depression, crime, and suicide were more widespread than some students of this subject have suggested.[32]

In adjusting the record, however, we ought not overstate in order to make the point. Jewish life in America, even from the beginning, was infinitely less marked by the pathologies that often scarred other groups. Irving Howe's analysis of the reasons for this is still relevant:

> Even during the first years of the immigration, which were marked by a quantity of social disorder, [the Jewish immigrants] filled out the social spaces between family and state with a web of voluntary organizations, the very kind that, more than half a century earlier, De Tocqueville had seen as distinctly American but which, in this context, were distinctively Jewish. Tacitly but shrewdly, the immigrant Jews improvised a loose pattern for their collective existence.[33]

The shocks of cultural dislocation for the early immigrants could and did in many cases contribute to social pathology or docility, but institutions formal and informal, part transplanted and part indigenous, reduced the jarring impact of "uprooting." And those who "kept faith," or those who were nurturing a new faith in radical politics do not in any significant numbers appear to have come undone. Fannia Cohn, a sensitive, somewhat irritable woman, concerned about making and keeping friends, apparently had to withdraw from the rough and tumble of everyday labor politics for a time. Yossef Bovshover at age twenty-six ended up in an insane asylum where he remained for seventeen years until he died in 1915. Elizabeth Hasanovitz, an educated girl who "had hope of doing something worth while," came to America alone, with a sewing machine, and tried to take her life by slitting her wrists.[34]

The great bulk of the Jewish immigrant socialists, however, show little obvious evidence of pathology—and certainly in no greater proportion than their nonradical counterparts. The socialists in this study were very much a part of the complex sustaining web of Jewish affiliation, social formation, and collective identity.

For the Jews more than for other groups, migration to America was a "family movement." The percentage of children under fourteen was more than twice that in the non-Jewish immigration; and almost half the Jewish immigrants were female, compared to 30.5 percent for the total immigration. The socialists conformed to this pattern. We have already seen how young they were, and of 76 for whom I could find this kind of data, 32 came to the United States with members of their immediate families, 5 with cousins or uncles, and 22 to relatives already here. Those few who traveled alone, and to no one they knew, often received institutional aid. In testimony before the United States Industrial Commission in 1901 it was stated that the Jews seemed to be more proficient than other groups in this respect:

> The United Hebrew Societies . . . have a representative at the Barge Office for the special care and protection of Jewish immigrants. . . . The poor of its faith that come in are visited and receive assistance if necessary. Those that are detained are visited by this agent, and if they need money to telegraph, or clothes, or any material assistance, it is given them.[35]

The vast majority, as we have seen in some of the illustrations, received assistance from "American" relatives in the form of shelter, money, and general guidance. This often extended to initial employment as well. At least 20 of the 170 Jewish immigrant socialists in this study got their first jobs through relatives, another 12 through *landsleit,* and several others with the help of the American Jewish Women's Committee (Ellis Island). A "*shul mensh*" took Hymie Cohen to his first job, and Rose Schneiderman, the fiery capmaker who rose to leadership in the world of radical labor, got help from

> the United Hebrew Charities. In those days poor Jews looked to them for everything. Someone from the organization took me to Hearn's Department Store on Fourteenth Street. . . . I got a job as an errand girl. . . .[36]

The workplace itself constituted a social formation—that is, a place wherein one could feel part of a larger group and sustain a positive sense of status and identity. Marcus Ravage, who "realized everyone [he] knew was a socialist," remembered in a remarkable memoir that

> the number of workers was small, so that everybody knew everybody else. During the lunch-hour we visited, and fell into violent arguments about the labor movement and socialism and literature, and mocked

good-naturedly at the "capitalist" when he ventured to put in a word (as he always did); and each of us, except the girls, took his turn in going for the can of beer. All this tended to preserve the human dignity and self-respect of the worker.[37]

Sometimes discussion would not wait for lunch-hour. When Morris Hillquit worked in a shirt factory (a somewhat less exacting job than others in the garment world), he got involved with a

circle of young Russian intellectuals . . . who spent at least as much time in discussing social and literary topics as in turning out shirts, and the whir of the sewing machines was often accompanied by the loud and hearty sound of revolutionary songs.[38]

Often the entire staff of a shop, including the boss (especially after 1900), were *landsleit*. Dora Solomon, a Socialist Party member and an active picketer and recruiter, worked in such a place. But she did not want to work on Saturday.

The foreman said "If you don't come in you don't have a job." So I came in on the first Saturday. I sat down by my place and as soon as I sat down I started to cry. I reminded myself that back home right now my father is coming in from *shul* and there will be a big family dinner. When the others discovered what I cried about they also started to cry—including the foreman! I had everybody crying—then I got used to it.[39]

Hyman Rogoff, who was in the United States no more than three months before he was out on strike,

came here because it was a dreadful regime in Russia. It was always bad for the Jew. We weren't allowed to live the way we should—there was no freedom. . . . I had a sister and an uncle here . . . and they accepted me very nicely and helped me arrange my life [including getting into a shop where] the atmosphere . . . was . . . brotherly; there was . . . communication. . . . Everyone loved the coming together to meetings. . . . We were very trusting of one another. We reported different things that happened in our families. Some made a better living, others lived worse, but in general it was that togetherness that the workers had that was unforgettable.[40]

The "togetherness" was reinforced by the proximity of the shops to the Jewish quarter. In 1900 nearly 80 percent of the garment industry was located below 14th Street.

These immigrant socialists, then, were people temporarily up-

rooted, dislocated, sometimes anxious but often together and involved in processes of interdependence and mutual solace through
their families and their workplace.

Almost immediately Jewish immigrants began to create synagogues (five hundred on the East Side alone before World War I) and
landsmanshaftn—social, fraternal, health, and mutual aid societies
whose membership was generally based on common residential origin
in a *shtetl* or region. Louis Wirth's description of the *landsmanshaft* in
Chicago is applicable to New York as well as to all the other cities in
which Jews settled.

> . . . ghetto life [is strong in] familial and communal ties, and in attach-
> ment to tradition, form and sentiment.
>
> These ties of family, of village-community, and of Landsmannschaft
> [help] the ghetto family . . . survive crises that would tear an ordinary
> family asunder. . . . [A] stranger who is able to call himself a Landsmann,
> not only loosens the pursestrings of the first individual he meets, but also
> has access to his home. Not only do the Landsleite belong to the same
> synagogue, but as a rule they engage in similar vocations, become part-
> ners in business, live in the same neighborhood, and intermarry within
> their own group. A Landsmannschaft has its own patriarchal leaders, its
> lodges, and mutual aid associations, and its celebrations and festivities. It
> has its burial plot in the cemetery. It keeps the memories of the group
> alive through frequent visits, and maintains a steady liaison with the
> remnants of the Jewish Community in the Old World.[41]

Only about a dozen of the socialists belonged to *landsmanshaftn*,
but the *landsmanshaft* principle carried well beyond the institutions
that bore the label. One important study has shown that in 1917, 1000
of 3600 Jewish organizations in New York were of a *landsmanshaft*
nature; when "these groups affiliated with a national fraternal order
they generally retained their landsmanshaft identity and not even the
socialist Arbeiter Ring significantly altered the pattern."[42] Almost
every immigrant Jewish family was in one way or another involved in
one or more of these organizations. The principle, as we have seen
with the socialists, also carried beyond the *formal* association of fellow
townsmen in the mutual aid that *landsleit* gave as a matter of course.

Despite what some of the more class-conscious socialists contended about the *landsleit* principle, it did not always erode militancy.
At Isadore Wisotsky's house

> All the boarders were *landsleit* which made the evenings lively. Everyone

discussed politics. . . . The major topics . . . concerned the unions, meetings and . . . strikes in the needle trade in which everyone worked.

During the cloakmaker strike of 1910, when Isadore was fourteen, his "house was packed with striking *landsleit*."

They talked and ate black bread and herring and drank beer for which I was sent. I told the saloon keeper that it was for greenhorns, so I obtained a full pitcher for six cents. For others, it was ten. . . .[43]

Saloons and barkeepers, *landsleit* or not, played an important role in maintaining networks in the immigrant community. Abraham Belson, a boot-stitcher in the old country and a reefer-maker here, complained that

it was a very hard existence . . . but a striker could get a piece of herring. You know the old times in the saloons. We came in for a glass of beer for a nickel, and got a free meal. And as the saloon keeper was sympathetic he would often tell the bartender to give us free beer and free lunch. That's how we got along. Most of us were not married; these were all young people. Those that were married really had a tough time. But family helped out and the movement helped a little.[44]

Not all went to the tavern for political discussion. Bernard Fenster insisted, "No politics: we spoke about a glass of beer, or a girl or such things."[45] In fact, the tavern was apparently popular enough with activists and others to worry some. M. Kuntz, the secretary of the New York Cloakmakers, appealed to the union members in December 1890 in an article in the *Freie Arbeiter Shtime* (The Free Voice of Labor, an anarchist newspaper) to stop wasting time in saloons and to devote more to education.

An important "education" was going on in the taverns, however, as well as elsewhere in the neighborhood. In New York City's Eighth Assembly District, the most crowded of the Jewish quarter, there were, in 1899, 140 groceries, 131 butcher shops, 62 candy stores, 36 bakeries, 20 cigar stores, 14 tobacco shops, and 10 delicatessens, among many other small mercantile enterprises. These frequently became social centers. Customers or simply visitors

exchanged news and gossip, made dates and arrangements between families, passed on word of job openings, complained about their children and the difficulties of adjusting to American ways. These small stores often served, too, as communication centers for disseminating information about strike meetings.[46]

Information was disseminated too by four Yiddish daily news-papers, a score of periodicals, theaters, and public forums, all offering the comfort of the familiar tongue. These media supplied a wide range of literature and political tastes, and framed issues in terms of a familiar, understandable, morally intense Jewish heritage.

Melech Epstein, one of the socialists who would contribute to this process by helping to establish the radical *Morgen Freiheit,* stood on the sidewalks of East Broadway two days after his arrival in America in 1913:

> What a sight! Here, on one block and within a few steps of each other, were three Jewish dailies, the biggest of them the *Forward,* a labor Social-ist paper, its modern ten-story building the highest on the lower East Side. The heavy traffic in and out of the building suggested clearly that 175 East Broadway had significance beyond being the home of the *Forward,* a vital institution in itself; it was the address of an entire move-ment. The animated movement of people on East Broadway was novel and stimulating. Yet it had a familiar ring.
>
> I was taken to Sholem's Cafe, half a block from East Broadway. There, under one roof, were more celebrities than one could find in many similar cafes in Eastern Europe combined. The freedom and com-posure of these novelists, poets, journalists, and labor leaders, sitting around little tables engaged in spirited discussions of world affairs, Jew-ish problems, literature, and art, excited my imagination. I wondered wistfully if I would some day find myself among those at the tables.
>
> No one has yet done justice to this famous cafe of the Yiddish literati, the birthplace as well as the grave of many explosive ideas. The second famous institution on the East Side, Cafe Royal, on 2nd Avenue and 12th Street, largely the gathering place of Jewish theater people, has also been rather neglected by the literature on the East Side. Non-Jewish intellectuals and Bohemians from Greenwich Village often showed up there, taking part in the discussions. The waiters at these cafes were characteristic types. They were on familiar terms with their customers, and some of them were in the habit of insisting on what the customer should and should not eat. It was in the old Jewish style.[47]

Despite confusion, even bewilderment, the Jewish immigrant socialists used the word "familiar" in the sense of "family," and the concept of familiarity, in the sense of well-known or recognizable, strikingly often in their memoirs. Jews certainly experienced, and were upset by, dislocation. Despite the fact that most of them made their exodus with relatives, uprooting and emigration and, to some extent, generational conflict broke family bonds. Many Jewish immigrants, however, attempted to restructure their families as soon as they arrived here. The central aim for vast numbers of them was to bring to America relatives still in Europe. Moreover, a new "familiarity" was becoming manifest in *landsmanshaftn, landsleit* cohorts, among fellow workers, in clubs and mutual aid societies, and in social and political movements.

As time passed, much unfamiliarity passed with it, not only for "American" veterans of four or five years but for the *grine* (greenhorns, newcomers) as well. New immigrants, those arriving after 1890, were no longer coming to a wholly alien world. They endured many of the same hardships as the first wave, but in a milieu even more structured, more shielding, more *familiar.* In addition, more who were now coming had spent at least a short time in cities. Of course, Vitebsk was not New York; it was not even Newark. But Jewish immigrants at the turn of the century were better prepared by experience for urban life than the Jews who preceded them, and better prepared than non-Jewish immigrants who came from rural backgrounds.

A complex, loosely structured but relatively self-contained Yiddish-speaking community and sense of family had been recreated and redefined in New York and other Jewish concentrations. And by the middle of the first decade of the twentieth century, the "East Side" spilled over into adjacent streets and had even established smaller versions of itself uptown in Harlem and the Bronx, and across the bridges into Brooklyn.

Out of the rich social formations, institutions, and network of overlapping group affiliations of this Jewish world came socialism, and eventually highly disciplined militant unionism. These did not grow out of a desperate anomie, pursued by dislocated persons searching for surrogate community.[48] Nor did socialism and radical unionism emerge out of poverty and hardship alone. The horrors of the sweatshop, the low wages and high risk of injury and death, the unrelenting routine, and the precariousness of the seasonal jobs, all illustrated above in the lives of the socialists, were real enough. Yet it is not clear that other groups of workers, immigrants or native-born, had it better. Were not sharecroppers, miners, construction workers, blacks, even more oppressed—at least equally oppressed? This is a difficult question because of the number and elusiveness of the variables involved in measuring oppression. But it is even more difficult to make the case that proletarianization, exploitation, and concentration *by themselves* explain the allure of socialism, when significantly oppressed non-Jewish groups, even in the same industries, generally failed to join radical movements in anywhere near the proportions that Jews did.[49]

Zalman Libin, the capmaker and radical Yiddish playwright, said:

> My muse was born in the gloomy sweatshop, it gave its first anguished cry by the side of the Singer machines; it was educated in the dark tombs of the tenements.[50]

No doubt. But without the midwife of Jewish community—its institutions and its values—Jewish socialism may well have been stillborn. One recent study, in fact, went so far as to conclude, ". . . the more solid and self-sustaining the Yiddish-speaking immigrant community, the greater the opportunity the Yiddish-speaking radicals had to vend their wares. . . ."[51]

4

Jewish Radicalism in the New World

When the *Am olam* groups began to emigrate, the news that Jewish "students" were going to America to establish agrarian communes ran ahead of them. Nicholas Aleinikoff, who came over with the first party, gave the following description of their reception.

> In Krakow, we were presented with a copy of *Das Kapital*, by Karl Marx. In Lemberg, orthodox Jews gave us a Torah and a large banner with the inscription *Degel Machne Yisroel* (Banner of the Army of Israel).
>
> Our journey from Brodi to Berlin was one continuous ovation. In every city we were met with a big reception.
>
> It was in the morning of May 30, Decoration Day, 1882, when the train brought us from Philadelphia to New York. We formed lines, took out the Torah, unfurled the banner and, with Russian revolutionary songs on our lips, marched to Castle Garden. Suddenly we heard music. We thought that America had also prepared a welcome for us. . . . Very soon, boys from the streets started running after us, throwing stones.
>
> Then we understood that America had not prepared any reception for us. We put back the Torah, folded up the flag, and found our way to Castle Garden, where we stretched ourselves out on the grass to get some rest.[1]

Rest was necessary. America would not be easy for any of the intelligentsia who came to the United States before 1900 dreaming of revolution. The majority were relatively unfamiliar with the working classes of either Eastern Europe or America, and only a minority had had actual experience in the Russian revolutionary movements. This latter group included Abe Cahan, Michael Zametkin, who was a regular at the Odessa police station by the time he was fourteen, and Louis Miller, already a "seasoned" revolutionary in Vilna at thirteen.

The intelligentsia embraced socialism and anarchism and a variety of combinations of the two. Often with different labels they belonged to the same organizations. Some moved back and forth in their "ideologies," or cooked up an eclectic stew of European ideas strongly flavored with the ethical and moral ingredients of their religious backgrounds. Cahan, after having been associated with the agrarian communalism of *Am Olam,* which he ultimately rejected as "Utopian," described himself as an anarchist *and* a socialist. For a while he preached the "propaganda of the deed" and advised the poor to "march with iron bars and axes on Fifth Avenue and . . . seize the palaces of the rich."[2] But after the Haymarket Affair, 1886–87, when seven radical agitators were sentenced to death for the murder of seven policemen killed by a bomb at an anarchist meeting, Cahan became convinced that the anarchists were "adventurers," and he committed himself more firmly to socialism.

So did many other early emigres, though there was in their socialism as yet no significant dimension of "going to the people," at least not to the masses of Jewish immigrants who were beginning to arrive in the United States. Loosely organized as the "Propaganda Association," many of the radical Jewish intelligentsia did aim to persuade Jewish immigrants not to scab, but they focused their attention on Russia. They continued to speak Russian to immigrants whose language was Yiddish. And they believed that

> though we find ourselves in a relatively free land, we dare not forget that great struggle for freedom which we experienced in our old home. . . .
> [There] our brothers struggle . . . or suffer in Russian prisons, our heroes, our martyrs. . . . From far we cannot do much but we can send money. We must support that holy movement.[3]

The attachment to the Russian movements and to the Russian context itself was very strong. Saul Yanofsky, for example, attended a meeting of the Russian Progressive Union despite the fact that the subject of the evening was of little concern to him. But, the fact that the meetings were held in Russian . . . interested me very much. [They] took me back, in my fantasies, to the old times, when I was still in Russia, when I had such beautiful and wonderful dreams.[4]

Many of these young people had had the opportunity to with-draw from small town parochialism, and to attend gymnasium or university. In the process they learned formal Russian and came to associate that language with liberated sentiment, and Yiddish with *shtetl* backwardness. On the East Side or in Chicago, where in the first two decades of the twentieth century the Jewish immigrants under-went massive proletarianization, this attitude toward the *folksmasn* and its "jargon" came to be self-defeating. Like the radicals who remained in Russia, at least up to the 1890s, these immigrant intellectuals failed to see the possibility of collective proletarian resistance emerging from within the Jewish masses. They often withdrew into a self-contained radical community. Morris Hillquit recalled how "unhappy and forlorn" they were in their workshops,

but at night on the roofs they again lived in a congenial atmosphere. Once more they were students among students. . . . Most . . . evenings were spent in discussion . . . science, philosophy, or politics. . . . Probably the most numerous group was . . . the socialists.[5]

Hillquit's view romantically glosses over some problems. Without a following, and therefore without even the hope of social power, his young men and women friends would grow less congenial. Sectarian-ism would generate intense squabbles and make many of them feel even more isolated, "unhappy and forlorn."

As early as the summer of 1882, however, Abraham Cahan, in the United States only a very short time, challenged the Russian-speakers by pointing out that the Jewish workers did not understand the propaganda that the intellectuals were disseminating. It was pro-posed, almost as a lark, that Cahan lecture in Yiddish; and relatively quickly this so-called folk vernacular became the primary medium of communication. For some time, however, the consensus continued to be that Yiddish was strictly an expedient in the conduct of socialist activity and not a value in itself. Many Yiddish-speaking socialists, especially those who came to the United States before the increasing infusion of Jewish values into revolutionary movements of Russia in the 1890s, insisted that they were not *Jewish* socialists. In revolt against traditional Judaism and very much enamored of progressive universalism, many of these men and women feared being associated with any form of "nationalism." Some, in 1889, even joined the anarchists in their attempt to prove themselves "modern" by holding parades and balls on Yom Kippur, the holiest day of the Jewish year.

The radicals may have been attempting to exploit the antagonism which the masses sometimes felt toward the "pious pillars of the synagogue and community," but certainly by "celebrating" in "their own way" while humming the haunting melody of the Kol Nidre, they also demonstrated "the extent to which traditional faith dominated [even] those who denied it."[6]

In any case, there was grave miscalculation, particularly by the anarchists, who continued to *publicly* ridicule religion long after most of the socialists had stopped. Elias Tcherikower, the leading historian of the early Jewish labor movement in the United States, concluded that:

> Even the Jewish immigrant who had relinquished strict religious observance and had become somewhat of a skeptic was still deeply rooted in religious customs and traditions. The violent attacks of the anarchists against religion were directed against the very core of his being and identification, and this could not be forgiven. There was, indeed, much talk on the East Side about the anarchists, but it only led to the increasing alienation of the masses. Some forty years later one of the organizers of the balls commented that the anarchists, whose major goal was to win the masses over to their side, had done what more than anything else was calculated to drive the masses from them. "The war against God [he said] played a great part in the decrease of anarchist influence in Jewish life."[7]

Socialists had not come to terms with religion either; they simply recognized that to attack it publicly was impolitic. Just as Yiddish was *adopted* as an expedient to communicate with the masses, so the "war against God" was *dropped,* as an expedient to prevent the alienation of those masses. Yet in the United States and almost simultaneously in Russia, this purely utilitarian orientation gradually diminished as the radical intellectuals became immersed in the Yiddish-speaking world and worked more closely with the evolving Jewish proletariat.

Exposure to intolerable working conditions increased the sensitivity of the intellectuals to the needs of the Jewish working class. Cahan and Zametkin, Miller and Libin, Hillquit and many others worked, at least for a time, in the shops. Nearly 40 percent of the nonproletarian socialists in this study had shop experience early in their careers. American conditions, which produced the first solid Jewish proletarian bloc, and forced the radical intellectuals into the factories, generated the belief, in some at least, that there *was* a Jewish working class, and that it could be organized into unions. The belief was reinforced significantly in the United States after 1885 by the increasing flow of Russian Jewish immigrants. This influx pulled the intelligentsia away from potential isolation and pushed them toward mass action. The Jewish Workingmen's Verein, formed in 1885, was the first systematic effort of the Jewish intellectuals to organize the proletariat, and was the first union to carry the label "Jewish."

DIFFICULTIES OF SUSTAINING A MOVEMENT

Keeping the Jewish proletariat firmly organized, however, proved to be a difficult task well into the first decade of the twentieth century. Some of this had to do with the intellectuals, some of it with the masses, and all of it was connected to economic conditions and general sociohistorical realities. The intelligentsia had proceeded, after all, "from Messianic politics . . . to trade union activities [for] which nothing in their radical background had truly prepared them. . . ."[8] Often, then, there was more attention to abstract labor and radical principles, and less to specific conditions of individual trades. This gave and would continue to give Jewish unions a special dimension of idealism, distinguishing them, as one union executive put it, from the "purely business proposition" of the American Federation of Labor. But early on there was a failure to keep membership together once strikes ended, or during the slack season.[9]

John Commons, the important American labor historian and economist writing at the turn of the century, added another view, which for the most part, proved to be absurdly hasty:

> The Jew occupies a unique position in the clothing trade. His physical strength does not fit him for manual labor. His instincts lead him to speculation and trade. His individualism unsuits him for the life of a wage-earner, and especially for the discipline of a labor organization. . . .
> With the continual influx of immigrants unaccustomed to unionism, with the employment of women and children, and with the prevalence of home work, the problem of [union] organization is indeed serious. . . . The problem has been the *nature of the Jew himself.* The Jew's conception of a labor organization is that of a tradesman rather than that of a workman. In the clothing manufacture, whenever any real abuse arises

among the Jewish workmen, they all come together and form a giant union and at once engage in a strike. They bring in 95 per cent of the trade. They are energetic and determined. They demand the entire and complete elimination of the abuse. The demand is almost always unanimous, and is made with enthusiasm and bitterness. They stay out a long time, even under the greatest of suffering. During a strike large numbers of them are to be found with almost nothing to live upon and their families suffering, still insisting, on the streets and in their halls, that their great cause must be won.

But once the strike is settled, either in favor of or against the cause, they are contented, and that usually ends the union, since they do not see any practical use for a union when there is no cause to fight for.[10]

Commons proved to be less than a seer, but he did identify some facts about Jews and early labor organization. There were more than twenty unions of Jewish workers organized in the 1880s, and by 1890 many came together in a new federation, the United Hebrew Trades, which had been established in 1888 in New York by the socialists.[11] But it *was* difficult to maintain union solidarity in the slack season or after a strike.

This had less to do with the Jew's "instincts" for trade, however, and more to do with particular socioeconomic conditions. It is certainly true that the Jews, denied purchase of land and proscribed from participating in a variety of occupations and fields, had worked in trades for generations and came to believe that a "*melokhe iz a malkhes*" (a trade is a kingdom). The ambitions, therefore, of Jewish immigrant workers often lay elsewhere than in the shop. Bernard Weinstein, who had been converted to socialism by Abe Cahan while the two of them worked in the shop, recognized this:

Many of the workers in those days wanted to become bosses. It was not very difficult. All one needed was a somewhat larger flat, and one could become a contractor. . . . Contractors, working as hard as their employees, would often argue that their interests were the same as those of the workers, for the real exploiter was the rich manufacturer.[12]

Though the contractor often fared no better than his employees, the immigrant's ambition to become an independent entrepreneur was encouraged by the fact that as early as the 1890s the industry began to pass from the hands of German-Jewish to Russian-Jewish manufacturers. The immigrant economist-statistician Isaac Rubinow wrote in 1905, "Almost every newly arrived Russian-Jewish laborer comes into contact with a Russian-Jewish employer, almost every Russian-Jewish tenement dweller must pay his exorbitant rent to a Russian-Jewish landlord."[13]

Israel Barsky, who came with the Odessa group of *Am olam,* complained that few workers were "class conscious"; each "wants to become a capitalist." Some of the workers would not have put it quite that way. They wanted to escape the torments of the shops; some thought they could do this individually. Labor activist Rose Cohen's father's dream was "some day to lay down his needle and thread and perhaps open a little candy store or a soda water stand."[14] And socialist Louis Glass's father, attempting to convince his son to be a peddler, said: "Louie, if you will take a job in a shop, you will never be able to crawl out of it. You will be buried in that shop."[15] Louis Glass did not take his father's advice; other sons did.

The horrendously oppressive conditions of the sweat-shop industry impelled workers to think about escaping. And the fluid, fragmented structure of the system contributed to an outflow of experienced workers into more tolerable if not more profitable forms of employment, and to a relatively steady influx of new immigrants. This did not lend itself to the maintenance of unions with stable membership. Also, Jews, as we have seen, belonged to other organizations of mutual aid and, quite simply, "union dues" were often resented as an additional burden. Unions were also not exactly encouraged by bosses and managers. A variety of techniques, sometimes repressive, sometimes merely manipulative, were used by employers to prevent unionization. Marsha Farbman, who fled the Kishinev pogrom in 1903, went to work in a New York factory making false braids:

> I spoke soon to all the girls. I said, "We can't work for such low wages. . . ." My Yiddish was not so good, but I spoke Russian. A few girls understood. . . . All the others spoke English and Yiddish, so we were able to get together to plan a strike. . . .
> The forelady spotted right away that I was a socialist. . . . She met with us and raised the wages to avert the strike and unionization. We got the few cents more on the braids and we went back to work. But the union was not organized.[16]

Despite all of this, and despite the depression which began in 1893, by the early 1890s, the immigrant socialists had demonstrated the possibility of organizing a mass following in New York. Twenty-seven unions and socialist organizations from New York, with a membership close to 14,000, were represented at a United Hebrew Trades Conference in 1890; and that organization was able to send Louis Miller as its delegate to the founding congress of the Second Socialist International in Paris, and Abe Cahan to the Second Congress in Brussels in 1891.[17] As late as 1906 the majority of Jewish workers remained unorganized—only 2,500 of 42,500 cloakmakers, for example, were unionized. But in fits and starts the combination of unionism and polemical journalism did provide a real connection between the socialists and the masses, even in these early years.

For a long time, socialism, like unionism, could not sustain a compact movement among immigrant workers, even for those who were already leaning leftward. Socialism was, however, a vigorous and vital theme in Jewish immigrant life almost from the beginning. The Jewish Workingmen's Verein in 1886 formally affiliated with the Socialist Labor Party (with its mostly German-American membership) and joined a coalition of liberals and socialists to support the New York mayoral candidacy of Henry George. Thousands of Jewish workers made their first entry into American political life this way, and they did it in association with the socialists. The very next year two "Jewish" foreign-language federations were formed in the Socialist Labor Party, section 8 for Yiddish-speakers and section 17 for the Russians. Fourteen more Jewish sections were added in the 1890s, and as early as 1889 the party press celebrated the rapid development of socialist influence among Jewish workers.[18]

Later, in 1901, Morris Hillquit would, along with Eugene V. Debs, become a "founding father" of the Socialist Party of America, and Jews would support the candidates of that party in increasing and disproportionate numbers.[19] The Workmen's Circle, or Arbeiter Ring, a fraternal society particularly important to the financing and institutionalization of Jewish socialism, increased its membership in New York from 5,000 to 10,000 between 1905 and 1908. In that latter year, Jews, approximately 39 percent of the Socialist Party membership in Manhattan and the Bronx, organized enormous campaign meetings on the East Side for Eugene Victor Debs, the socialist candidate for President.[20] This is not as impressive as what Jewish votes would do a little later for the Socialist Party but it was possible for an

American journalist to believe in 1909 that "most of the Jews of the East Side though not all acknowledged socialists are strongly inclined toward socialism."[21]

When John Commons and others declared the Jews incapable of sustained collective action, it was less than a decade away from the maturation of Jewish socialism as a mass movement and from an enormous, durable growth of union membership in the Jewish trades. As late as 1910, the Dillingham Commission reported that southern and eastern Europeans were "unstable" in their industrial relations and tended to "demoralize" labor organizations. Commons and even those later observers, perhaps partially blinded by ethnic prejudice, were way off the mark.[22] Isidore Schoenholtz, who came to America at the age of sixteen in 1906, just before the decade of mass labor struggles and victory in the American Jewish world, put it well:

> Some did not believe that . . . [Jewish workers] could be organized. . . . Time showed just the opposite. These were false prophets.[23]

MOBILIZATION

On November 22, 1909, 20,000 shirtwaist makers, mostly Jewish girls and women between the ages of sixteen and twenty-five, went on strike. Only the tiniest minority of them were members of the ILGWU. In the year following this general "uprising," Local 25 alone counted over 10,000 members. The largest strike by women in the United States to that time, the shirtwaist makers' rebellion stimulated subsequent struggles and victories that led to the formation of stable, enduring, powerful socialist unions.

Conditions in the shirtwaist factories were somewhat better than in other parts of the garment industry. The shops tended to be newer and cleaner. The women, however, were victimized by sex discrimination as well as by class exploitation. Male workers did "inside contracting" by employing "girl helpers" as "learners" at three or four dollars a week.[24] Often kept "learners" long after there was little left to learn, these women formed over 20 percent of the work force. And all the female workers worked long hours, and were required to pay for their lockers and even the chairs on which they sat.

The following tune, sung by the women, was often heard even over the clatter of the machines in the shop:

As soon as I go to bed
Then I must rise once more,
To work I go
with bones weary and sore.

To God will I weep
With a loud cry!
Why was I born
A seamstress, why?

I'm forever hungry,
with nothing to eat.
Demands for more money
Bring only defeat.[25]

In 1909 the Triangle Waist Company, one of the largest manufacturers, had fired a number of workers suspected of unionizing activities. Local 25 of ILGWU called a strike against the firm in September. The Leiserson shop also went out. Weariness and demoralization set in among the strikers after a month of hunger, beatings by hired thugs, and bullying by police. At a meeting of thousands of workers at Cooper Union on November 22, Local 25 proposed a general strike. A debate ensued which dragged on for about two hours.

One of the strikers from Leiserson's, "a wisp of a girl," who in eleven weeks of picket-line scuffles was arrested seventeen times and had six ribs broken, asked for the floor.[26] The daughter of an Orthodox Jewish scholar, Clara Lemlich addressed the audience in Yiddish:

I am a working girl; one of those who suffers from, and is on strike against the intolerable conditions portrayed here. I am tired of listening to those who speak in general terms. I am impatient. I move a general strike—now!

The enthusiasm of the crowd was tumultuous. The chairman, Benjamin Feigenbaum, who would later write a book on the labor laws of the Talmud, grabbed the young woman's arm, raised it, and called out in Yiddish, "Do you mean faith? Will you take the old Hebrew oath?" With a sea of right arms raised, the crowd recited, "If I turn traitor to the cause I now pledge, may this hand wither from the arm I now raise." The general strike was on.[27]

Clara Lemlich was no stranger to radicalism and strikes. From the time she was ten in the Ukraine, she had been reading Turgenev, Gorky, and revolutionary literature. She fled, like Marsha Farbman and several others in this study, the Kishinev pogrom of 1903, and spent some time in England. Here, before coming to America in 1904, she apparently attended several anarchist meetings. Within a week in the United States, fifteen-year-old Clara Lemlich was at work in New York's shirtwaist industry. She was a skilled and relatively well-paid draper, saving money for medical school, when in 1906, as she put it, "some of us girls who were more class-conscious . . . organized the 1st local."[28] Lemlich was one of seven young women and six men who founded Local 25 of the ILGWU. She participated thereafter in a number of strikes that led up to the major conflict of 1909, by which time she had become well known in activist trade unionist and Socialist Party circles.

Clara Lemlich was part of a growing and important cadre. In many shops there were women like her who influenced significant numbers of others. They did this through persistent discussion, by invoking a sense of sisterhood, and by example. The influence of their example was not limited to women. Surely the men's Great Cloakmakers' Revolt in 1910 was at least partly a result of the new sense of combativeness and commitment demonstrated by the women. In July 1910, after careful preparation, approximately 65,000 workers, mostly male, left their workbenches in the cloak and suit trade, and walked the picket lines.[29]

Abraham Rosenberg, who had come to America in the 1880s, and moved from sweatshop tailor, up the ranks of the union hierarchy, to become president of the ILGWU (1910–1914), described the walkout:

> By half-past two, all the streets in New York from Thirty-eighth Street down and from the East River towards the west, were parked with thousands of workers. In many streets cars and wagons had to come to a halt because of the crowds. Many of our most devoted members cried for joy, at the idea that their long years of labor had at last been crowned with success. I thought to myself such a scene must have taken place when the Jews were led out of Egypt.[30]

The great mass struggles and victories, starting in 1909 and lasting at least five years, began in part because of the economic recovery following the depression of 1907–1908, in part because the post-1905 immigrants with experience of "going to the people" began to assume leadership in the unions, and in part because hopes for the revolution in massively repressed Russia waned, moving more radicals to perceive America as "home." None of this should slight, however, the accumulation of grievances over more than a decade, or the groundwork laid by the socialist politicians, attorneys, and journalists—the Cahans, Hillquits, Feigenbaums, and Londons—who persisted in attempts at recruitment, organization, and dissemination of propaganda.

Perhaps no single development galvanized Jewish immigrants for militant unionism and socialism more than the Triangle Shirtwaist fire of 1911. Almost no one of the dozens of the Jewish socialists in this study who were in the United States at the time of the event fails to mention that the tragedy, which killed more than 140 women, made the deepest impression on them. Indeed, the news reached into the *shtetlekh* of Lithuania and deep into the Ukraine where relatives, friends, and neighbors knew one or more victims. Rose Pesotta's sister had worked in the Triangle Factory to 1910 and wrote to her family in Derazhnya in 1911 that two young girls from that provincial town had perished on the sidewalks of New York. The Yiddish press repeated the harrowing details of locked doors, inadequate fire escapes, burning bodies. Louis Waldman, the socialist labor lawyer, was an eyewitness. On his way home from Cooper Union, where he was studying, Louis

> looked up at the [ten-story] burning building, saw girl after girl appear at the reddened windows, pause for a terrified moment, and then leap to the pavement below, to land as mangled, bloody pulp. . . .
> We all felt that the workers who had died in the plant of the Triangle Waist Company were not so much the victims of a holocaust of flame as they were the victims of stupid greed and criminal exploitation.[31]

Waldman went to hear Morris Hillquit's address in the aftermath of the fire.

> The word "Socialism" kept recurring throughout Hillquit's speech at the Triangle fire memorial meeting. Of course, I had heard the word before and I had often listened to lesser socialist speakers at various street corners on the East Side. But Hillquit's personality and his plea for the victims of the fire aroused my enthusiasm and sent me off on a pursuit of knowledge . . .[32]

Clothing Workers' strike
Brown Brothers

Socialists elected in New York City, 1917. *Upper row, left to right:* Beckerman, Wolff, Braunstein, Lee, *Baruch Charney Vladeck, Adolph Held,* and Calman. *Lower row, left to right:* Claessens, Feigenbaum, Rosenberg, *Louis Waldman,* Whitehorn, *Jacob Panken, Abraham Shiplacoff, William Karlin,* Orr, Garfinkle, Gitlow, and Weil.

From the Archives of YIVO Institute for Jewish Research

and ultimately to a lifetime of association with labor and socialist politics.

Even those who had been radicalized in the old country credit the Triangle fire with reinforcing their activist commitments. Revolutionary refugee David Dubinsky, who would go on to help build the ILGWU into one of the nation's most powerful unions, recalled:

> Two weeks after I started working [early in 1911], I went to East Broadway to join the Socialist Party. But I was just a listener at its rallies until the horrible fire in the Triangle Shirtwaist Company.[33]

And Fannia Cohn, who in "Russia . . . imbibed and participated in the revolutionary spirit," said, "it was the triangle fire that decided my life's course."[34]

At protest meetings after a stirring mass funeral for the victims of the fire, organizers and activists, like Rose Schneiderman, hammered home the message:

> I know from . . . experience it is up to the working people to save themselves. The only way they can . . . is by a strong working-class movement.[35]

The period from 1909 to 1914 was one of increased activity among working-class people throughout America, but the militancy of Jewish workers was particularly intense. In many major cities, tens of thousands of Jewish workers struck for higher wages, better conditions, and union recognition. In New York, the United Hebrew Trades experienced a phenomenal growth. There were 61 constituent unions, with 65,000 members in 1910. By 1914 there were 104 unions in the federation, with 250,000 members. The American labor movement was growing, but the Jewish trade unions grew faster. The garment union's 68 percent increase between 1910 and 1913 was a rate of growth greater than any other labor union in the country.[36]

In the same period Jewish socialists deepened their roots in the East Side. Many not only had actively participated in the organization of the unions, but they recruited an increasing Party membership and helped garner votes for Socialist candidates. Between 1910 and 1914, Jewish assembly districts in New York delivered 10 to 15 percent of their votes to Socialist office seekers, and after 1914 the figure climbed past 35 percent. Jewish votes in 1917 were responsible for the victories of ten Socialist state assemblymen, seven Socialist aldermen, and a Socialist municipal judge.[37]

THE AMERICAN CONTEXT

Socialism was also on the upsurge in America itself and reached a peak of influence between 1912 and 1916. Jewish socialists felt that they were part of a movement that in the not too distant future could emerge victorious. This was not a function of confusion, fevered imagination, or a desperately designed fantasy to resolve the problems of marginality. It was an understandable miscalculation based on rather firm realities.

As early as March 1900, the Socialist Party could claim the support of 226 branches in thirty-two states, and in November of that year there were Socialist candidates on the ballot in thirty of those states. Party membership in the United States went from 15,975 in 1903 to 118,045 in 1912, more than a 700 percent increase.

In 1910 the Party elected its first congressman, the Wisconsin German-American Victor Berger. It also won control in twelve cities and towns and had elected nineteen members to various state legislatures.[38] In 1911 there were seventy-four Socialist mayors and other major municipal officers and by 1916, twenty-nine Socialist state legislators in eighteen states. This was not simply the foreign-born's "tempest in a teapot." Socialists received significant proportions of the vote in several "American" towns. In Hagerstown, Maryland, in 1917, where only 1.5 percent of the population was foreign-born, 15 percent voted Socialist. In Reading, Pennsylvania, a constituency with 9 percent foreign-born gave a third of its vote to Socialist candidates. And 44 percent of the voters in Hamilton, Ohio, where only 6.7 percent were foreign-born, supported the Socialist Party.[39]

Because of repression in the south and west, and the continuing influx of immigrants, especially Jews, the vast majority of whom entered the working class, the foreign-born would provide a growing proportion of Socialist Party membership. Over 50 percent of Socialist Party members in 1919 belonged to the various foreign language branches. But in 1912, when Party membership was at a high point, only 13 percent were in the language federations.[40] And it was not unusual either for the top leadership of local socialist groups to be native-born, even when a majority of the rank and file were foreign-born. The native-born, moreover, often leaned more to the left. Wisconsin, Pennsylvania, and New York, all with heavy concentrations of immigrants, tended to produce "right-wing" socialism, whereas Ohio, Indiana, and Michigan, with many fewer immigrants, were states identified with the "left wing."[41] The most militant of revolutionists within the Party were generally American—William Haywood, Jack London, Frank Bohn, for example. The leading "conservatives," Morris Hillquit, Victor Berger, and John Spargo, were all immigrants.[42]

This is not an attempt to substitute a myth of native radicalism for the older myth of immigrant radicalism. After all, native-born Americans were not a monolithic group, and new immigrants were strikingly heterogeneous. Neither group comprised an ideologically homogeneous entity. But Jewish immigrant socialists could receive supportive, encouraging signals from at least some members of the host American culture. Adolph Held sensed this. "The Americans that came to us," he said, "were always more radical than we were."[43]

There were other, less supportive signals, too, from a culture that was basically antiradical. The death sentence for the Haymarket anarchists in 1886–87 and the popular association of anarchism with foreigners no doubt had a "chilling effect" on many who contemplated espousing "dangerous" views. There was a growing anti-immigrant sentiment at the turn of the century, reflected in a series of "restriction" laws, and by 1903 Congress passed a bill that allowed for the deportation of immigrants deemed subversive. Furthermore, repression of worker militancy in factory and mill towns like Homestead, Pennsylvania, and Lawrence, Massachusetts, was incessant from the 1880s through to the second decade of the twentieth century.[44]

In some of the metropolitan areas, however, particularly New York and Chicago, where the Jewish working population was significant, there were also innovation and reform. Indeed, in the years 1906 to 1915, a period known as the Golden Age of Yiddish Socialism, American urban Progressivism was reaching high tide. Native-born Protestant Progressives, mainly interested in restoring security, morality, and prosperity to American life, pointed to the abuses of modern urbanism and capitalism, and they were often vividly descriptive. Many supported tenement and child labor reform and the regulation of working conditions in factories.[45]

The Progressives, unlike the socialists, generally opposed a class analysis of society. Many were interested in controlling what they saw as the pathologies of immigrant life and often they ministered to the lower classes in condescending fashion. Organized labor, including the ILGWU, recognized and resisted the paternalism inherent in Progressivism and was considerably wary of efforts by social Progressives to eliminate workers' "problems" through extensive legislation. But some Progressives went beyond *noblesse oblige* and beyond the framework of legislative reform. Gertrude Barnum, the daughter of a prominent Chicago Democratic family, moved from genteel middle-class reformism to the rough and tumble existence of an organizer for the ILGWU. She represented the less numerous but more militant reformers who actively entered the trade union area.[46]

John Dewey, the Progressive philosopher-educator, and Charles Beard, the activist-Progressive historian, had aims that were much broader than philanthropy or legislative reform. They advocated the right of workers to organize in unions to achieve their own formulated goals.[47] This was true, too, for the middle-class membership of the New York Women's Trade Union League, which contributed to strike funds. One of the League's more socially prominent and influential members, Mary Dreier, was arrested for participating in the shirtwaist strike of 1909, and evoked widespread publicity and sympathy for the strikers. Jane Addams, founder of the Hull House Settlement in Chicago, was also an advocate of worker organization. Addams and her cohort preferred to eliminate unemployment and gross inequality rather than to give charity. Abraham Cahan spoke kindly of settlement work and settlement people, and even anarchist Emma Goldman had positive things to say about Lillian Wald, the nurse who founded the Henry Street Settlement and came to be known and adored throughout the lower East Side. All of this supports the conclusion of a recent study that there were clear, supportive links between Progressivism, progressive education, settlement houses, and the Jewish radical labor movement.[48]

REBELLION, ADAPTATION, AND "OLD WORLD" STANDARDS

The Jewish immigrant socialists were involved in political and economic movements of *rebellion* against dominant social conditions in the New World. At the same time, however, during the Progressive

Era, when so much activity by native-born American Protestants was invested with religious and moral significance, these Jewish movements could, by using traditional *Old World* standards, particularly religious values, serve as ways of *adapting* to currents of that new world.

Even in the early period of union organization before Progressivism, the interests of workers and Old World Jewish traditions, especially in the secular atmosphere of America, seemed not merely compatible but almost inseparable. As early as 1873, a "respectable, Orthodox" writer, in announcing the formation of a society to help poor Jewish workers find inexpensive, healthy dwellings, used the language of the prophets in criticizing "blood sucking, exploiting landlords."[49] The first socialist brochure in Yiddish, published in the 1890s and entitled *Di geule* ("Redemption"), was translated by the author as "The Remedy." It closed with Isaiah's message:

> Then there will be no rich and no poor. No poverty . . . only equal, blessed and contented folk.[50]

In the mid-1890s, Bernard Weinstein, as a representative of the United Hebrew Trades, was invited to a cleaners local to help settle the arguments that persistently broke out at their rather lively meetings:

> When we arrived, we saw everyone sitting around a table facing the chairman. All the members wore *yarmulkes* [skullcaps] except a few younger members with hats. Most were dressed in long smocks resembling caftans. Every Jew had a glass of beer in hand, and before him slices of herring and chunks of dark bread.
>
> The hall was half dark from the smoke of pipes and one could have been deafened by the clattering of glasses. A few Jews waited on the tables and continually served full mugs of beer, with everyone shouting "l'chaim!"
>
> The chairman stood on a platform in the middle of the room . . . and when he noticed our committee—we hadn't known where to sit among the hundred or so members—he summoned us with three resounding raps of his hammer, to the head of the table. Everyone rose and as the chairman recited our "credentials" we were heartily toasted with the clinking of glasses. . . .
>
> The tumult was practically incessant. They began a Simkhat Torah melody. Fresh glasses continued to come to the tables from a barrel nearby. . . . Finally I asked my bearded, bespectacled neighbor, "What's the occasion?"

"How should I know," he answered. "Every meeting is like this. . . .
That's how we are—sometimes we kiss each other from happiness, sometimes we fight."

At the end of our speeches, they all cried out the words, "Long live
the union!" and the Orthodox Jews applauded and bumped glasses.
Meanwhile a few started to move aside the tables and began dancing to a
Hasidic tune. . . .

In our report to the UHT, we called this group the Simkhat Torah
Union.[51]

In the same period, the *shames* (caretaker) of a small synagogue
on Norfolk Street, also an active member of a pressers local composed
of *landsleit* from Galicia, invited Bernard Weinstein to a meeting at his
shul. Here it was hoped that Weinstein, as a representative of the
United Hebrew Trades, could help with the work of making converts
for the union. Weinstein listened to the president of the local, who
had a long beard and *peyes* (side curls): " 'The first walking delegate
among the Jews was Moses and the Sanhedrin was the first executive
board.' " The president's speech went on "overflowing with wisdom
from the Torah."

His examples were wonderful and simple and went straight to the hearts
of his listeners. All of his comparisons led to the union. The people in
the skull caps became warmed up and showed their enthusiasm by clap-
ping and stamping their feet.[52]

Social strain, hardship, and discontent of Jewish workers had to
be made meaningful to potential recruits for collective economic and
political action. Union organizers, intellectuals, journalists, and political activists constantly wove biblical references and Talmudic aphor-
isms into their appeals.

Abe Cahan was one of the most successful at this technique. In
the first issue of *Neie Tseit* (New Times) in 1886, he used the theme of
Shevuot (the festival of weeks, associated with the receiving of the law)
to illustrate socialist principles, and he remained interested throughout most of his career in using Jewish tradition and folk-religious
forms in this way. He understood and applauded the fact that the
rigid mores of Jewish Orthodoxy had already undergone a loosening
in Eastern Europe and that in America, the *tref medine* (unkosher
land), there was further erosion. But Cahan knew how thoroughly
Jewish values and traditions were embedded in the Jewish imagina-

tion, even in that of a professed atheist like himself. Ethnic attachments, in the richest sense of that term, operated even upon those
who thought they had discarded them as "backward," and certainly
were meaningful to the average Jewish worker who read Cahan's
journalism.

In 1890 in the *Arbeiter Tseitung* (worker's newspaper) Abe Cahan
began a weekly column known as the *Sedre,* the portion of the
Pentateuch read each week in Sabbath services. He would begin with a
formal element in the liturgy, but soon took off into a discussion of
socialist matters.[53] A workman leaving his job on *erev shabos* (the eve of
the Sabbath) and looking forward to a day of rest left us this anonymous response to Cahan's writing:

> One Friday, going home from work and considering what paper to buy, I
> noticed a new Yiddish paper with the name *Arbeiter Tseitung.* I bought it
> and began to read it, and remarkably, this was the thing I wanted. It was
> [a] Yiddish, socialist newspaper. Although till then I never heard about
> socialism and its doctrine, still I understood it without any interpreta-
> tion. I liked it because its ideas were hidden in my heart and in my soul
> long ago; only I could not express them clearly. . . . That paper
> preached, "Happiness for everyone" [and] "new changes for the better-
> ment of the people. . . ." This I could sign with both hands![54]

Cahan's pieces proved so popular that even the anarchists tried to
imitate them in the *Freie Arbeiter Shtime* (Free Voice of Labor) with a
column called *Haftorah*—the segment from the prophets used to
elucidate the weekly portion.

Yiddish newspapers, by providing a literate audience, attracted
some of those intellectuals previously alienated from the Yiddish language—even from the Jewish people. Many, including David Edelstadt, the labor poet and one-time buttonhole maker, and Leon
Kobrin, dramatist and erstwhile cigarmaker who had known little or
no Yiddish, studied to become "Yiddish writers." Soon some of them
were added to that small but growing group of radical Jewish intellectuals who regarded the preservation and revitalization of the people's
language, culture, and tradition as essential to group identity *and*
revolutionary fervor. Edelstadt might, in 1890, a few days before Yom
Kippur, attack the Orthodox as defenders of obscurantism with a
poem in the *Freie Arbeiter Shtime,* but in the same poem he would use
traditional vocabulary and concepts:

Each era has its own Torah
Ours is one of freedom and justice.
. . . .
We also have new prophets—
Borne, Lassalle, Karl Marx;
They will deliver us from exile.[55]

The people saw their modern grievances aired in their own
tongue and framed in terms of a morally intense Judaic tradition, and
were more readily organized. Kobrin believed that the Jews

found a new festivity . . . in the anarchist and socialist ideals, and in the
raptures of a battle . . . and that this type of Jewish worker was to be the
chief material of the entire labor movement.[56]

Much sociological and anthropological work suggests that mobili-
zation of wider support for new interests at least partly depends on
whether those interests can be reconciled or legitimized by communal
values of the traditional culture. The radical acting as a leader in
organizing the subordinate group "often helps to revive the traditional culture and to modernize it."[57] Even Benjamin Feigenbaum,
who had rebelled against hasidic parents, fiercely attacked the supernatural, and wished for speedy assimilation of the Jews, would frequently make some socialist concept clear and more acceptable by
relating it to Jewish ethical precept. This was no mere expedient on
Feigenbaum's part. He himself maintained a deep moral commitment
organically connected to Jewish commandment.

Despite its cosmopolitanism and class-war vocabulary, the
"liberated" upper leadership of the Jewish radicals and labor militants
did not secede from the ethnic community. And the great majority of
Jewish socialists in this study, at whatever level of participation in the
movements, remained deeply rooted in Jewish tradition. At the same
time that they drew upon Old World values, they voted for socialist
candidates, were members of the Party, belonged to socialist unions
and helped recruit for them, read the radical Yiddish press, and
looked forward to the new world they believed they were helping
bring about.

In 1904 *Di Tsukunft* (The Future) carried an editorial which read
in part: "It often occurs that we encounter people who are socialisti-
cally inclined and at the same time you see them attending slichos
[pre-High Holy Day prayers], fasting on Yom Kippur, etc."[58] Indeed,

on the socialist East Side the congregations could not accommodate those who wanted to attend High Holy Day services. As late as 1917, 343 "temporary synagogues" were created for Rosh Hashonah and Yom Kippur with a seating capacity of close to 164,000.[59]

Harry Golden's father was a socialist but he continued to go to *shul* quite consistently. When Harry chided him about this seeming contradiction, the elder Golden answered, "'These people are my brethren, they are the people among whom I was raised and I love them. Dudja Silverberg goes to *shul* to speak with God, I go to *shul* to speak with Dudja.'"[60]

Many of those who no longer went to synagogue even on the holiest days were also affected by a persistence of religious values. Joseph Rapoport, the 1920s radical knit-goods industry organizer, peppered his conversation with biblical references, parables, and stories from Jewish folk culture. These he combined with allusions to Russian literature and Marx.[61] A great many others spoke of "fulfilling a holy duty," or of "being filled with the spirit of [a] sacred struggle. . . ,"[62] mirroring images in the *Shulken aruk* (the standard code of Jewish law) and the Prophets. Perhaps no one of these did this as consciously as Elizabeth Hasanovitz:

> My soul is blazing with indignation. . . . Let us then unite our voices in a mighty chorus. Let us blow . . . our trumpets far and wide—shake up the world, smash in dust the sinful structures of present society, cleanse the earth of evil and wake the people, wake them to consciousness, appeal and sing for the glory of brotherhood, of equality and love.
> . . . it was so clear—so sure to come! . . . Ours is the struggle for that wonderful dawn—and to us shall belong its glory.[63]

The struggle to create new identities out of traditional materials in a modern context was not always conscious, nor simple. But it was made a good deal easier between 1905 and 1910, when large numbers of Bundists reached New York after the collapse of the 1905 Revolution in Russia. The Bundists hailed the breakup of religious hegemony, in America as well as in Europe, but strongly resisted further assimilation. They desired to remain Jews—atheists, socialists, but Jews. They brought with them to America sophisticated ideological defenses for this position, and they articulated them with spirit and dedication. They were effective. By 1906 there were three thousand members in Bund branches in America, more even than the enrollment in the Jewish branches of the Socialist Party.[64] The news-

Sidney Hillman soon after he arrived in the United States in 1907.
From the Archives of YIVO Institute for Jewish Research

papers, the activists, the socialists, and even more so the Bundists furnished the language and the terms of the discourse that kept immigrant workers, who were on their way to becoming Americans, "balanced between an ancient past come to life, and a nearer past falling to pieces."[65] They were effective because they were tapping into and refurbishing something that was still alive in Jewish workers—Jewish culture. Seventy-eight percent of the immigrant socialists in this study had had significant exposure to Jewish tradition and almost 35 percent of them had been deeply immersed in that tradition as sons and daughters of rabbis, cantors, teachers of Talmud, or as students in advanced Jewish studies themselves (see table 1).

Sidney Hillman, one of those students and eventually the president of the Amalgamated Clothing Workers Association (ACWA), in 1916, after nine years in this country, married Bessie Abramowitz, who was to become vice-president of the same union. Bessie Abramowitz did not have a strong religious background and had no parents in America. She married Sidney Hillman in a synagogue. Though Sidney had been training in the old country to be a rabbi, he had "put this behind him" over a decade since. He too had no parents here. Yet *something* drove them to that synagogue. Immediately following the religious ceremony, the couple went straight to march at the head of the unions' annual May Day parade!

Lucy Lang, the daughter of Orthodox parents and an anarchist for a time, who knew Emma Goldman and Jack London, had Jewish "friends in conscious revolt against religion. [They] deliberately flouted Orthodox Jewish customs in a way that shocked and embarrassed" her. Yet she was "irresistibly drawn to [these] radical friends." Years later when Lucy Lang's faith in a "beautiful tomorrow" remained undiminished, she wrote: "Who knows whether this blind faith is not part of my make-up . . . because I am a granddaughter of Reb Chaim the Hospitable, whose faith in Messiah was handed down to him through the centuries."[66]

Lucy Lang and Sidney Hillman were contemporaries of the Progressive Era and the Settlement House movement. In fact, Hillman's social attitudes, style, and pragmatism were in part reflective of the thought of Progressives John Dewey and Charles Beard. And Lucy Lang, along with several others, including Bessie Abramowitz and Bella Dvorin, were frequent visitors at Jane Addams's Hull House in Chicago. This brings us back to the point that while Jewish immigrant socialists were in *rebellion* against dominant conditions, they were at the same time adapting, at least to the Progressive currents of the New World; and in both instances they were often using Old World values and religious culture.

The use, conscious or otherwise, of religious values was not, in this period, a monopoly of the Jewish immigrant socialists nor of Jews generally. Between 1880 and 1920 the moral vision of evangelical Protestantism produced in the United States a "civil religion of American mission," and it provided the essential thrust of the Progressive ethos. Many Progressives invested their chosen fields with the religious and moral significance earlier generations had attached to the ministry. John Dewey declared at the start of the era: "What we need in education more than anything else is genuine, not merely marginal faith in the existence of moral principles." And Jane Addams, through her Hull House—a cross between the social science of the University of Chicago and the evangelicalism of the Protestant churches—was "a living example of applied Christian thought."[67] In his autobiography, Frederick Howe, the prominent Cleveland Progressive, wrote that though he had disentangled himself "from the embraces" of his strict Protestant upbringing,

> Physical escape from . . . evangelical religion did not mean moral escape. From that religion my reason was never emancipated. By it I was conformed to my generation and made to share its moral standards and ideals. . . . [The persistence of religious values] is, I think, the most characteristic influence of my generation.[68]

Jewish religious values, reshaped, persisted in this era, too, as we have seen. And for the immigrant socialists these cultural values were no compromise of class values. They were an enrichment and an articulation of class reality.

CLASS STRUGGLE AND CLASS CONSCIOUSNESS IN THE JEWISH COMMUNITY

At least two classic ingredients for the development of a working-class consciousness appeared to be in place by the early 1900s. There were large numbers of exploited workers, and they were geographically concentrated. Moreover, in the case of the Jews, the concentration went well beyond place, and included common language, ethnic homogeneity, and shared experiences, recent and historical. All of this was reflected in a growing institutional infrastructure on the East Side and other large cities. Class and ethnic factors then were mutually reinforcing. And if we use C. Wright Mills's definition of class consciousness, i.e., awareness and identification with one's own class interest, rejection of other class interests as illegitimate, belief in some basic Marxist doctrines, and readiness to use political means to achieve shared goals, the Jewish labor activists and certainly the socialists were class conscious.[69]

Jewish unions and the American and Jewish socialist movements came into being at approximately the same time. In fact, Jewish socialists were the very ones who organized the Jewish unions. This is very different from what happened in the older American labor movement, which has been generally conservative. "The American Federation of Labor . . . is like an insurance company," according to Morris Feinstone of the socialist United Hebrew Trades. American unionism

> is all a purely business proposition. The improvement in wages and hours is bound to come as a matter of course. The Jewish locals want their unionism on a higher plane. They want emphasis on idealism, class-consciousness rather than merely betterment in wages.[70]

The class consciousness of the Jewish workers as well as their struggle for better wages collided with the class interest of Jewish manufacturers. The factory and shop owners and contractors were persistent in their attempts to destroy organization. They hired spies, fired activists, played home workers off against disgruntled factory workers, used a combination of bribery and threat, and finally brute force. Abraham Belson, a boot-stitcher in the old country and a reefer-maker in the new, tells the following story:

> I came to New York in 1907. A woman from my old home had a son who got me a job in a factory where he worked making children's coats. We had what you might call the beginning of a union—local 17, reefer makers. . . . The union, established in 1905, was still very weak, but we were preparing for the time when we could make demands. In February 1907 we demanded that we no longer be required to bring our own machines. The bosses made a lockout.
> Until 1907 the manufacturers really thought that local 17 was only a temporary nuisance in the trade, and that just like other Jewish unions up to that time, it would disappear in the slack season. . . . When this didn't happen they decided to destroy local 17 with kindness.

‑פון די ריזער סייזערס, וועלכע די א געדוננענע באסס פון די די באסעם האבען צו'הרג'עט אין ציבל=בי=ג=

A group of striking reefer makers injured by hired goons.

From the Archives of YIVO Institute for Jewish Research

The bosses started to make parties and give out beer. They tried to organize a company union which would supply sickness benefits, even cemeteries for the workers,—they shouldn't need it God forbid. . . . They promised everything . . . but these maneuvers did not help.

The climax came at one of the parties thrown by Weinstein Brothers, one of the biggest firms of that time. . . . The hall was richly decorated . . . and the tables were laden with beautiful foods. . . . Big chunks of bread with huckleberries . . . herring and corned-beef. . . . German beer was continually poured out to the thirsty Jewish workers. . . .

One of the bosses got up and made a heated speech about organizing a "society" to provide us with a good future. This "herring conspiracy" ended, however, when a union committee walked in and destroyed the whole celebration. We all went into the street and out into the quiet of the night, our palms upraised for the Bundist oath. . . .

When the manufacturers decided to make a lockout [in response to our demands], we went on strike. The young ones led the marches, the older ones went along in a happy mood. This was new times. The Jewish immigrant worker in that moment showed America that his soul was uplifted. . . . The reefer makers strike became the center of the struggle of the whole Jewish labor movement. . . . [It] set a pattern for the future strikes.

[But] it was one of the bloodiest strikes. . . . Many workers were injured. It looked like a hospital with bandages and more bandages. The bosses had hired two gangsters who broke heads or stabbed with knives.[71]

Many of the strikers in this era, including women and children, suffered violence. During one strike Elizabeth Hasanovitz

watched young brave children in the picket line, not fearing the policeman who would chase them . . . nor the gangsters hired by the bosses, who would stain with blood many a young girl's face when she dared to speak to a scab who was under their protection.[72]

Flora Weiss could have been one of those young girls:

More than once they broke my glasses on the picket lines, and struck my head so that I needed medical attention. I was brave; I was idealistic. I didn't want to do physical battle. This was not in my nature or in my blood, but I felt as if I were fulfilling a *holy duty* when I ran after a scab . . . I felt . . . as if I were on the barricades in a *revolution*.[73]

These representative illustrations indicate a significant struggle between classes in the Jewish community and a genuine class consciousness among the Jewish workers. We can also see, however, in the case of Abraham Belson, for example, that sometimes class and ethnic attachments reinforced one another. And from Flora Weiss, who makes that classic synthesis of fighting a "revolution" and fulfilling a "holy duty," we have yet another demonstration that class consciousness can be partly rooted in and enriched by traditional values.

Ethnic groups have characteristically included more than one class, and the Jews were no exception. The Jewish workers struck against factory owners who were Jewish, and, increasingly, Russian-Jewish. This included Reuben Sadowsky, one of the largest cloak manufacturers in New York City. Prior to the Great Cloakmakers Revolt, Sadowsky, partly to encourage industrial peace, not only closed on the Sabbath but encouraged weekday services in his factory. Actions like this could of course blunt class consciousness, as the writer of a letter to the *Jewish Daily Forward* suggests:

> I am a Socialist and my boss is a fine man. I know he's a capitalist but I like him. Am I doing something wrong?[74]

It is also probably true that when the trade unions called their strikes, they partly counted on the traditional charitable instincts of the *entire* community. They, furthermore, accepted the mediation offered by the "uptown" German Jews in settling with the downtown manufacturers.[75] And their settlements, which included the Joint Board of Sanitary Control, the "impartial chairman," and a great deal of shared decision making, were pioneering events in union/ management cooperation. Some would say collaboration, because much of this seemed to blur the distinctions between capitalism and socialism, and to take the sharp edge off of class consciousness.

There were certainly discomforting cross-pressures. And years after the struggles of the second and third decades of the twentieth century, Louis Painkin, the militant cutter and son of a "great Hebrew scholar," still felt the pain:

> I had a relative who was in the raincoat business; he gave me a chance to learn the trade and subsequent to that I struck against him. . . . [W]e put him out of business. . . . He died of aggravation; And I was practically the leader of it. I was dedicated . . . [but] also too young to appreciate anything . . . done for [me]. You are involved in a cause, and the cause is paramount.[76]

Class consciousness and the cause remained paramount for

many, despite the cross-pressures, and Painkin in the 1960s was still saying, "I am not afraid of the word revolution." Jacob Levenson spoke for a good number of Jewish immigrant socialists in this study when he said recently:

> The religious background was there. . . . We had orientation to Jewish life; but we tended more to the class-conscious struggle.[77]

This class consciousness broadened not only because of the militant struggle between Jewish classes but also by the fact that Jewish workers often crossed ethnic barriers to forge links with other working-class groups. Italian, German, and Jewish silk workers struck in Paterson, New Jersey, in 1913, and the support they received from New York City came overwhelmingly from Jewish workers. Irish transit workers struck in Harlem in 1916, and crowds of Jews besieged the trollies and tossed out scab conductors. There was a promise that year from other unions, mostly Irish-based, for a sympathy strike, but only the Jewish unions saw the promise through.[78] The great steel strike of 1919 received approximately $300,000 in support from other unions: $175,000 came from the Jewish-dominated garment unions, $100,000 from the Amalgamated Clothing Workers alone.

These Jewish workers who transcended ethnic barriers to help other groups of exploited people were not necessarily transcending their own ethnicity thereby. Indeed, the very opposite is suggested by the fact that this transethnic class consciousness was apparently peculiarly characteristic of Jews relative to the insularity of the Finns, Hungarians, Poles, Slavs, and even Germans.[79]

Class and ethnic attachments—perhaps a better word here would be values—have often worked at cross-purposes; but at least into the 1920s for Jewish radicals, class and ethnicity—whether or not overtly identifiable—appear often to have been mutually reinforcing.

There are several intriguing examples of the interplay between class and ethnicity. Some of the "uptown" philanthropists in the German-Jewish community, in line with at least one dimension of Progressive thinking, encouraged from the beginning communal self-help endeavors of the "downtown" Russian Jews. They assisted the Hebrew Sheltering and Immigrant Aid Society and the Hebrew Free Loan Society, which were immigrant-supported bodies. Some uptown leaders, as we have seen, even endorsed nonradical goals of the Jewish labor movement. Others, reflecting another side of Progressivism, condemned "duplication" and the "inefficiency" of unprofessional immigrant organizations. If the immigrants were left to minister to themselves, these critics warned, they would perpetuate the "ghetto" and its vices: 1) superstition—by which uptown Reform German Jews meant Orthodoxy, and 2) radicalism.[80]

The Educational Alliance, a mixture of night school, settlement house, gymnasium, and lecture center, embodied the desire of some German Jews to integrate the newcomers unobtrusively—to clean them up and to quiet them down. And the *kehillah* (communal council) movement, 1908–1922, was an invocation to community, a naïve hope on the part of the German Jews that by centralizing the actions of Jewish institutions and by appealing to Jewish peoplehood, class war and the pathologies of social dislocation would disappear. The Alliance and the *kehillah* had some significantly positive consequences. But the social control dimensions of the efforts of the German Jews came up against the size, energy, institutional and communal experience, *cultural pride,* and *class consciousness* of the immigrant.

The German Jews "called us . . . *ostjuden* [Eastern Jews]," Joseph Schlossberg remembered. "They had nothing but contempt for us. . . . They established Jewish charities," but they did this as if they were people "belonging to a superior race, and we the recipients, belonging to an inferior race." This was not "progress" or "relief." Only "the socialist movement brought that."[81] And so despite their efforts the Progressive German Jews and the Jewish manufacturers— sometimes they were the same—found themselves overwhelmed by continuing industrial tumult.

The interplay of class consciousness and ethnic interests was also evident during this period in the congressional elections on the lower East Side. Morris Hillquit, the "Americanized" lawyer who tried so hard to be a socialist without being a Jewish socialist, lost his bid for the Ninth Congressional District seat in 1908, and his defeat was unexpectedly heavy. He was replaced as the Socialist Party candidate in 1910 by Meyer London, whose father was a Talmudic scholar and whose mother was a devotee of the old faith. London was sent to Congress three times—in 1914, 1916, and 1920. Ethnic interest no doubt played a role here. Morris Hillquit in 1908 at the first rally of his campaign had said:

If elected to Congress, I will not consider myself the special representative of the alleged special interests of this district, but the representative of the Socialist Party and the interests of the working class of the country, so understood and interpreted by my party.[82]

This he put forth at a time when East Side denizens were upset by the Police Commissioner's report implying that Jews were responsible for 50 percent of the crime in New York City, when the "special interest" issue of immigration restriction was being hotly debated in Congress, and when the position of the Socialist Party on that issue, favoring some restriction, did not seem positive to East Side Jews who still had relatives desiring to escape from pogrom-ridden Russia. Like the English conservative Edmund Burke over a century earlier, who ran as a representative not of his constituents but of the "realm," the radical Morris Hillquit was roundly rejected.

Meyer London, an erstwhile colleague of Cahan and Hillquit in the socialist movement, openly identified as a Jewish socialist and allied himself with the interests and vital movements of the East Side. Though failing of election in 1910, London outran his own Socialist Party ticket two to one. And by 1914 he was victorious.[83]

Does this mean that ethnic interests were more important than class consciousness? Or could it be that here again they were at least potentially compatible? London told a crowd of 15,000 after his election, "I hope that my presence will represent an entirely different type of Jew from the kind that Congress is accustomed to see." But in the same speech, and apparently met with the same enthusiasm, London also said, "We shall not rest until every power of capitalism has been destroyed and the workers emancipated from wage slavery."[84] And he went on in the House to introduce bills described as "wild socialist schemes" by his congressional colleagues. "When I made my first speech," London remembered,

one of the most extreme of the Republicans made his way across the House and peered into my face as if to discover what kind of a weird creature from some other world had found its way to this planet.[85]

Meyer London did not substitute ethnic interests for class interests; he combined them. Morris Hillquit would soon be doing the same. When he ran as a Socialist for Mayor of New York in 1917, some representatives of the German-Jewish community advocated voting against him. If Hillquit were "elected by Jewish votes," they thought, "who can doubt that . . . [the American] tradition of tolerance will be imperilled?"[86] Hillquit responded:

> This is the old subtle trick of the ruling classes. It is the same old trick Booker T. Washington worked on the Negroes. . . . "Don't assert yourselves or else you will incur the hatred of the ruling classes. . . . Be gentle slaves and you will be all right."
>
> And I say to you as a citizen to citizens, as a Jew to Jews, you don't have to be good; you have the right to be as bad as the rest of the world.[87]

Another case illustrating the point of the complex relationship of class and ethnicity is Jewish behavior within the Socialist Party organization. In 1912, mainly through the exertion of the Bundists, the Jewish Socialist Federation was formed, uniting all the Jewish branches in the Socialist Party. It was "virtually a Jewish Socialist Party within the . . . Party."[88] Most Jewish socialists did not belong to the Federation. Many strongly disapproved of it, including Abe Cahan and the members of the Forward Association, which was in a sense a rival center of influence. On the one hand the Forward Association types, with their desire to "Americanize" the Jewish labor and socialist movements, may be viewed as emphasizing class consciousness over ethnicity. On the other hand, the sixty-five branches of the Jewish Socialist Federation, with its membership somewhere under three thousand, "soon became a real force among the *more radical* Jewish workers in America" and was significantly "to the left of the American Socialist Party."[89] The Federation's personnel, moreover, were active and articulate and they furnished much of the future bureaucracy of the socialist garment unions. And despite their differences, the Forward Association and the Jewish Socialist Federation were able to cooperate in party work, the Workmen's Circle, and many other activities of the movement.

Both groups had visions of proletarian solidarity. That the vision blurred over time was not so much connected with attempts to sustain Jewish identity as it was related to *diminished* Old World tradition, a changing American economic milieu, and increasing upward mobility for Jewish immigrants and the sons and daughters of those immigrants.

5

SELF-IMAGES
AND
REFLECTIONS

The Radicals
Explain Themselves

The attraction to labor militancy and socialism needed no
elaborate explanation for Max Deutschman. To him it was
"very logical."

> I was sitting and working like all the other children. . . . At that time in
> the city they didn't know about democrats or strikes, or other things like
> that. Someone came down from Minsk, a young man. He tried to orga-
> nize a strike . . . and got attached to me. He told us we can work eight
> hours a day and have enough to eat. . . . Since I worked fourteen hours a
> day . . . and I had a big appetite . . . I became enthusiastic.[1]

By the time Max Deutschman arrived in the United States at the age
of twenty-one he was a veteran of radical politics.

For Pauline Newman, who came to America when she was ten,
with no political experience, the reasons for "becoming involved" in
the movements were also "rather simple." "Conditions in the shops
. . . dirty, dark, cold in the winter, hot in the summer, long days."[2]

Almost every one of the immigrant socialists, wherever they were
radicalized, and whatever other reasons they gave, stressed specific
conditions and low pay as motivating factors. Often, however, even

those who believed their interest in the labor and political movements lay solely and directly in "bread and butter" issues, found themselves moving toward larger concerns. Joseph Schlossberg, Secretary-Treasurer of the ACWA (1914–1940), who was in the sweatshops of New York City by the time he was thirteen, was one of these.

> My immediate interest . . . was relief from the sweat shop. Like all others, I suffered . . . bitterly. . . . My father was [also] a sweat shop worker. The earnings were very small; the work week was without a beginning and without an end. No matter how early I came to the shop, there were already people working.[3]

Schlossberg had specific grievances, but

> the spokesmen, the interpreters of our grievances . . . brought with them from the land of persecution high idealism and youthful enthusiasm. They were Socialists. The foundation and background of their socialism was the struggle against Czarist autocracy in Russia. . . . Those people spoke for us, wrote for us and worked for us. Thus each of our gatherings, whatever the immediate object, was an occasion for spirited propaganda for social justice in the broader sense.

Though Joseph Schlossberg had not been involved in the revolutionary activities against the Czar, his participation in the Jewish labor movement soon "filled [him] with the spirit of that sacred struggle."[4]

The concentration of Jews in the garment industry and on the lower East Side made it likely that large numbers of newly arriving nonpoliticized immigrants like Schlossberg and Newman would have some exposure to the radical ideology, which played an important role in shaping their politics. Proletarianization was essential, but oppressive conditions alone did not impel people to become socialists. "Conditions in those times were outrageous," Abe Hershkowitz reminds us. But it was not until he "got acquainted with socialist friends" who gave him advice, that he joined the Socialist Party.[5] Oscar Feuer, who quipped that "the cost of living was very cheap, but wages were even cheaper," was motivated by speeches he heard "from trucks on Rivington Street demanding . . . that immigrants join the workers' unions."[6] Marie Ganz worked "in a sweatshop for 13 hours a day under a speed up system [and heard] many a street orator . . . denouncing the rich." Her emotions "had been stimulated . . . by the sufferings of sweatshop slavery" but she "had been taught to think by the followers of the red flag," who were so much in evidence on the lower East Side.[7]

A recent study has suggested that socialism on the lower East Side, "was a state of mind rather than an ordinary political movement," and that a Jew here became a socialist "just as naturally as, in other sections of the nation, one joined the Republican Party, went to church and read the *Saturday Evening Post*."[8] This is obviously an exaggeration, since most Jews on the lower East Side, or for that matter anywhere, never became socialists, but it is a plausible exaggeration nonetheless. "Socialism was in the air among Jews . . . particularly among the working people," was the way Jacob Levenson put it.[9] Abe Sherer, who came from a small town in Galicia, recalled:

> In those times the Socialist Party was active on the East Side; they held meetings very often. . . . Once walking home from work I saw a placard on Avenue A . . . advertising that Abe Cahan, the editor of the *Forward* was going to lecture that evening. And I was interested in hearing this. . . . I went and Cahan made a great impression on me. That was the first time I ever heard a person speak at an open assembly in America.[10]

Friends, street orators, public lectures, and often family brought individuals into political organizations and unions or out on strike. Pauline Newman recalled:

> Some of my relatives who were already Americanized would say "I'm going to a meeting; you want to come along" and you came along.[11]

> . . . a relative who worked with me at the Triangle Waist Company took me along to . . . classes [at the Socialist Literary Society] . . . that really . . . started me in the movement. . . .[12]

One afternoon Rose Cohen's father showed her

> a little book with a red paper cover which he took from his breast pocket. "This" he said, "is my Union book. You too must join. . . ."[13]

And after hearing several "stirring" speeches at a meeting, to which her father had brought her, Rose Cohen joined the union.

Jacob Panken, who was elected on the Socialist Party ticket by his East Side constituency in 1917 as judge on the Municipal Court, had worked for his father, who manufactured purses.

Florence and Jacob Levenson, who "met at a lecture on Marxism and have been together ever since."

Courtesy of Gene Levenson

New York Socialist Literary Society, 1905.
From the Archives of YIVO Institute for Jewish Research

When the union was organized and a strike was ordered, the few people my father employed struck. The old gentleman came to my bench. I shall never forget it for it was a lesson in solidarity . . . and fraternity with those who were workers, taught me, that moment, by my father. He said to me, "You cannot work here . . . while your fellow workers are on strike. You cannot and dare not be a 'black leg.'" He did not have to repeat that to me. I struck against my father with the rest of the employees.[14]

Often, as with Joseph Schlossberg's or Jacob Panken's experience, it was within the unions and organizations or out on strike that radicalism was learned. Clara Lemlich remembered that the more experienced workers talked constantly about trade unions. There were even lunch-time discussion groups in some shops on trade union theory. Louis Waldman, the labor lawyer, on the picket line eleven weeks in 1910, said: "Since I was now on strike I joined the union [and] I was soon drawn into the maelstrom of union activity."[15] "I didn't get into the union," said Bernard Fenster, who had joined to get a job, "it got into me, into my heart and soul."

It is more than likely that Waldman was such a ready recruit and that Fenster's "heart and soul" were so receptive because they had been deeply prepared long before. Waldman was proficient at Talmudic interpretation and a reader of books "sacred and secular," and Fenster "did not work on Saturdays [because he] was religious. . . ."[16]

Nearly all the immigrant Jewish radicals had been intensively socialized in the traditional culture, a culture permeated with Jewish ethical and spiritual values. Even those who emphasized poor working conditions and pecuniary considerations as motivation for radicalism, agreed that militant unionism "was a question of humane living . . . of recognizing a person to be a person," and that "the labor movement was never just a way of getting higher wages. What appealed . . . was the spiritual side . . ." and the satisfaction of helping people.[17] A militant strike leader for the Amalgamated Clothing Workers, who learned Talmud from her father, described herself as a "good Jew" and said:

> Keeping kosher isn't [being] a good Jew. . . . You [have] to be good and [practice] *tzedaka*. *Tzedaka* means to help a person. . . . In our heritage the first thing is *tzedaka*.[18]

Fourteen-year-old Feigl Shapiro, responding to the same *shtetl* norms, wanted to learn about what one could do as a union member about the needs of the poor and what one *must* do for the worker and for the people's sake.

A few months after her arrival in the United States in 1914, Feigl Shapiro "got active in the union. . . . By 1916 [she] was a member of the Socialist Party."[19] Jack Sperber also came to America when he was fourteen. He brought with him the skills in tailoring his sisters had taught him, and with these he landed a job in a shop. Sperber also brought, in his words, "the shtetl principles of justice and mutual help," and with these he was prepared to be "greatly influenced by the lectures of Emma Goldman and Alexander Berkman," to which he had been taken by his anarchist brother-in-law.[20]

We have already seen in chapters 3 and 4 that the Jewish radicals along with the great majority of their fellow immigrants were attached, affiliated, and significantly bound up in a web of important social formations which helped reduce the jarring, atomizing impact of "uprooting." The illustrations here, when added to the statistical evidence cited earlier indicating how deeply immersed these radicals had been in Jewish tradition, suggest once more that the socialist Jews, in addition to being part of the rich network of communal relations and institutions, were still very much in touch with and moved by Jewish cultural and religious norms.

The radical associations and modern organizations these Jews built did not emerge on the complete wreckage of traditional culture. They grew instead out of the vitality and strength of that "damaged but still viable" culture, to which the socialist Jews continued to be bound.

MARGINALITY AND "SELF-HATE"

The Jewish radicals of the immigrant generation, seem to have responded in several different ways to their "marginality." The great majority fail to fit very precisely the category "marginal person," if we mean by this, having one unsteady foot in each of two relatively antipathetic cultures, and demonstrating several or all of the classic psychological attributes—confusion, anxiety, compulsion, inconsistency, and general irrationality. I could identify no more than nine of ninety-five (9.5 percent) who were "ambivalent"—i.e., neither quite in the rich matrix of group-affiliation ("marginal culture") that made up the Jewish lower East Side, nor in some part of the American or East European "mainstream,"—before their respective commitments to activist socialism.

Perhaps Fannia Cohn, Secretary of the Education Department of the ILGWU, falls into this category. She wrote to a friend:

> We are born into a social group, with its customs, traditions, ideals, loyalties and habits. We breathe in all these values. They leave an impress upon our entire being. Suddenly, we come in touch with another world, with the life of a social group whose spiritual values and whose conceptions of good and bad, just and unjust are different from our own. But in the end we must find ourselves. We must find where our real sympathies lie. And, even then, when it seems to us that we are no longer sitting between two stools, even then do we have our internal conflicts.[21]

Fannia Cohn, however, was soon to find herself firmly rooted in a Jewish socialist milieu, which was not so much a surrogate community as a partially transplanted one, built at least in some measure with significant materials from the old. "Yes," Fannia Cohn could write, "we are not only what we are, but also what we 'were.' "[22]

Abraham Cahan, editor of the extraordinarily influential *Jewish Daily Forward* exhibited some of the same internal conflict. In a series of letters written between 1883 and 1884 he said: "I debate, I argue, I get excited, I shriek and in the midst of all this, I remind myself that I am a vacant vessel, an empty man." He complains of a lack of "orientation"; he intensely desires a "firm foundation" and is apparently tormented by his "divided mood."[23]

By 1886, however, Cahan, who understood how strong a hold Jewish religious values had even on a nonbeliever like himself, was using biblical and Talmudic reference in his writings, and by 1890 he had developed a synthesis of Jewish religious culture and socialism in his newspaper columns that was the envy of his political and journalistic rivals. In 1891, when Abe Cahan as a delegate of the United Hebrew Trades came to the Brussels congress of the Second International, he explained that the federation of unions he represented had "nothing to do with religion or nationality" and that the word "Hebrew" was adopted "only because of the language spoken by all its members." At the same time, however, he introduced a resolution condemning antisemitism:

> The Jews are persecuted, hounded; they have been made into a special class. This class wants to fight and asks for its place in the ranks of Social

Democracy. . . . The Russian press constantly attacks the Jews and asserts that we are hated even by the worker-socialists. I want you to declare that this is not true.[24]

In April 1903, when the news of the Kishinev pogrom reached Cahan in Connecticut, he was bird-watching, a hobby he had developed as a break from writing. He immediately rushed, field glasses and bird manual in hand, for a New York train. "I felt an urge to be among Jews," he explained.[25] Partially in response to the Kishinev pogrom, Cahan wrote his little known novel *The White Terror and the Red,* which was published in 1905. The story, set in the early 1880s, explores the conflicts of young Jewish revolutionaries and deals critically with their destructive attitude toward the Jewish people and the pogroms that victimized them.[26]

Later when Cahan and the Forward Association were attacking the Jewish Socialist Federation, which was founded in 1912, as "nationalist," the *Forward* editor was greatly agitated by the Leo Frank trial, a significant episode in American antisemitism. Frank, the owner of a pencil factory in Georgia, was accused, then convicted, in a gross miscarriage of justice, of the rape and murder of a young employee. After the commutation of the death sentence, a mob abducted and lynched Leo Frank.[27] Cahan had traveled to Atlanta several times in 1913 to cover the trial proceedings, and devoted almost the entire last volume of his memoirs to the case.

Jewish "crises" continued to agitate Abe Cahan. After the 1929 anti-Jewish riots in Palestine, which a handful of radicals applauded as the beginning of "revolution," Cahan rushed to cover the impact of the events on the Jewish community there. Although he did not consider himself a Zionist, he no longer doubted that he was deeply committed to the Jews of Palestine.[28]

Abe Cahan never completely transcended the "divided mood" he referred to in his youthful letters. He was, after all, a refugee from Russia, observing revolutionary sacrifice from afar, and an assertive assimilationist wedded to Yiddish journalism. Cahan as a socialist could integrate his old and new selves. But Cahan the exile never fully came to terms with his becoming something of the "successful American." The ambivalence he continued to experience shows clearly in his semiautobiographical novel, *David Levinsky,* published in 1917. David is also a "success," but reflects:

I cannot escape from my old self. . . . David, the poor lad swinging over a

Talmud volume at the Preacher's Synagogue, seems to have more in common with my inner identity than David Levinsky, the well-known cloak manufacturer.[29]

In addition to the nine socialists including Cahan and Cohn who appear to have been ambivalent, another seven were explicitly hostile toward Jewish identity. Yet there was no one among the radical immigrants in this study quite like Victor Adler, for example, leader of the Austrian Social Democratic Party, baptized, with no special sympathy for his former co-religionists, and with a highly equivocal attitude toward antisemitism; nor were many like Leon Trotsky and Rosa Luxemburg, who were hostile to any form of Jewish separatism.[30] Instead, among the Jewish socialists in America there was Benjamin Feigenbaum, a giant presence in the cultural and political life of the lower East Side, who often wrote and spoke variations of the following theme: "May the process of assimilation follow its course for it bestows the greatest blessing upon people, especially the Jews."[31] And Feigenbaum, like some of the early anarchists, made war upon God. But he maintained a deep interest in Jewish law and was a moral conservative, who continued to refer to socialism as the "Messiah."

Morris Winchevsky, the patriarch of Jewish socialism, was also "antireligious."

My greatest pleasure had been in proving that Moses did not write the Torah, that Joshua did not rearrange the course of the sun and the moon, that David was not a very nice man and Solomon not always wise.[32]

But Winchevsky, whose disbelief approached fanaticism at times, could say:

. . . for almost everything I write I have to thank that poet-preacher [Isaiah] who entered my heart and mind with love for orphans and widows and other defenseless and oppressed people . . . with his hatred for everything that stands for robbery and murder and deceit under whatever mask it parades. . . . I am grateful . . . not to him alone, but also to Amos and Hosea before him and Micah after him.[33]

In addition to the sixteen "ambivalent" or "hostile" Jewish socialists in this study, ten others were primarily advocates of cultural assimilation; yet hardly any of these would go so far as to actively deny their Jewishness. Morris Hillquit, one of American socialism's most influential writers and tacticians, came closest to denial. He rejected any form of religious practice, took part in the early Yom Kippur balls, and made every effort to be a socialist without being a Jewish socialist. He opposed, however, any antireligious appeal. "The socialist movement," he contended, "is primarily an economic and political movement. It is not concerned with institutions of marriage and religion."[34] Moreover, Hillquit's power in the Socialist Party depended significantly upon support from its Jewish constituency, and so he would soon sprinkle his addresses with the phrase "as a Jew" and would soon adopt a motif that ran:

> I prefer to see the Jew proclaiming his equality with the other nations of the world rather than seeking to deny his race in implied admission of national inferiority.[35]

At the very most then, twenty-six of these ninety-five Jewish socialists could be characterized as hostile, ambivalent, or assimilationist. But even here, as we have already seen, in some if not all of the cases, these were persons struggling, often creatively, to synthesize new identities. They were not simply marginal persons exhibiting the negative psychological characteristics of that condition.

One of the negative psychological characteristics of marginality is alleged to be self-hatred. According to several social scientists, self-hatred is an affliction very common among the marginal Jews of the modern age, and particularly among Jewish radicals attracted to socialist universalism. Marxism, with its emphasis on religion as opiate and on nationalism as reactionary false consciousness, tended to preclude respect for culture and the rights of national minorities. The Jew who espoused Marxism, then, was, according to some analysts, engaging in self-hatred and along with "the pathological anti-Semite . . . desired the ultimate disappearance of the Jew."[36]

Conflicts with regard to their own Jewishness existed for many Jews attracted to socialism, and some were, as we have seen, indifferent or hostile toward Jewishness. But embracing socialism, unlike religious conversion, did not require denial of ethnic origins and most of the Jewish radicals in this study are not easily identified as engaging in self-hatred. This is partly because self-hatred is a vague concept, can take many forms, and is often difficult to detect. This is especially so if we accept the contention that positive Jewish identification, in some, can be a defense mechanism against self-hate, and that for the small minority of socialist Jews who feared being charged with "nationalism," self-hate could serve as a defense mechanism against positive identification. Georgii Plekhanov's Jewish wife spoke for this latter group in Russia and in America when she said in the 1880s:

> Deep down in the soul of each one of us, revolutionaries of Jewish birth—there was a sense of hurt pride and infinite pity for our own, and many of us were strongly tempted to devote ourselves to serving our injured, humiliated and persecuted people.[37]

Most important, the vast majority of Jewish socialists were not only *tempted* to identify openly with, and serve the cause of the Jewish people, they did it. They did it as Bundists, Socialist-Territorialists, Socialist-Zionists, all of which were syntheses of Jewish nationalism, in one form or another, and universalist Marxism.

The radical Chaim Zhitlowsky, who often stood alone outside of any organized group, was a "nationalist" from as early as 1884. He went on to become the chief theoretician of diaspora nationalism and yiddishism. Socialism, he said,

> does not intend to abolish nations. To knead them into one dough and to make from that dough, one large loaf—mankind.[38]

The idea that self-hate could signify repression of positive Jewishness is lent credence by the fact that in many cases initial adventures in apparent self-hatred ended in return to the cultural traditions, and with no diminution of radicalism or class consciousness. "The very word 'religion' came to be discredited by many liberal people," Morris R. Cohen reflected, "because no distinction was drawn between ritual and religious convictions and feelings."[39] Joe Rapoport was one of those liberal people.

> Throughout my boyhood I shared a room with my grandfather, and he tyrannized me. He forever was scaring me with stories of the *dybbuk,* the devil. We were forever doing things to ward off evil spirits from our room. He made me do honor to my right foot when I put on my pants by using my right foot first. The same thing with putting on my boots and washing my hands. There was a morning prayer, [and] a noontime prayer that he made sure . . . I did every day or he would punish me. When he died I felt liberated from this imposed worship. I not only stopped following it but I hated it.

It was not long, however, before Joe Rapoport realized that he persistently made allusion to Talmud and Yiddish folk stories, and that his conversation and beliefs had the rhythm and substance of prophetic texts.[40]

And Morris Winchevsky, the great satirist of the supernatural, wrote:

> Step by step I return to my foundations . . . the prophets, Jewish history and Jewish legend. I become a Jew. Again a Jew. This does not undermine my commitment to international socialism, because a non-Jew, a non-gentile, just an ordinary "person" cannot be a real socialist. . . . I become a Jew. The *Tanakh* (Bible) on the table again, with a new commentary, but the old *Tanakh.*[41]

If a combination of antisemitism outside the home and repressive modes and strains of Judaism in the home is the formula for the growth of self-hate, then one would imagine that a woman like Emma Goldman ought to have been a prime candidate. She was exposed to the most brutal Russian antisemitism, and her father was a strict, formalistic practitioner of Judaism. He was also an autocrat with a ferocious temper. Emma suffered his violence as well as the frequent beatings of a Hebrew teacher. Nevertheless, she was, her biographer tells us, a product of "the prophetic tradition and the folk literature of the Bible. . . . [The] gorgeous imagery and thunderous accounts of renunciation and bravery had an inevitable effect on the sensitive intelligent little ghetto girl."[42] Emma Goldman, herself wrote:

> . . . at the age of eight I used to dream of becoming a Judith and visioned myself in the act of cutting off Holofernes' [an Assyrian general] head to avenge the wrongs of my people. But once I had become aware that social injustice is not confined to my own race, I had decided that there were too many heads for one Judith to cut off.[43]

Emma Goldman's recognition of the pervasiveness of injustice, however, did not mean a rejection of the Jewish cultural and religious values to which she frequently alluded in her writings. Nor did her universalism prevent her from speaking about the particular wrongs Jews suffered in an antisemitic world.

Self-hate may have led some Jews to Marxist universalism, or anarchism, which would eliminate all religious and national distinctions—though it certainly seems that conversion was a less risky, more viable, and faster route to Jewish disappearance than any form of radicalism. And furthermore, socialism and anarchism would also subvert Christianity, and unjust antisemitic Christian societies,

Emma Goldman at the age of seventeen, in 1886.
Alfred A. Knopf

TABLE 5
Socialists: Jewish Orientation (N = 95)

	percent	
Active identification	35.0	⎫
Passive identification	22.0	⎬ 73.0 percent
Dual orientation	16.0	⎭
Assimilationist	10.5	⎫
Ambivalent	9.5	⎬ 27.0 percent
Hostile	7.0	⎭
	100.0	

thereby quite possibly serving something very different from self-hate.

This becomes even more credible when we see that some 35 percent of the Jewish socialists identified actively and intensely as Jews, saw themselves, as indeed they were, as members of a marginal culture, but hardly as marginal men and women. Another 22 percent were predominantly Jewish in orientation and identification, and are probably best described as "passive," that is, as exhibiting no fear for the survival of Jews as a group, but investing little or nothing in fostering socialist *universalism,* and showing no desire to assimilate.[44]

Fifty-seven percent were consistently, unambiguously, and often assertively identifying as Jews. An additional 16 percent were imbued with a "dual orientation"—with some degree of Jewish consciousness peacefully coexisting with the belief that Jews would gradually acculturate. This dual orientation need hardly have been a source of conflict or disintegration; indeed as Georg Simmel and others have taught us, "multiple group-affiliations can strengthen the individual and reinforce the integration of his personality."[45] Over 70 percent, then, were imbued with positive Jewish consciousness. The great majority were significantly caught up in a web of overlapping institutions, affiliations, and Jewish social formations. Residential concentration, the family, mutual aid societies, educational alliances, theater groups, reading clubs, the congregations, and *landsmanshaftn,* the workplace, the unions, were, as we have seen, important forms of group affiliation. So were the informal social networks the Jewish socialists participated in—the community or neighborhood itself, the block, the rooftop, the *landsleit* cohort, the tobacco store, and the tavern.

The Jewish socialists were not marginal persons. They were not

alienated from their community, nor did they appear to be disproportionately suffering serious personal maladjustment, because of "uprooting."

Samuel Gompers, reflecting on a lifetime of leadership in "bread
and butter" unionism, wrote:

> Un-Americanized workers proved especially susceptible to Socialist
> propaganda [and] according to my experience . . . Socialism accom-
> panies instability of judgment or intellectual undependability. . . . The
> . . . Socialists have uniformly been men whose minds have been
> warped. . . .[46]

The Jewish immigrant socialists, however, make it appear that Gompers and the social scientists who have followed his lead have not done
a very close or careful analysis of their subject.

ENERGY, IDEALISM, AND PERSONAL AMBITION

The spiritual energy involved, for these Jewish immigrants, in
the rejection, rebellion, synthesis, and creativity necessary to forge
new identities was remarkable, if not always successful. They were
not, after all, "birds of passage" looking to make a bit more money
and then to return to the roost of the "home" country. It was clear for
most of them, particularly after the failure of the Russian Revolution
of 1905, that America was the last frontier. A life would have to be
made here. And to this they dedicated themselves.

Morris R. Cohen writes that despite the difficulties of a strange
language and a strange environment, the Jewish immigrants

> brought to the tasks which the New World presented a force that was
> more than the force of any single individual. It was as if a great dam had
> broken and the force of water accumulated over many years had been let
> loose. This mighty force permeated every nook and corner of human
> endeavor.[47]

The Jew in Eastern Europe had been raised on the concept of
tachlis. The word comes from the Hebrew root meaning "accomplish"
or "fulfill." As it was used by East European Jewry, *tachlis* meant an
orientation to ultimate outcomes, rather than to immediate benefits.
A person realized his or her full significance only in having accomplished something. There could be "neither meaning nor satisfaction

in simply living one's life;" one had to achieve something.[48] After the hegemony of the religious-traditional conception of *tachlis* had been partially eroded, and Jews began to transfer their search for *tachlis* to the secular world, great numbers of them collided with anti-Jewish restrictions. Many emigrated, in part, for the opportunity of self-realization.

The socialists were no exception to this general pattern of energy and aspiration. Elizabeth Hasanovitz, one of a number of young women who went on hunger strikes to persuade parents to let them go to America, wrote:

> I had my hopes, my plans. . . . The hope of doing something worthwhile, hopes unexplainable, but so promising. . . . If I cannot accomplish anything, what is life for then?[49]

Abe Cahan in a letter to a colleague in the 1880s asked: "What can be done to change oneself to rise to the stature of a perfect human being?"[50] And Sidney Hillman was described from early on by intimates as "believing in his star." This leads toward a somewhat complex point. Even as these immigrants clung to the militant class-feeling and the social idealism of the movements with which they were involved, many were imbued with a desire to rise in the world. Social idealism and personal ambition were, at least for several decades, not mutually exclusive. On the contrary, they often reinforced each other.

David Dubinsky came to the United States with experience in radical politics and wanted very much to be a doctor. Full of energy he went to work to earn money for his education, but soon got caught up in socialism and union affairs.

> [W]ith double pay for overtime, I was making as much as $50 a week. But making money and making soapbox speeches at night for the Socialist Party didn't keep me busy enough. I began to get active in the union.[51]

He gave up his job as a cutter and took a full-time union position. "I wanted the job because there was so much to be done." Union leadership would be a larger arena for Dubinsky's energy and ambition. At the same time, Dubinsky claimed,

> union politics were not my only concerns, nor was the Socialist Party. Not long after I started as an apprentice at Boston Cloak Company, I joined nine friends (all Socialists) in starting a cooperative restaurant on Tenth Street, between First and Second Avenues. We each contributed ten

dollars to get started and we served meals for a quarter each. Leon Trotsky would come in for lunch. We had a lot of customers.[52]

Pauline Newman believed she was "rather fortunate in having the opportunity to serve others . . . most of us rejoiced in the ability to serve others." But in addition she

found a great deal of satisfaction in being called upon from time to time to serve in other [than organizing] capacities such as speaking . . . even scribbling. [This was] a great satisfaction to me because it was something I wanted to do very much, to give expression to my thoughts, . . . my feelings.[53]

And Bernard Fenster, after a time in union activities, wanted to take a greater "part . . . in the movement," because he wanted "to be a *ya-taka-dom* [big shot]."[54]

At least forty of the Jewish immigrant socialists, almost all of whom had been shop workers, made careers in the labor movement. Many of them, however, including Fannia Cohn, David Dubinsky, Max Zaritsky, and Adolph Held, had had opportunities to succeed materially elsewhere. Socialist trade unionism appears to have offered the Jews what the Catholic Church and politics had offered the Irish: the opportunity for the achievement of common goals *and* personal promotion.

A proportion of the workers who considered themselves socialists also had the urge to rise *out* of the working class.[55] When Jewish workers listened to the speeches of Morris Hillquit, who had gone from indigent cuffmaker to prosperous lawyer in less than two decades, some in those large audiences must have been dreaming of repeating that meteoric rise. The dream was reinforced not only by the dreadfulness of the jobs they held, but by the fact that in the garment trade, where most of them worked, contracting, which was not inaccessible, appeared to be a relatively successful route to upward mobility. Adolph Held said, wistfully, in this regard: "You know most of our strikes were against people who were formerly workers."[56] Yet of 110 Jewish immigrant socialists, 100 stayed in the movement in one way or another for long periods of time, most of them for their whole adult lives.

Jewish immigrant desire was strong and unrelenting, and full of shadings and complexities. It is easier to feel the intensity of all of this than it is to explain or analyze the various choices that were symptomatic of that intensity. But the foregoing suggests that just as Jewish socialism was a creative synthesis of older cultural values and the newer requirements of an industrial order, so participation in socialism for some Jews was an energetic merging of collective idealism with individual ambition.

6
ᴛhe
WOMEN
World of Our Mothers and Others

T he radicalism of Jewish women grew out of the same sources as male radicalism—proletarianization and the secularization of the Jewish religious values in which they were steeped. The integral and vital role played by women in Jewish immigrant radicalism is apparent in the previous chapters. Working women's radical consciousness and militant collective action, however, emerged in the face of extraordinary obstacles and deserve special attention. Jewish working-class women often lacked marketable skills, and were therefore more economically vulnerable. In their attempts to organize they came up against general indifference and even outright hostility from organized labor and the Socialist Party. They also came up against the competing claims of feminism and socialism and significant cultural prescriptions about the proper role and place of women.

THE OLD WORLD

Jewish young women in Eastern Europe were deeply immersed in traditional culture but shared in the changes experienced by the general Jewish community in the late nineteenth century. An increasing number appear to have been working women. The Russian census of 1897 indicated that 15 percent of Jewish artisans were female.

Other women earned income in a variety of ways, including storekeeping, peddling in the marketplace, or going door to door selling items they had bought in cities or baked or made themselves. The conservative estimate is that 21 percent of Jewish women were employed as artisans or peddlers.[1] Most of the female radicals in this study came to America by the time they were fourteen or fifteen years old, and only four had had any experience with proletarianization. No more than another handful had worked or "helped out" in family businesses before their emigration. Most, however, were aware of the growing numbers of women workers and had female friends and relatives who worked, including, often, their mothers. It is striking that while only 13 mothers of 67 male radicals were clearly "gainfully employed" (19 percent), 9 mothers of 28 female radicals were contributors to family income (32 percent).

Rose Schneiderman's mother sewed, and Clara Lemlich's mother kept a store. The mother of Pearl Halpern worked in a cigarette factory, and Clara Weissman's mother had a stand in the marketplace. The number of Jewish families in which the mother was basically "business-oriented" and the father primarily "scholarly" has probably been exaggerated, and in any case does not represent the general family constellations for the Jewish radicals.[2] A greater proportion of females than males, however, had mothers who worked, and at least two socialist daughters lived in families where the mother was indeed the primary bread-winner.

Even more striking is the number of female radicals who received education in the old country. Fifteen of twenty-six (58 percent) about whom data were available had schooling beyond informal instruction by their mothers at home. At least five had gone to private schools and eight more to Russian elementary schools and gymnasia. This did not always happen without a struggle.

When Emma Goldman's father insisted on her leaving school to comply with an arranged marriage, she protested,

> begging to be permitted to continue my studies. In his frenzy he threw my French grammar into the fire, shouting: "Girls do not have to learn much! All a Jewish daughter needs to know is how to prepare a gefüllte fish, cut noodles fine, and give the man plenty of children." I wanted to study, to know life, to travel. Besides, I never would marry for anything but love, I stoutly maintained.[3]

Some women worked as artisans. More were peddlers, often with a "stand" in the market.

From the Archives of YIVO Institute for Jewish Research

Fannie Shapiro's mother, "a very primitive woman, religious and naive," refused to let her daughter go to school; but Fannie, sensing change all around her, and with brothers off in cities in schools, insisted, "I want to learn. I want to see a life, and I want to go to school."[4] Others had it easier. Fannia Cohn's mother encouraged her studiousness and diligence and she had secular and Talmudic instruction in a private school.[5] Rose Schneiderman's father wanted her to be a teacher and her mother "was determined that [Rose] learn Hebrew so [she] could read and understand the prayers recited at home and in the synagogue."[6] And Lucy Sperber's mother insisted on a gymnasium education for her daughter.[7]

In East European Jewish families, the male child was "officially" preferred, particularly the eldest boy; and girls were generally discouraged from studies and ambitions beyond marriage. However, in the families of girls who would become radicals, it appears as if mothers, and sometimes fathers, as with Rose Pesotta and Rose Schneiderman, were willing to contravene *shtetl* tradition. Perhaps it is better to say these parents were, in the late nineteenth century, willing to "modernize" and use one *shtetl* tradition—the pursuit of learning— to overcome another—the inequality of the daughters.[8] Moreover, the women in this study were raised within family constellations which were more likely to produce independent daughters with activist ideologies. Eighty percent of the girls who went on to socialism were nurtured by two parents for the greater part of their adolescence. And in most of the families there appear to have been relatively egalitarian marriages in which neither parent dominated.[9]

The external impingement upon and the internal changes within *shtetl* culture were increasing aspirations for all, perhaps most, for previously hemmed-in young girls. This showed up clearly in the political arena. Significant numbers of women were evident in the Jewish revolutionary movements as they developed in Eastern Europe. Young unmarried women appear to have constituted one-third of the Bund's membership and apparently they held the organization together after the mass arrests of 1898.[10] In the 1900s, increasing and disproportionate numbers of Jewish women were arrested for political activities. Almost 50 percent of the women in this study who were twelve or over at the time of their emigration to the United States were radicalized in Eastern Europe. This included Social Democrat Rose Pesotta, Bundist Flora Weiss, Socialist-Territorialist Marsha Farbman, and Social-Revolutionary Fannia Cohn.

As with the men, when hopes for revolution in Russia ebbed or pogroms intensified, desire for refuge and opportunity in America increased. The intensity of desire for independence that America appeared to offer was extraordinary. Fannie Shapiro told her parents: "If you're not going to let me go to America, I'm going to drown myself."[11] Emma Goldman also promised to throw herself in a river, and Elizabeth Hasanovitz threatened to starve herself to death unless permitted to emigrate. Rose Pesotta wrote:

> After months of argument and cajolery, I persuaded my parents to let me . . . go to the United States. I [saw] no future [in Russia] except to marry . . . and be a housewife. That [was] not enough. . . . I kept repeating to myself: "I must find a way out. I must find a way out."[12]

IN THE PROMISED LAND

The aspirations of these young women were reflected in the numbers who pursued education after their arrival in the United States and while they were working ten or more hours a day in the shops. At least fifteen went to school, mostly at night, and seven more took classes or studied on their own at Hull House, Henry Street Settlement, the Educational Alliance, the Socialist Literary Society, and the East Broadway Library.[13]

Mollie Linker came home from a job in a glass factory at seven,

> and school started at seven-thirty and there [were] a few blocks [to walk]. So I had just time enough to wash up and change a blouse. . . . I had two blouses. And with a sandwich I went to school.[14]

Most of the young unmarried Jewish women worked in the garment industry, and the socialists and future socialists among them were no exception. Twenty-five of thirty-one whose work could be determined were employed in dress and shirtwaist manufacture. These women, going to school at night, and working for wages, could dream of self-sufficiency. Even though a good part of their wages often went to supplement family income, to support brothers in higher education, or to help bring relatives across the Atlantic, the women could hope for eventual independence.

Flora Weiss had such a dream. She came to America at age fourteen with schooling, political experience in the Bund, but no skills. Her sister took her

> into a factory to learn to be a dressmaker. I wasn't able to thread a needle. . . . But I learned it. . . . and became self-sufficient [though] I suffered a great deal.
>   I wanted to earn a lot of money . . . because I wanted to support myself [and] I wanted to organize the workers around me . . . to do something for mankind. . . . I thought . . . I would see a better world.[15]

Jobs in the garment industry, however, were oppressive and demoralizing, and threatened Flora Weiss's dream of self-sufficiency. The seventeen-year-old went to school at night for several years, but:

> There were times in the school that I actually fell apart because the conditions in the factory were so horrible; besides the long hours of work, the hygienic conditions were burdensome. . . . I really broke down physically, and the family thought that they would have to send me to a sanitarium.[16]

Bosses often took particular advantage of girls, most of whom they assumed were timid and green. Females were paid less for the same work, they were timed when they left to go to the toilet, and they were subjected to speedups. Marie Ganz remembered, "At the end of each week the girl who had turned in the least work was dropped off the payroll."[17] Fannie Shapiro had to leave her job because "the boss pinched" her. She "gave him a crack and he fell. He was very embarrassed; so the whole shop went roaring."[18] Shapiro's story has its humorous edge, but sexual harassment was a serious problem; it is reported in a significant number of the memoirs, and once women were organized and union grievance procedures established, charges of sexual abuse were prevalent.[19]

WORK AND MARRIAGE

Many women wanted out. Rose Cohen, who had joined the union with her father's advice and encouragement, asked him:

> does everybody in America live like this? Go to work early, come home late, eat and go to sleep? And the next day again work, eat, sleep? Will I have to do that . . . always? "No," he said smilingly. "You will get married."[20]

Many women looked forward to this solution. Indeed, a tune first sung in Eastern Europe was now heard in the New York City sweat-shops:

> Day like night, night like day,
> And sewing, sewing, sewing;
> Dear God, help me—send
> My handsome one soon,
> To save me from this toil.[21]

Marriage, however, would at least threaten the goal of independence held by women whose aspirations had been raised in the old country and which had been intensified by emigration. This was true not only for those who had been radicalized in Eastern Europe but for thousands of their sisters who had been aware of the political and economic activities of European Jewish women and who would go on to activism themselves here in America.

One socialist woman who thought she could marry and still work told her husband:

> Let's not have any babies. Let's both work and . . . make as much money as we can. . . . I want to help [my parents] come to this country. . . .
> I was naive to life. . . . So before I looked around I gave birth to my baby. And did I have a struggle until I was able to . . . leave him with a friend and . . . go back to the shop to work.[22]

That this woman returned to work after having a baby—indeed, that she continued to work after she married—was exceptional. Only 2 percent of East European Jewish households reported working wives in 1880. And only 1 percent by 1905.[23] This figure is undoubtedly an underestimation, particularly if we include in "working wives" all those women who were partners in small businesses, took up push-cart operations, kept lodgers, looked after other women's children, took in laundry, and did piecework at home.[24] But the number of married women working in factories or shops was indeed very small, particularly when compared to other ethnic groups. In 1904, William Z. Ripley wrote in the *Atlantic Monthly,* "The Jew will not permit his wife to work in the factory." And this appears to have been the case.[25] In 1916, for example, it was reported that only 3.7 percent of female Hebrew wage earners were married, while 38.6 percent of Italian women in the work force were married, and in the total female labor population, 19.3 percent were married.[26]

Jewish radical women or those who were on their way to radicalism did not conform to this pattern. Twenty-four of thirty-two married, and the great majority continued to work afterwards. But marriage was nonetheless restrictive. Those women who were most active in the labor movement, by and large, remained single all of their lives. Rose Schneiderman's mother had a negative attitude toward her daughter becoming a trade unionist: "She kept saying I'd never get married because I was so busy—a prophecy that came true."[27]

Although she had romantic flirtations with men throughout her life, Rose Schneiderman shunned marriage, believing its rigors would prevent her from achieving her goals in the labor movement. She told a group of working girls,

> If you think you will be a grand lady after you leave the factory and are married, you are sadly mistaken, for you will have to work yourself to death.[28]

And although those activists who did marry often married radical men, there were problems. Women were still expected to fulfill customary roles. Hutchins Hapgood saw here, perhaps too easily, a positive synthesis of activism and tradition:

> Many of these women [he wrote] so long as they are unmarried, lead lives thoroughly devoted to "the cause," and afterwards become good wives and fruitful mothers, and urge on their husbands and sons to active work in the "movement."[29]

We can read something else in what union activist Hyman Rogoff said:

> My wife, every chance she had, she helped me so that I should be able to take part in the workers movement—that I should be active and have *the freedom I always wanted*.[30]

And Meyer London's daughter believed her father's work

> was helped immeasurably by my mother's understanding and encouragement. It was her feeling . . . that life was worth while only if one lived it for a useful purpose—primarily to help those who need help. *She asked for nothing for herself* that would have in any way subtracted from the . . . causes.[31]

Theresa Malkiel
J. Lopez/State Historical Society of Wisconsin

Some women were able to stay relatively active themselves. Bessie (Hillman) Abramowitz was one of these, though she had to drop out for a while in 1917 and 1921 when she had her babies. Theresa Malkiel was one of the very few who was able to couple activism with the customary responsibilities of wife and mother.[32] Nonetheless she understood the difficulties involved in that combination. She made the following entry in a fictionalized diary she published in 1910:

> See, Jim is mortally afraid that I'll remain a rebel after I'm married. . . . It's pretty tough on a girl to be striking, quarrelling with her family and be on the outs with her beau at the same time.[33]

One woman, a reader of the *Freiheit,* a Yiddish communist paper, was forbidden by her husband to have the paper in the house. He was a reader of the socialist *Forward.* The wife had a woman friend who faced a similar situation, but "she hid her copies [of the *Freiheit*] under the mattress."[34]

Children, in addition to the normal demands they made upon women's time, also created a variety of cross-pressures on activist mothers. One mother, when she came home from being arrested on the picket line in 1910, was confronted by her small boy: "I wouldn't let you go to work any more. Maxie's mother don't work, she stays home."[35] Marriage and motherhood could be and was troublesome for women activists. But women who chose to remain single were not thereby free of troubles.

THE LONELINESS OF THE SINGLE ORGANIZER

Unlike married male activists, who had wives to encourage and support them and to do the chores, women often found union organizing difficult and destructive of the possibilities of any significant personal life. Rose Schneiderman

> found out that organizing is a hard job . . . and often very frustrating. You work and work and seem to be getting nowhere. Just when you feel that it is no use going on, something happens.
>
> You organize a group and set up a local. Then you have to nurse the members along so they won't get discouraged and quit before the union is strong enough to make demands on the employers. All this could be terribly discouraging if you didn't have faith in trade unionism and didn't believe with every cell in your body that what you were doing in urging them to organize was absolutely right for them. . . .

Lucy and Jack Sperber at the ILGWU's Unity vacation retreat, ca.1924.

Courtesy of Martin Sperber

Organizing also means hours and hours of standing on corners in all sorts of weather to distribute handbills to the women as they come from work. I must have given out millions in my lifetime. It means calling an endless number of meetings and never knowing if anyone will show up. And on top of all this, you never have a life of your own, for there is no limit to the time you can put into the job.[36]

Pauline Newman, the first female organizer for the ILGWU, in the period after the "uprising" of 1909 wrote to Rose Schneiderman:

I could not help coming to the conclusion, that while my life, and way of living is *very interesting*—it is at the same time a very lonely life. Always alone. Except when you are out doing your work. I made a hit in St. Louis. I am sure of that; no one to share it. I have so many plans to carry out, so much work to do—work that shall live after I am gone—Yet no one to help me, no one to advise me. Always alone. It is dreadful. Yet it seems that there is no way out of it—at least for the present.[37]

It was lonely for these women not simply because they had no spouses. The men in the unions for a long time regarded the women workers, and especially women organizers, with suspicion and hostility. A contemporary student and a woman who corresponded with some of the female organizers wrote:

Men officials of the union have objected to women organizers in the same fashion and for the same reasons that they have objected to women in industry. "The woman organizer can't stand the strain of living away from home and being constantly on the job. It's a man's job," stated one official.[38]

And discrimination was rampant. Although women in the ILGWU, for example, developed leadership qualities, initiated and successfully carried out strikes, and were responsible for the formulation of union policy, the locals' executive positions continued to be monopolized by men.[39] Even those who achieved some distinction, like Fannia Cohn, would say:

My life was not easy sailing. It is not easy for a woman to be in a leading position, especially in the labor movement. . . . But I *think* I live a full, interesting and satisfying life. The appreciation of my efforts which I get from the membership and the local leadership is my reward.[40]

Fannia Cohn wrote to correspondents that despite the rewards she was not without "inner pain, worry and spiritual humiliation." And to overcome this she had to "be in constant touch" with her friends.[41]

Men in the unions, at least at first, were unresponsive to women's demands. "What do girls know?" one woman remembered a man asking; "They want to dance—instead of a union they want to dance."[42] The need for mutual support was strong. It helped build, among the women of ILGWU Local 25, a movement that created an important and effective educational department and then a highly successful vacation retreat.[43] The increasing solidarity of women was not only psychologically sustaining for themselves, it led to significant long-term accomplishments for the whole union movement and membership.

LESS CLASS-CONSCIOUS SISTERS

The Jewish women organizers also faced barriers in their work with women of other ethnic groups. Minnie Rivkin was called "Christ-killer" and "communist" by Italian women with whom she worked. Rivkin tried, with some history, to destroy the charge of deicide, and then went on to tell the women that socialism was acceptable because Jesus was a communist who said, "Heal the sick and feed the poor." But Italian girls, Minnie Rivkin believed, "belonged to the union because they felt they *had* to. . . . Outside of that, they had no interest in what takes place."[44]

In order to generate interest among non-Jews, Flora Weiss was asked by the union to work in nonunion shops.

> They thought I would be able to organize the workers and bring them into the union—It was regretfully not so. The majority of the workers in that time—I was originally in Chicago—were of Polish origin. It was an element that did not lend itself to organization.[45]

> We spoke friendly, we smiled to each other and immediately they reported us to the Bosses. . . . I suffered plenty from that . . . and was not able to obtain work very easily. . . . But it didn't stop me from talking to the workers. Because I held it my dedicated duty to do so.[46]

No doubt some of this opinion on the unorganizability of non-Jewish women had to do with ethnic chauvinism. One Jewish girl said, "If [the Italian girls] were more civilized they wouldn't take such low pay. But they go without hats and gloves and umbrellas."[47] But there was some objective basis to the view that Italians and Poles were slower to come to unionism and from there to socialism. The Women's Trade

Union League annual report for 1908–1909, published just prior to the "great uprising," stated in part:

> The Jewish women are quick to organize and the league has found in several trades that the membership of unions was wholly Jewish, while the other nationalities working in the same trade were non-union.

And an Italian seamstress later recalled that:

> Jewish girls . . . were much more advanced than the Italians. . . . They fought for us Italians. The chairlady in my shop, she was Jewish. She goes up to the boss and she says, "Look at this girl! Why are you paying her so little?" She was talking about me! Oh, they were very advanced. . . . Later on we got our own union and were advanced too.[48]

Ethnic attachments and values seem to have played a role in preventing the emergence of class consciousness among Italians and Poles. But in the case of the Jewish women, as we have already seen with the Jews generally, ethnicity and class consciousness appear to have been complementary, if not mutually reinforcing.

Getting through to the native-born Americans in the garment industry was apparently not much easier for the class-conscious Jews. One Russian-Jewish female milliner, in this country six years, who tried to organize a union, told an investigator of the millinery trades:

> . . . it's no use trying to organize the American women. They don't care about anything but making dates. It's all men and dances, and they don't care about organizing because they expect to get married and stop working. It's no use talking to them. When you begin on unions they call you a socialist, and that ends it; or if you talk about woman's suffrage, they laugh at you. Why should they laugh?
>
> There is something fascinating about America. But they are not thinkers here. It's all money. They don't think—but then not many people do in any country. American women are not disturbed enough. You have to be disturbed to think. Russian women [think] . . . because things have been hard for them.[49]

In 1910, Pauline Newman took great joy in the fact that she and her co-workers had

> at last succeeded in organizing an English-speaking branch of the waistmakers union. And . . . not with ten or eleven members—but with a good sturdy membership of forty. Now what will you say to that![50]

And as late as 1935 Rose Pesotta complained about

> the 100% American white daughters of the sturdy pioneers. They are all
> members of . . . card clubs [and] lodges. . . . Class-consciousness is . . .
> remote from their thoughts.[51]

FEMINISM AND SOCIALISM

Many of the women in this study, because of the prejudice and
insensitivity of male leadership, felt isolated from the mainstream of
the labor movement. They felt somewhat divided, too, from their less
class-conscious sisters. And sometimes they were uncomfortable even
with the Socialist Party, which took a long time to support women's
unionism without reluctance, and even then failed to understand the
"Woman Question." Many of the women were members, active
recruiters, and Socialist candidates themselves, like Esther Freedman,
who ran for the New York State Assembly several times on the Socialist Party ticket. But they did this *despite* the fact that, for the most part,
Socialist Party posture toward women was marked by disinterest and
condescension.[52]

It was understandable, then, that many of the Jewish women
would, in their struggles, accept intervention and financial support
from a middle-class, feminist group like the Women's Trade Union
League. Several class-conscious activists, like Theresa Malkiel, Rose
Schneiderman, and Clara Lemlich, even became members and went
on to become officers of the League. They experienced the tension
inherent in the attempt to synthesize feminism and socialism. The
Women's Trade Union League, like most Progressive organizations,
did not adhere to a class analysis of society and social problems. Indeed, most of the members were feminists who saw promoting the
organization of women and women's suffrage as ways of transcending
class lines.[53] A male correspondent warned Rose Schneiderman about
her work in the feminist movement:

> You either work for Socialism, and as a consequence for the equality
> of the sexes, or you work for women['s] suffrage only and neglect Social-
> ism. Then you act like a bad doctor who pretends to cure his patient by
> removing the symptoms instead of removing the disease itself.[54]

Some of the class-conscious activists were exhausted and sickened
by "the keeping sweet all the time and pleading for aid from the 'dear

ladies' and the ministers," and they were suspicious of the League's loyalty to Samuel Gompers and the antisocialist leadership of the American Federation of Labor.[55] Because the fundamental purpose of the Women's Trade Union League was, however, to stimulate organization among working women, and because it succeeded in drawing public attention to conditions and gave direct aid, it proved itself a valuable ally. Socialist Party stalwart Theresa Malkiel, union organizer Rose Schneiderman, and several others continued to work indefatigably for the League.[56] The unions persisted in soliciting the League's support and the ILGWU maintained its policy of sending women to the League's Bryn Mawr Summer School.

These women did not, however, become feminists, at least not to the extent of putting the issue of the oppression of women above all else. They stayed with socialism, even though the Party continued in the main to treat women's issues as epiphenomenal. They stayed with radical trade unionism even though their union brothers continued to be chauvinistic, albeit less openly. They initiated education, health, and recreation programs despite the doubts of male colleagues. And they made strikes over the objections of male leadership. They stayed, in short, with class consciousness.

This decision, though that is too precise a word, was made within the framework of traditional Jewish values and recent Jewish experience. It is true that these activist women, particularly those who stayed single, were in rebellion against parts of the tradition; and it is also true, as Henrietta Szold put it, that: "To the Jew, accustomed from time immemorial to regard Jewish women as symbols of loyalty, a daughter's insubordination is nothing short of catastrophe."[57]

But the Cohns and the Schneidermans and the Rivkins were not only rebelling; they were responding to traditional norms reworked in a modern context. Ninety-two percent of the women had strong religious backgrounds, and 21 percent had been deeply immersed in Jewish tradition and culture. Most of these women continued to bear their Jewish heritage proudly, and most continued their activism within a predominantly Yiddish-speaking constituency with its host of organizations, institutions, and informal networks. Their class consciousness, their well-developed ethic of social justice, and the terms within which they couched the labor and political conflict were well understood in the Jewish community. Their idealism in seeking a "beautiful tomorrow," their energy in aspiring to self-sufficiency and

to "do something for humanity" were familiar in the Jewish population concentrations rife with the tradition of *tachlis* and the socialist
spirit. It is important to remind ourselves here, too, that these were
women who, as young girls, had had some encouragement from one
or both parents to pursue learning and had begun to think of themselves as truly capable.

Fannia Cohn continued to respond to the norms of *shtetl* culture
even as part of her became someone new. Reflecting on over forty
years in America, Cohn wrote:

> I came to the United States in search [of] freedom, rather than for
> economic advantages. . . . One thing I promised my family was that I
> would continue my studies in the "New World," as my mother wanted
> her children to be no less than professors.
>   In New York, I lived with my cousins, who were very wealthy and
> offered to assist me while I continued my studies. I refused to accept this
> offer as it conflicted with my "sense of independence." Coming as I did
> from a revolutionary background, I was eager to be here with "the
> people." . . . .
>   I wanted to really understand the mind, the aspirations of the work-
> ers. . . . Therefore I went to work in a shop.[58]

Much earlier Cohn had written: "I learned in the school of experience
that true happiness comes not from what we get, but from what we
strive to do."[59] Cohn strove, with remarkable energy and persistence,
to help provide the laborer with education. The purpose of workers'
education, she wrote, is to fulfill

> the desire on the part of the working man for a richer and fuller life
> individually and collectively. . . . [I]t aims . . . at a progressive reconstruc-
> tion of society. . . . a better social order.[60]

Fannia Cohn, with many of her radical sisters, continued, in the new
industrial world, to place good deeds, learning, and justice higher on
the scale of values than material wealth.

TOWARD SYNTHESIS

In the old country, for Jews generally and increasingly for Jewish
women, the inconsistency between an exalted religious and historical
status and a low political and economic condition—a discrepancy
which became greater with modernization and proletarianization—

heightened recognition of injustices, which in turn intensified desire for remedy. One young woman and radical-to-be expressed this "status-inconsistency" directly:

> Members of the human family, people with brains and ambition, we were not citizens; we were children of the cursed Pale, with our rights limited, the districts in which we could live and the trades and professions we could follow, all prescribed for us.[61]

In the new country there were many fewer legal prescriptions, but there were anomalies. Women with rising expectations, dreams of independence, and ethical sensitivities finely honed in the world of Jewish tradition, found themselves oppressed, exploited, victimized by gross unfairness. Anna Margolin, the modern Yiddish poet, in an ode to these daughters of the old country, wrote:

> O Jewish daughters of the factories! In your gaze I see hidden the charm of the small Jewish town, the glimmer of the faraway home.
> . . . .
> And when I observe you more closely, I behold much more: the ancient crowns of millenniums are shining through the yoke.
> For princesses are you all, nobility rests calmly in your gaze. How enslaved have you become now! Who shall bring you back to the King?[62]

Who indeed? Some women thought: a husband. But for most of the women in this study, it was socialism, and radical trade unionism. And many of the socialists and trade unionists, after a time, found a middle way. They participated in the extensive Jewish organizational network that was spawned by socialism and communism as these movements grew and drew in thousands of families. For women, participation in the network combined family-community obligations with some dimension of personal independence. Former working women (and future working women, too) found jobs and "special places in the children's camps, shules, consumer organizations and tenement committees, foreign relief societies, labor defense and hundreds of other societies."[63] This was not direct political participation, but it represented an extraordinary, significant, long-term contribution to the labor movement and social welfare. And it offered the Jewish woman a temporarily viable synthesis of her desire for self-sufficiency, her energy, her idealism, her class consciousness, and the traditional culture out of which these aspirations and attitudes at least partly emerged.

7
biography
as social
history

No person's life is as neat as the effort to define it; but the following biographical sketches help illustrate parts of the social and cultural history which helped form the radical consciousness of the individual subjects. There are things here, too, which illuminate and reinforce the point that the immigrant socialists were rooted in a rich, sustaining Jewish community and culture, and were continuing to respond to prophetic injunctions, messianism, and new versions of *tsedaka* and *tachlis*.

ISADORE WISOTSKY

Isadore Wisotsky was born in 1895, not far from Kiev in a *shtetl* "sunk in mud and poverty."[1] His father was a "normal Yidishe worker," who sold hats and caps he made by hand.[2] The elder Wisotsky "kept all the Jewish holidays and went through the Jewish rituals," but "he was not Orthodox." Isadore's mother "saw to [the Orthodoxy], she was pious, religious, strictly kosher."[3]

Until he was eleven, Isadore Wisotsky went to *heder*, where "saying prayers and learning Torah [still] afforded us the opportunity to 'shmoose' on politics or on world events, and cursing the tzar was a must." It was at *heder* that Wisotsky, after reading Kropotkin's *Mutual Aid*, heard about "a fellow [who] got a couple of smacks from his father for not believing that it's up to Messiah to free the Jewish people from bondage."[4]

Wisotsky got a few smacks himself:

My father would smack me, my mother would smack me, the rabbi would smack me, all the Jews smacked me. Everyone wanted to make a mensch out of me—Itzick—but Itzick did not amount to much as a child.[5] . . . In any case, they liked me, would you believe it?[6]

By the time he was twelve, Isadore Wisotsky was working to help support his increasingly impoverished family. The decreasing opportunities for Jewish artisans and the intensified competition from peasant handicraft industry and factory production impelled his father to leave Russia in 1908. He brought the whole family over to America in a year and a half. We "came, all the immigrants came," Wisotsky believed, "to run away from distress and hunger, from Russian poverty."[7]

The trip across in steerage was on a "small, stinky steamer, overcrowded . . . and [with] food you could not eat."[8] There were ten days of this and Wisotsky's mother grew ill.

I then became the mother of my two smaller younger brothers and little sister, until I got seasick. Then some good neighbor took care of us until we arrived at Castle Garden.[9]

Immediately upon arriving on the lower East Side, where Isadore Wisotsky's father had taken a flat, the family was visited by a host of relatives and *landsleit* from Lipovitz. They brought presents to the greenhorns. And Mrs. Katz, a "kind-hearted neighbor," taught Mrs. Wisotsky to shop and fix up the house "in the American manner."[10]

Soon, the "grinding of our daily lives began, with worries of earning a livelihood."

Father was an . . . operator. He learned this trade at his cousin's shop on Stanton Street and worked for four dollars a week as an apprentice. Since he was a relative, the boss allowed him to sleep in the shop, to save rent money [before the rest of the family arrived]. The boss thereby saved the wages for a night watchman.[11]

Wisotsky's father worked sixty to seventy hours per week. But there were many weeks of unemployment in the slack season. It was during these weeks that Itzick became the "breadwinner" by hawking newspapers. Soon, in order to help further supplement his father's earnings he dropped out of school and worked full time. And still it was necessary for the Wisotsky's to take in boarders.

Several of the boarders, Wisotsky remembered, were desperate to avoid the sweatshop. Moishe, who said "No bosses for him," earned his living by going to Slavic neighborhoods throughout the country, enlarging portraits of family members and painting them. The footloose Moishe escaped the shops and the bosses, but he ended up a "hoarse-voiced, glass-eyed, wandering drunk" who left his wife and children. Years later, Isadore Wisotsky heard that Moishe, "homeless and penniless . . . was found dead on a street in Buffalo, New York."[12]

Shimon, too, did not "want to die working seventy hours a week in a sweat shop . . . to get TB, spitting [his] lungs out in blood." He put himself through a period of intense prolonged work in order to save his money and, like some of the "birds of passage" of other immigrant groups, to return "home." Shimon dreamed of Lipovitz and about buying a butcher shop there. "I will go back," he said, "to have my Sabbath, my holidays. *You* live like mules here." Shimon did go back. He was drafted soon after he arrived and was killed during the First World War.[13]

Wisotsky's father tried a different way to battle the oppression of the sweatshop. "He joined the union right away."[14] He was soon involved in the cloakmakers strike in the summer of 1910, only a few months after his son arrived in America. Isadore Wisotsky, now fifteen, took part with his father in several demonstrations, and during the course of the strike the Wisotsky house was packed with striking *landsleit* eating black bread and herring and discussing politics and the unions.[15] During the crisis, people helped each other. Responding to the *shtetl* norm of mutual aid, the saloon keeper gave a discount on beer for strikers; and the "strikers borrowed from their landsleit friends who worked in other trades or peddled."[16]

The political discussions and the mutually supportive behavior were part of the "education" of Isadore Wisotsky. Rivele, another of the Wisotsky household boarders, also contributed to Isadore's education by taking him to lectures on "revolutionary trade unionism," given by Saul Yanofsky. "I did not understand much of the discussion," Wisotsky admits, "but my sympathies were with Rivele's ideas and thoughts."[17] Wisotsky remembered too that

> the socialists blasted the streets with propaganda for their candidates and promised that they would save the East Side from Tammany Hall and graft.[18]

Even on those "hot stuffy summer evenings" that Isadore Wisotsky "spent on the Williamsburgh Bridge . . . to cool off," people came, "sang songs of their native lands [and] discussed" politics.[19]

The congestion in the Wisotsky rooms, and Isadore's inability to get "a half-decent job" to help the family, made him uncomfortable enough to move out. But he took with him what he learned; and soon he was part of a "commune," which occupied "one room with nothing . . . and called itself facetiously, the 'Don't worry group.'" They argued all the time:

> The main subject was the social revolution and how to make it. And these debates lasted till dawn, [by which time] we were all breathless and hoarse.[20]

Isadore Wisotsky spent many more years discussing the social revolution. Between prayers and learning Torah as a boy, he had started his political career in the old country by "cursing the tzar." In America he moved through strikes and demonstrations into a significant period as a member of the Industrial Workers of the World (IWW), and remained active in the radical labor movement for most of his adult life.

ROSE PESOTTA

Rose Pesotta was born in 1896 in Derazhnya, a provincial town in the Ukraine served by a railroad. Because the town was a trading center, and because her father owned a flour and feed store there, Rose Pesotta saw a great deal of activity, some of which was political. She witnessed her father in political discussion often. He was outspoken, she said, had the courage of his convictions, and rarely lost the opportunity to do something for the good of the community.

Rose Pesotta was a voracious reader, and like Clara Lemlich often nestled in a corner of her attic with revolutionary literature. Her parents, acting against traditional norms, encouraged her education and sent her to private school:

> Among our studies were the Hebrew language and Jewish history. These were taught surreptitiously, not being specified in the curriculum for which [the teachers] had a permit.[21]

When her father took ill, Rose was taken out of school and had a private tutor at home. The teacher was a young woman who continued Rose's lessons in Hebrew, history, and literature. The point of most of the instruction, Rose Pesotta remembered, was that "the people came first. It is their actions that bring about changes in society."[22] Her mother took over at the flour and feed store and with a little help from Rose managed quite well. Rose Pesotta added to her self-esteem by contributing to the family income, and she had, in her mother and in her tutor, models of capable, confident, relatively modern Jewish women.

In her father, too, she had a model of political commitment and modern vision. He talked about equality for *all*, Rose Pesotta wrote, and he practiced it conscientiously.[23]

Rose Pesotta's most powerful model, however, was her sister Esther. In 1906 Esther Pesotta had visited an aunt in Odessa and "returned aglow with a new passion . . . the revolutionary movement."[24] She joined a "circle" in Derazhnya and recruited ten-year-old Rose to serve as a carrier of leaflets.

> I was then a fledgling of the underground and listened avidly to all that was discussed, chewing green apples or berries and linking up any information gained there with what I had read in the garret.[25]

After Esther Pesotta left for America, Rose continued through her teens to take part in the underground revolutionary movement. This meant for the most part organizing discussion groups, in neighboring "industrial" cities, among seamstresses, tailors, shoemakers, and factory workers.

Her activities in the underground and her studies with her tutor complemented each other.

> What information I did not get at the meetings of the circle, because I was afraid if I asked too many questions I would be silenced, I managed to glean from my tutor in a roundabout way. I devoured the contents of . . . books [and] periodicals.[26]

Eventually, among her radical friends there developed a sharp factional cleavage, and Rose Pesotta found herself pulled between the Bundists and the Socialist Zionists. Zionist literature, published abroad and explaining plans for resettlement in Palestine, was widely circulated among her associates. Though the Pesotta family did not themselves plan to go to Palestine,

Father purchased . . . bonds . . . issued by the Jewish Colonial Trust
. . . in the name of each of his children. We took pride in that possession,
which meant—as our dad explained—that we owned part of the future
Jewish nation.[27]

Educated, activist Rose Pesotta found in 1912 that despite its
railroad, its trade, and its political activity, provincial Derazhnya
palled upon her.

I felt that I must do something constructive with my life. Contacts
with the visiting workers in the underground, who traveled widely and
who were serving mankind, aroused me and made me feel useless.[28]

It was just at this point that Rose Pesotta's parents, despite their
modernity, arranged a "match" for their sixteen-year-old daughter.
She determined that no such marriage would take place. The evening
she had discovered her parents' "high-handed plan," Rose Pesotta's
circle met. There she read aloud revolutionary essays, some of which
were written by impassioned young women who had forsaken marriage and family for the work of liberating the Russian people.

I visualized myself as one of them, giving up everything to aid in
creating a new society based on freedom of thought . . . universal education, work for all without coercion. . . .[29]

None of this was possible, Rose Pesotta thought, if she stayed at
home. She wrote in desperation to her sister Esther in America:

Please write to Father urging him to let me go. Tell him you're
lonesome . . . and want your sister with you.[30]

Rose Pesotta ended her letter by threatening to "take carbolic acid and
end it all" if she did not hear from her sister favorably.

Her parents, after nine long months of debate, finally gave Rose
Pesotta consent to go. And her father in 1913 escorted her across the
Ukraine and Poland to the German border.

In America, Esther Pesotta, a shirtwaist maker in Local 25 and a
participant in the "Great Uprising" of 1909, got her sister Rose a job
in a shirtwaist factory.

Esther and some of my co-workers showed me tricks that enabled
me to attain facility; by the end of a year I could keep pace in any shop.[31]

While she learned sewing during the day, she went to school to learn English at night, and her hunger for education kept Rose Pesotta in courses at Bryn Mawr Summer School, the Brookwood School, and Wisconsin State School for Workers from 1922 to 1930.[32]

Rose Pesotta had an abundance of energy. In addition to educating herself, she joined, soon after she began working in 1913, the "up-and-coming Waistmakers Local 25." And for two decades Rose Pesotta alternated between work as an organizer and negotiator, and garment worker.

In her union activities, Rose Pesotta moved around quite a bit. She organized in Los Angeles, San Francisco, Seattle, Portland, Puerto Rico, Buffalo, and Montreal. Her friends called her a "flitting, happy little whirlwind." But reflecting the turmoil of being an activist woman in a male-dominated labor movement, Rose Pesotta confided to her diary in 1931: "Nobody knows how many cheerless sleepless nights, I have spent crying in my loneliness."[33] She was divorced twice and found herself in interludes afterwards with one married man, and then another. "Alone—again, alone," she wrote in her journal in 1932.[34]

In 1933 she became a full-time organizer of women workers and abandoned the negotiating process to men—partly because of the attitudes of leaders like former union president Benjamin Schlesinger, who apparently told Rose Pesotta "to stop this kind of business and go home and get married."[35]

In 1934, though she believed "the voice of a solitary woman on the General Executive Board would be a voice lost in the wilderness," she accepted a nomination for a vice presidency.[36] In July of that year, Rose Pesotta, struggling with the problems of a single, professional woman, recorded the following reflections in her diary:

> I am not among the respectable women, no home, no family, to care for.
> It is a difficult life full of hardship . . . but in the long run what does it matter. . . .
> My mother like millions of others . . . toiled a lifetime raising a large family, how many sleepless nights and agonizing days has she spent . . . watching over them, and now? Gone, to the four corners of the world— and she is left alone—the price of raising a family.[37]

Rose Pesotta paid a price for her choices, too, but the girl from the railroad town of Derazhnya, raised by a progressive Jewish family and educated in Hebrew, revolutionary literature, and Jewish history, stayed in the front line of the battle for ten more years, saying: "The World is my Country and to do Good is my Religion."[38] "The principle for which I stand will keep me always alone—I shall not become a slave of a man who does not share it with me."[39]

CHARLES SASHA ZIMMERMAN

When sixteen-year-old Sasha Ubsushone arrived at Ellis Island in 1913 an immigration official welcomed him to the land of the free by changing his name to Charles Zimmerman. It was probably the first and last time that Sasha would allow someone to impose upon him in such a fashion.

After less than a year in the United States, Zimmerman led a strike of knee-pants makers and helped form a union local. In 1916 he joined the International Ladies Garment Workers Union and soon thereafter the Socialist Party. He went on to become one of the most influential labor leaders in the garment industry and a long-time activist in the struggle for civil rights and socialism.

Charles Zimmerman, however, had come to the United States with no political experience. Indeed, before emigration he had never left the *shtetl* of Talna in the Ukraine, where he was born in 1897. But he did bring cultural baggage. In the old country, like so many of his fellow Jews who went on to become radicals, Sasha had been nurtured in the moral commandments of Torah, Talmud, and *tsedaka*.

In the United States Zimmerman would grow indifferent to religious *ritual,* but there is no mistaking the fact that Jewish community and culture—including religious *values*—were as critical to the formation of his radical consciousness as were economic hardship and proletarianization.

The most important part of his "education," Zimmerman claimed, was his grandmother, who raised him.

She was the person closest to me. She was an extremely Orthodox woman. But she applied her orthodoxy with common sense and intelligence. She made me do my homework even on *shabos* if I were behind in school. Over my objections she would say, "For education it is allowed." She was very clever; but more than that, she had a moral understanding, a feel for people. The strongest picture in my mind is my grandmother sitting at the window on *shabos* at twilight time reading the *Tanakh.* She

Charles Sasha Zimmerman, in 1939.
Courtesy of Rose Zimmerman

taught me important things from that book and from her life. She taught me a lot.[40]

Zimmerman's father had died when Charles was seven, and his widowed mother opened a combination candy and grocery store to support the family, which now consisted of herself, three children, and Charles's grandmother. The store, which was "only as big as a telephone booth," provided just enough income to keep the Zimmermans alive. Nonetheless, Charles did manage to gain some formal education in addition to the informal transmission of values he experienced at his grandmother's side. This included three years of Talmud Torah (preparatory for yeshiva) and two years of Russian schooling. To enter the Russian gymnasium, which already had its quota of Jews at the time of Charles's application, he had to make what he called "his first civil rights fight." With the help of a doctor in town, he managed to win.

Because Charles was literate, a young man connected with revolutionary organizations in Odessa and Kiev asked the twelve-year-old to write communiques for him:

> Apparently he didn't want his handwriting to be on it. . . . I asked him questions. . . . [He said] when you will grow up, you'll understand. But whether I understood or not, it was bound to leave some impression. There was the revolutionary movement in town . . . and the kids knew all about it, and there were meetings.
> All these things had an effect. . . . At the age of eleven and twelve you are no longer a child.[41]

At fifteen, Charles Zimmerman was at work in a piece-goods store as a sales person earning ten rubles for a six-month period. This, in 1912, was the best job he could find to increase the family earnings. His sister, trying to do her part, had already left for America that year and was a shirtwaist maker in New York City. She worked hard, saved her money for a *shifscarte* (ship ticket) and brought Charles Zimmerman to the United States.

> I was not anxious to come to the United States. I didn't want to be a garment worker. I knew if you came to the United States, you became a garment worker. [But] I left because we could not economically exist any longer in the small town.[42]

In America in 1913 Zimmerman avoided the garment shop but only temporarily. Two days after moving in with his sister, his uncle's

family, and several boarders, he found a job in a piece-goods store on
Ridge Street only one block from the flat. He was expected to work
until 10:00 p.m., but he wanted to go to night school. The memory of
his grandmother and his own experience with Talmud Torah and
gymnasium fostered in him a desire to continue his studies. Zimmerman tried to convince his employer to allow him to work only until
6:00 p.m. This was not accepted and Zimmerman quit, but his uncle
supported him while he attended night school and looked for a job
during the day.

On one of those days, the anniversary of his father's death, Zimmerman went to the synagogue to say *Kaddish*. At the door, the beadle
asked him for a quarter.

> I didn't have a quarter. So he didn't let me in. I never went into a
> *shul* again. I probably would have stopped anyway as I progressed to-
> ward atheism in the radical movement.[43]

No longer formally immersed in his religion, Zimmerman was
still rooted in Jewish community. In his tenement on Ridge Street
lived a "bunch of *landsleit*," all of whom worked in a knee-pants shop
in Williamsburg. They not only got Zimmerman a job, but they taught
him to do "section work." And he became a "front maker"; that is, he
made the fly of the pants and one part of a pocket. He had come to
America. He had become a garment worker.

The shop in which Zimmerman worked had a "wooden staircase
and wooden floors . . . oil all over . . . motors. . . . It was actually a fire
trap." It was also a nonunion shop, and Zimmerman as a "learner"
had worked three full weeks without pay.[44]

> We were a bunch of young fellows; we read the *Forward,* we knew
> what was going on. And we were all *landsleit* besides. We decided on our
> own to strike.[45]

The strike lasted three weeks and the settlement included recognition
of the union.

> There was no question about the desire of . . . the workers to be
> union members. They all agreed . . . they all stuck together, because they
> were all friends and *landsleit.*[46]

Zimmerman had won his "second civil rights fight," and it was
hardly his last. A manager from the United Garment Workers in New

York came to the shop, which was serviced by a Brooklyn business agent, to compliment Zimmerman and the others on the fact that they had struck and unionized the shop. He said their reward was the lower dues of $2.25 that they were being charged, instead of the usual $7.25.

These *landsleit,* however, had been giving the business agent the full fee, and realized they had been cheated. Zimmerman and the others ran to the union office shouting:

> "A *gonif* [thief] in the union, a *gonif* in the union." We didn't know at that time what kind of a bunch were running the Williamsburg office. We didn't know enough to be afraid of yelling: "The *gonif* must be thrown out."[47]

Seventy members led by Charles Zimmerman went to the very next membership meeting, and when the meeting started—

> We didn't know you had to ask for the floor. . . . We all got up and started yelling, "There is a *gonif* in the union and he must be thrown out." . . . We finally forced this corrupt business agent to resign. . . . We didn't know anything about the internal politics [of the union]. The fight took place as a matter of our resentment against a *gonif* in our union. The union was something holy to us.[48]

When asked to run for the union executive board, Zimmerman, believing "there wasn't enough time for activities," refused. Even after the shop was unionized, Zimmerman had to work from seven in the morning till six in the evening.

> It was just about enough [time] to grab a bite and run to night school. I used to go to meetings . . . but I didn't want to take any official position.[49]

In 1914 Charles Zimmerman was layed off and his uncle took him into the factory where he was a foreman and taught Zimmerman carpentry. The job was in Astoria and paid $7.00 per week. After carfare Zimmerman brought home only $5.80.

> On this we had to live—the whole family. And not only the family, the *landsleit* too. . . . My mother [whom Zimmerman had brought over in 1914] would cook a big pot of potatoes and buy a herring or two. [The *landsleit*] would come in and have herring and potatoes and tea and sing David Edelstadt's songs. . . . We sang as if the world was ours because we had herring and potatoes. . . . We were a very happy bunch.[50]

In less than a year Zimmerman was again unemployed, and after a short stint with military coats in a New Jersey factory, his sisters brought him once more into the garment shops of New York City. In 1916 he joined the ILGWU and after a few weeks was elected chairman of his shop.[51] The very next year, while still going to night school, Zimmerman joined the Socialist Party.

> I was a socialist all along and despite the fact that I was busy with school I joined the Party. . . .
> I became a member because that was what I believed in and that was part of our life. . . .[52]

After the Russian Revolution Zimmerman gave up school altogether.

> I said, what is the use of studying for anything? We are going to have a new society. . . . I gave up school and became more active [politically].[53]

Except for brief periods—one, a year-long "hobo trip" across the United States in 1921–1922—Charles Zimmerman remained active in radical labor and civil rights movements into the 1970s despite blindness that had resulted from a stroke in 1966. The activity was intense and varied. In 1918, while a member of the Socialist Party, he joined the Industrial Workers of the World and worked closely with the anarchists. In 1919 he joined the Communist Party. Someone quipped about his apparent ideological eclecticism that "for Zimmerman you need a whole separate party."[54]

He continued throughout to be an independent spirit. In 1926 Zimmerman helped organize a general strike in the cloak trade. He did this somewhat reluctantly, because it looked as if any strike in the garment industry that year could not succeed. The striking workers, with the help of Charles Zimmerman and Louis Hyman, did elicit a favorable offer. The Communist Party, however, over Zimmerman's vehement protestations, forced a continuation of the strike, which ended in a disastrous defeat. "I learned the danger," Zimmerman said, "of a political party controlling a Union." By 1929, after the expulsion of the Lovestoneite faction from the Communist Party—a faction with which Zimmerman was closely tied—he determined that the Communists were not a political party, but "robots," and Zimmerman resigned. "Robots," he said, "can not make a revolution or build a new world."[55]

Charles Zimmerman returned to the ILGWU and headed Local 22 of the union in New York for twenty-five years, until 1958, when he became manager of the Joint Board of the Dress Waistmakers Union. He was also chairman of the AFL-CIO's Civil Rights Committee. And in 1972 Zimmerman was elected co-chairman of the Socialist Party Democratic Socialist Federation (now Social Democrats U.S.A.).

Charles Zimmerman was born in a *shtetl* and was raised mainly by a loving, Orthodox grandmother who had a "moral understanding [and] a feel for people." He experienced economic hardship and proletarianization. He was nurtured, aided, and sustained by his relatives in the old country and in America—as were vast numbers of Jews to whom family ties and community were essential. His sisters, his uncle, and his *landsleit,* still operating on the *shtetl* norms of communal responsibility and mutual aid, found him jobs, and provided moral and political support. And all "these things had an effect." Charles Sasha Zimmerman, like the biblical prophets his grandmother had taught him about, developed a vision of a new and better world, and he pursued it for more than half a century.

CLARA WEISSMAN

Clara Weissman was one of the very few in this study to emigrate from Russia unaccompanied by close relatives.[56] She did, however, like most, come to family already in the United States. She lived for a time in Newark, New Jersey, with her older sister, who had sent her a *shifscarte* in 1914.

Clara Weissman had found it necessary to leave Kishinev, where she was born in 1900, because of the deteriorating economic condition of her family. Her father had been a moderately prosperous builder, but Clara, one of six children, was deprived of his support when he was killed in a pogrom in 1906. Her mother, "a very religious woman," took a stand in the market, trading city-made goods for produce to try to sustain the survivors. And Clara's eleven-year-old brother was sent to work in a cigar factory. But income was scarce and America beckoned. Clara Weissman's sister had already left in 1912, and Clara followed two years later.

In steerage she brought with her a package of herring and cookies. Two days into the ten-day trip she could not distinguish the fish from the confection and tossed the package overboard. Clara

Clara Weissman
Courtesy of Clara Weissman

Weissman arrived hungry and lice-ridden, and at Castle Garden found no one waiting. Her sister had apparently misunderstood the day or time of arrival. It did not appear to be an auspicious beginning for the young girl, who "half believed that there was gold in America's streets." An agent from the Hebrew Immigrant Aid Society, however, helped ameliorate some of the disorientation and took Clara all the way to her sister's apartment in New Jersey. Here Clara Weissman found her sister with a new-born; her brother-in-law, "a *luftmensch* from the old country," had been disabled by an accident at work; and Clara herself had virtually no skills.

She did manage to get a job in a cigar factory. The workers were mainly immigrants and blacks, and the two groups worked in separate sections of the shop. During the half-hour granted for lunch, however, Clara Weissman "mixed," and the black workers taught her English. For a long time, she says, she spoke English with the accents of Eastern Europe and the American South. During this time she also continued her education in night school.

Eventually friends brought Clara Weissman into the garment industry and taught her dressmaking. Here, Weissman said,

> We were at the mercy of the contractors, who paid as little as they could for piece work. [The girls were also under pressure from] bosses who always tried to take advantage of the young ones. The sons and even the old men tried to make every girl.

In 1918 Clara Weissman was on strike and immediately thereafter joined the union.

> I joined the union because it was the right thing to do. I joined because I was brought up on it.
>
> I was brought up by progressives. My father was dead, my mother was incredibly busy holding together a family of seven. And I was in a school set up for children orphaned by the pogroms. But the Russian government was stupid. They set up these schools, and for teachers they gave us revolutionaries they had exiled from the cities. Naturally, they taught us progressive things.
>
> The priest used to come once a year to see whether we were taught religion and loyalty to the regime. When he came in we were supposed to sing, *"Bozhe Tsarya Khrani"*—God protect the Czar. Instead we say, *"Bozhe Tsarya Khoroni"*—God bury the Czar. But, of course, the priest didn't catch it. These revolutionaries instilled in us progressive thinking. This I brought with me.

Clara Weissman's progressive thinking led her to the union and therein to a position of shop stewardess. She was also involved in socialist circles and activities, though she never joined the Socialist Party. This she "left to her husband." Reflecting some of the tensions of an activist who marries, she said,

> I could have joined 150,000 times because I agreed with the progressive ideas. But my husband whose political life began when he beat up his teacher in Russia for calling him a "dirty Jew," belonged to twelve different organizations, including the Socialist Party. I had two children. I brought them into the world and believed that I had to raise and take care of them. And I did a good job.
>
> I didn't want to become pregnant, but in those years, what did you know anyway? I worked through my sixth month. *That* was very unusual. In those days you married, you stayed home, and you got a dining room set.

Clara Weissman was a homemaker raising her children from 1921 to 1932, but she was not interested in a dining room set. Throughout those years she stayed active in political discussion groups, tenants' rights groups, and other organizations. And in 1932, after bringing her mother to this country and into her home, Clara Weissman returned to work, "got her union book back," and for twenty years more was active in the radical labor movement.

BERNARD CHASANOW

Bernard Chasanow, like Clara Weissman brought "progressive thinking" with him to the New World. In addition, like Rose Pesotta, he had had actual experience in radical politics in the old country. He was born near Vitebsk in 1886 in a *shtetl* that had six synagogues. His father was a Hebrew teacher and his mother, with the help of five other children, baked *latkes* (potato pancakes) to sell. But despite their efforts, the family could not earn enough, and Bernard was apprenticed to a tailor at the age of ten.

> There was no limit to the working hours. We only knew that we had to start work when the shepherd led the goats and cows to pasture [and continue] until pitch darkness. . . . When the holidays came between Purim and Passover we had to work all day and all night. Thursdays we also worked all night because Friday we had to stop before candle lighting. . . .

I ate at the house of my boss. My night's lodging was on top of the stove which was cold during the week and burning hot on Saturday night. . . . That's the way I worked day and night, freezing and burning on top of the stove for two years. . . . These were difficult . . . days of drudgery, meagre food and sleeplessness.[57]

In 1898, Chasanow heard of a *kruzokh* (circle)—a group of boys and girls who called themselves "democrats." Chasanow did not know the meaning of that word.

We only knew that this group made a *Yid achad* [Jewish Alliance]. They [gathered themselves in the *shtetls*] held hands and marched in the street, where the Russian Police used to, on *shabos,* take chained political prisoners through to St. Petersburg.[58]

It did not take long for the authorities to forbid the "stroll." But the group continued to gather in the forest and tell stories and political allegories, and recite the poems of David Edelstadt. From these boys and girls, Chasanow learned about strikes of workers in several cities, and that, in one instance at least, a twelve-hour day had been won.[59]

In the summer of 1898, the bosses in the town decided that in the week before Rosh Hashonah, the workers—tailors and milliners—would work nights as well as days. Chasanow and several tailors, some of whom were from other towns, determined not to work after sundown. On the first night of the "strike," he invited his friends to the Chasanow household, though there were only two rooms. "We nestled together on the floor." When they went to work the next morning the strikers were fired. Chasanow, however, was kept on because the boss would otherwise have had to return the fifty rubles he received from Chasanow's father for the son's apprenticeship.[60]

The boss brought in his nephew, called sarcastically in the town *chusen,* or bridegroom, because he had spent his whole dowry on a fancy overcoat. Chasanow developed a hatred for him because he was a "scab." And when Chasanow got back together with his group of "democrats," they pleaded with him to bring the boss's nephew for a talk in the park. The nephew refused to come along, however, for fear that the activist teenagers would beat him up. Chasanow's friends advised him to get "revenge" on the boss, but he "had no bad feeling" toward his employer. The boss's wife and daughter worked in a cigarette factory to make ends meet, and Chasanow believed the family was in a struggle for survival. Apparently he did not want to get involved in what Abraham Liesen described as the Jewish clash of "pauper vs. pauper."[61] The guilty one, said Chasanow, was the nephew. And on him he would get "revenge."

Chasanow and the *chusen,* one *shabos* morning, readied themselves for synagogue. It was raining and the nephew wanted to wear his old coat, but Chasanow persuaded him to wear his good one. Near the end of the reading of the Torah, Chasanow went to the anteroom of the synagogue, where all the coats were hung. He found "the dowry" and poured acid on it, and went back in to pray. After services, the nephew and everyone else noticed smoke coming from the coat. Chasanow came to the "rescue," and with a scissors, cut the burning pieces from the coat. In defense of his *shabos*-violating action, he said, "It's just as much a *mitzva* [obligation, good deed] to save a garment, as a person."[62]

With that, Chasanow's apprenticeship as a tailor was ended. And he was sent to a factory in Vitebsk, where his brother was already working.

> As soon as I got to Vitebsk I discovered my brother had joined a workingmen's group. After a Passover stroll . . . he introduced me to the Social Democrats and the leader of the Bund.[63]

On the first of May in 1899, Chasanow, in Vitebsk, was part of a massive workers' demonstration. Thus began a career in politics which he carried with him to the United States in 1909.

Here he lived with his brother for a while, worked at cloaks and suits, joined Local 11, and in 1910 was out in the cloakmakers' strike. He continued to be involved in the labor movement and in left-wing politics for several more decades. Chasanow, from a *shtetl* with six synagogues, described his boyhood tailor's apprenticeship as his "first university," and his experience with the "democrats" at the age of twelve as the beginning of his radical activism. It turned out to be a long career.[64]

I. E. RONTCH

I. E. Rontch was one of the very few radicals whose family came close to fitting the East European Jewish stereotype. Rontch's "extremely Orthodox" father was a scholar and very active in the synagogue, but "could make no living." His mother ran a millinery store that sustained them all, including four daughters. Rontch was named for a great rabbi, Itzak Rochonen; and grand rabbinical ambitions were nurtured in him.

> My job was to study day and night, but I was more interested in the workers in Birnbaum's factory, which was near our house.[65]

At the age of seven in 1907, during the post-revolutionary repression in Russia, Rontch had witnessed strikes and had seen police beat up strikers—even kill one young worker. "That made me closer to the movement for the workers."

If Rontch were impelled to resolve any ambivalence about his masculinity that his "weak" father is classically supposed to have engendered in him, one would think that the son would have chosen to side with the powerful authorities and not the victimized workers. On the contrary, however, at nine years of age Rontch was distributing radical proclamations that he had hidden in his *Gemara*. These he was given by a fourteen-year-old girl, a member of the Young Bund. She, Rontch recalled, "had an influence on my life."

At eleven, Rontch himself was a member of the *kleinem Bund*. He cut his *peyes*, put on a uniform, and went to gymnasium, thereby dashing all parental hope of a rabbinical future. His mother screamed and cried, saying, "You are not my son anymore," but that did not last very long. And his father on his deathbed told the twelve-year-old Rontch, "I want you to promise me to be a Jew. . . . I don't care if you will not be very religious. . . . Honesty is more important than religion."[66]

Rontch was very proud of his father, who had been a substitute *hazan* (cantor) for the many poor *shtibelekh* (informal *shuls*) where "plain Jewish workers came to *daven* [pray]." His father, Rontch said, did not do the prayers as if they were songs; instead, he "talked to God." Although Rontch no longer formally pursued Jewish studies, he did go to synagogue after his father died to say *Kaddish* for a year, and he continued to "read the Prophets at home by [himself]."

> I was so taken by the words—they inspired me so—especially . . . Elijah.[67]

In 1912 Rontch went to America and stayed with his uncle in Rochester, New York, for a short time. Then, over a four-year period he worked in secondhand clothing stores, a necktie factory, a printing shop, and a piano factory—all the while nursing ambitions to be a writer. In 1915, at the age of fifteen, he had a poem accepted for publication in *Der Kundes* (The Prankster), a Yiddish journal of literature and humor. In 1917 he went to Chicago, where he published regularly under the by-line Itzak Rochonen, his rabbinical namesake. Soon he was teaching for the Workman's Circle schools, and he came to be regarded as a great, innovative educator.

All through these years and into the 1920s, the former rabbinical aspirant and *kleinem Bund* member's "sympathies [were] with the left-wing movement"; and he joined the *Freiheit* (Yiddish Communist paper) in 1921. Between 1929 and 1933 Rontch experienced a period of disillusion over Communist Party discipline; and he felt, with several others, including Kalmon Marmor, "like moving away . . . to a little town to become a *melamed* [schoolteacher] and forget about all." Except for this brief interregnum, however, Rontch continued to be a vital and politically committed poet and historian who "sits with the masses." And he told an interviewer in 1980, "the words of the prophets continue to influence me to this day."[68]

8

CONCLUSION

The Persistence of Culture

The vast majority of Jewish immigrant socialists were men and women rooted in the culture of *Yiddishkeit* and Jewish ethical tradition and religious values. The socialism many of them pursued was not theoretically fine-tuned, and "ideological" eclecticism was the order of the day. Yossef Bovshover could believe he served the cause by dividing the stock of the grocery store his brother had given him, among his unemployed friends; Morris Hillquit could persistently cite Marx's belief that in America workers can achieve their goals through class struggle but *auf friedlichem wege* (peacefully), while Isaac Hourwich complained that "in America there never was and still is no revolutionary movement."

Some were members of the IWW, others continued to consider themselves anarchists. Several stayed for a long time with the Socialist Labor Party; more were founders of the rival Socialist Party of America. The majority remained with the Socialist Party after 1919; a minority went with the Communists. Many dropped out of the Communist movement somewhere between 1922 and 1956; a few held to the Communist course their whole lives.[1]

Ramshackle and not centrally directed, Jewish socialism, like socialism everywhere, was a political movement dedicated to building a thoroughly new society. Fannia Cohn held "the opinion that the future social organization will be the worker's independent commonwealth,"[2] and most of her colleagues and cohort agreed with her. In this regard and others, Jewish socialism were part of an international phenomenon that began in the nineteenth century. But the Jews, upon entering modern history in Eastern Europe and on the East Side, made a unique response to socialist propaganda, and brought to socialism a Jewish dimension.

Much of the evidence presented here suggests that we cannot understand this response if we continue to insist, from an overly narrow Marxist perspective, that class was the single most important determinant of modern Jewish affinity to radicalism, and that Jewish cultural and religious values played little or no role in predisposing its adherents toward support for socialism. Proletarianization was critical but it was not, by itself, powerful enough to make Jews socialists. Large numbers of workers from other ethnic groups were exploited in equivalent degree or worse, but they did not in the same proportions as the Jews join radical movements. Often class consciousness and ethnic consciousness are mutually diluting; but sometimes, as we have seen with the Jews in the period from 1880 to 1920, they could be reinforcing.

Rose Pastor Stokes said:

> I believe that the Jewish people because of the ancient and historic struggle for social and economic justice, should be peculiarly fitted to recognize a special mission in the cause of the modern socialist movement.[3]

And she was right. The great bulk of the Jewish men and women who came to socialism had been saturated in Jewish tradition and Jewish culture. To them socialism, though a political movement, was more than the mere program of a political party. To them socialism was more than an economic or sociological doctrine, it was an ethical system.[4] Even atheists like Cahan and Feigenbaum and Winchevsky proved by their words and their actions that Jewish ethical precepts and religious values still had a strong hold on them, and that their upbringing and training prepared them to be more receptive to radical ideology.

The words, idioms, ideals, and visions of the prophets surfaced time and again in the conversation, speeches, and writings of these men and women, and a great many of them appear to have been impelled by the religious imperative of *tikn olam* (improvement of the world), and by messianic passion. Here we need to remind ourselves not only of how often versions of secular messianism appear in the thought patterns and language of the Jewish immigrant socialists, but of just how "secular" Jewish messianism really is. Spiritual and sup-rahistorical elements are obviously part of Jewish messianism but it has always contained a this-worldly, historical and quite political dimension. The Hebrew term *olam haba*, sometimes translated as "hereafter," is often used to refer to a coming world and not necessarily to the "other world."[5] "Inspired men," not gods, would be saviors, and the inspiration would come from flesh and blood prophets with their ringing demands for social justice on this earth.[6] Jews, of course, have no monopoly on messianism. Christianity, in its Protestant, Catholic, or Eastern Orthodox versions, built on ideas of Jewish messianism. And in its early stages there was a pronounced futuristic note. But the conviction that the "end" had already come in Jesus Christ, or, later, that the Kingdom of God is virtually identifiable with the Church, generally muted messianic passion.[7]

Benjamin Feigenbaum may have been exploiting what he thought others believed when he said to Jewish audiences, "Socialism is the Messiah," but Morris Shatan was entirely sincere when he said after hearing socialist propaganda, "I thought Messiah had come." Others, though not necessarily as explicit, talked about sacred struggles and holy duties, and visions of a more beautiful world. "Even when things were terrible," Pauline Newman said, "I always had that faith."

To specify and corroborate the transmission of values from one generation to another, and the movement and reshaping of those values from one historical context to another, is difficult because the evidence is often fragmentary and elusive. But a relatively cohesive sense of Jewish peoplehood, and the centrality of religious values to the definition of Jewish culture, were clearly still extant in the period from 1880 to 1920. And the preceding pages represent a small portion of the material available to reinforce the thesis that Jews did not become radicals irrespective of the content of that culture.

In addition, adherence, conscious or otherwise, to Jewish cultural and religious values did not, as we have seen, necessarily mean a diminution of class consciousness. Jews often crossed or tried to cross ethnic lines to forge working-class alliances. And ethnic attachment was not the force that turned some Jewish people away from class loyalty; we are better off looking at economic, occupational, and even social mobility if we want to understand that particular dynamic.[8] Even here as Jews moved out of the proletariat, a radical, or at least a reformist perspective was sustained by organizations and institutions and networks of political socialization, created by the Yiddish-speaking working class and its radical socialist leadership. Indeed without that *Jewish* fraternal network it is likely that upward mobility, assimilation, and further secularization would have eroded class consciousness much faster.

We should also point out again here that the great majority of the 170-member subject group stayed in the movement for the whole of their adult lives. Dozens fulfilled individual aspirations through careers in the union bureaucracy, and many turned down lucrative opportunities elsewhere. Even some who left the movement continued to give support. Abe Hershkowitz, who stayed, remembered Hyman Schneider, one of the leaders of the garment strike in 1913, who left:

> . . . In 1915 Schneider moved to Indiana. And now [1965] he is one of the richest men in that section. He has a department store. He is still a socialist and supports all the socialist undertakings. And that is how it was with a lot of people who went through the movement.[9]

Few of the people involved, whether they left the movement or stayed in, expressed regret about their investment of time and energy in labor and socialism. One activist said, echoing a host of others,

> If I could do it over again I would do it over and over again for the Union and for the labor movement as a whole.[10]

Participation for another

> gave meaning to the long hours and low wages and the horrible living conditions. When you were cold you were warmed by the idea that someday it was going to get better.[11]

And to Morris Hillquit

> the socialist movement with its enthusiasm and idealism, its comradeships and struggles, its hopes and disappointments, its victories and defeats, has been the best life has had to offer.[12]

Many of these men and women, very late in their lives, believing that what they had done had been worth doing, still saw socialism as the answer to oppression and inequality. Many expressed disappointment, however, with the behavior of contemporary workers and so-called socialist states. "I'm a little discouraged sometimes," one veteran said,

> when I see workers spending their free hours watching television—trash. We fought so hard for those hours and they waste them. We used to read Tolstoy, Dickens, Shelley, by candlelight, and they watch the "Hollywood Squares." Well, they're free to do what they want. That's what we fought for.[13]

And Joe Rapoport, reflecting the feelings of many of his contemporaries, said recently:

> From when I was a little boy in Stanislavchik . . . when I heard stories about socialists like Sasha the bagelmaker in the 1905 Revolution . . . I believed in the promise of socialism for the Jewish people. . . . I joined the radical movement in America with the belief that socialism would bring salvation for the Jewish people and for all humanity. . . . That is why my . . . visit to the Soviet Union . . . was shocking.
>   Despite that disappointment, I continue to believe that socialism . . . more than any other system of society, promises to end the social divisions and to unlock the creative genius of the people. . . .[14]

"We had a vision," Pauline Newman remembered,

> that justice and freedom and everything else we desired would be there under socialism, and that your job was to help bring it about, and you did what you could.[15]

The immigrant socialists did what they could. Between 1908 and 1915 they established a stable and enduring radical union movement in the garment industries. They constituted, in the same era, an important pillar of the Socialist Party in the United States, and in New York helped elect Socialist aldermen, assemblymen and even a congressman.

Jewish socialists contributed significantly to keeping the concepts of human interdependence and government responsibility for social welfare in the political dialogue. And they shared responsibility for several decades of reform legislation. These men and women, in addition, created a wide-reaching web of fraternal associations which transmitted the values of the Left to succeeding generations.

In their own generation the immigrant socialists were an important and articulate minority giving a tone and a shape, a meaning and a hope to the Jewish community of which they were so much a part.

And they were a prophetic minority too—not because they accurately predicted the future, but because they worked at educating and mobilizing the best in people, and at sustaining loyalty to the highest ideals of social justice. They worked, like Isaiah and Amos and Micah and Hosea, with whom they were so familiar, at hastening the coming of a just, peaceful, and beautiful world.

The 170 people who constitute the group upon whom the collective biography is based are named below. To be included on this list these men and women had to have been born in the old country or had to have emigrated before they were six years old; and they had to have been activists, but not necessarily leaders, in socialist unions or in socialist politics in the broadest sense.

Even if some, like Emma Goldman, who flirted with socialism for a time, or Rose Pesotta, who began as a Social Democrat, ended up as anarchists, they were included on the list because they stayed with radicalism. The same was true for the process in reverse: Abraham Cahan could be said to have been an anarchist early on, but he was soon firmly in the socialist camp. On the other hand, men like Morris R. Cohen and Marcus Ravage who called themselves socialists for a period are not on the list, because the commitment was short-lived.

The original list, devised mainly from the major histories of the Jewish labor and radical movements, biographical dictionaries and encyclopedias, The Encyclopedia Judaica, and the YIVO archive and Tamiment Institute Library catalogs, changed over time as some names yielded no more information than the fact that the individual was a socialist. Other names were unearthed and added that fit the criteria, and for whom relevant information was available.

Abramowitz, Bessie
Aleinikoff, Nicholas
Baroff, Abraham
Barondess, Joseph
Barsky, Israel
Belson, Abraham
Boudin, Louis
Bovshover, Yossef
Braff, Bernard
Braslowsky, Abel
Brise, Theodore
Brownstein, Abraham
Cahan, Abraham
Cantor, Herman
Caplowitz, Philip
Chanin, Nochem
Chasanow, Bernard

Cohen, Hyman
Cohen, Isadore
Cohen, Rose
Cohn, Fannia
Cooperman, Max
Davis, Samuel
Deutschman, Max
Doroskin, Jacob
Dubinsky, David
Dubnow, Jack
Dvorin, Bella
Edelstadt, David
Edlin, William
Entin, Joel
Epstein, Melech
Farbman, Marsha
Farbman, Moishe

Feigenbaum, Benjamin
Feinberg, Israel
Feinberg, Morris
Feinstone, Morris
Fenster, Bernard
Feuer, Oscar
Fichandler, Alexander
Freedman, Esther
Ganz, Marie
Geliebter, Philip
Gerber, Julius
Gershin, Julius
Ginzburg, Lyuba
Gittelson, Haskel
Glass, Louis
Gold, Ben
Gold, Joseph
Goldman, A. L.
Goldman, Emma
Goldreich, M.
Goldstein, Ike
Goldstein, J.
Greenberg, H.
Gross, Aaron
Gutterman, Joseph
Hait, N.
Halpern, Gershin
Halpern, Pearl
Hasanovitz, Elizabeth
Held, Adolph
Hendel, Timothy
Hershkowitz, Abe
Hillman, Sidney
Hillquit, Morris
Hoffman, Ben Zion
Hourwich, Isaac
Hyman, Louis
Ingerman, Anna
Jacobson, Charles
Kadar, Esther
Karlin, William
Kasimirsky, M.
Kaufman, Morris
Kobrin, Leon
Krantz, Philip
Krindler, Charles
Kuntz, M.
Lang, Lucy
Lemlich, Clara
Levenson, Florence
Levenson, Jacob

Libin, Zalman
Liesen, Abraham
Linker, Mollie
Litwin, A.
London, Meyer
Magidow, Jacob
Malkiel, Leon
Malkiel, Theresa
Margolin, Abraham
Menaker, Shleme
Mendelowitz, Abraham
Mikol, David
Miller, Abe
Miller, Leon
Miller, Louis
Mintz, Moses
Nadelman, M.
Nagler, Isidore
Nelson, Louis
Newman, Pauline
Novick, Paul
Olgin, Moishe
Painkin, Louis
Panken, Jacob
Pesotta, Rose
Pine, Max
Pinski, David
Price, George
Rabinowitz, Benjamin
Rapoport, Joseph
Rappaport, Anna
Raynes, Rose
Rivkin, Minnie
Rogoff, Hillel
Rogoff, Hyman
Rontch, I. E.
Rosenberg, Abraham
Rosenfeld, Morris
Rubin, Sam
Salutsky, J. B.
Schlesinger, Benjamin
Schlossberg, Joseph
Schneid, Hyman
Schneiderman, Rose
Schoenholtz, Isidore
Schveid, Mark
Segal, L.
Serdatzky, Yente
Shapiro, Fannie
Shapiro, Feigl
Shatan, Morris

Shein, Jacob
Sher, Zelig
Sherer, Abraham
Shiplacoff, Abraham
Shul, Anna
Sigman, Morris
Slutzky, Harry
Solomon, Benjamin
Solomon, Dora
Spector, Nathaniel
Sperber, Jack
Sperber, Lucy
Stokes, Rose Pastor
Trachtenberg, Alexander
Vladeck, Baruch Charney
Waldman, Louis
Walinsky, Ossip

Weinstein, Bernard
Weinstein, Gregory
Weiss, Flora
Weissman, Clara
Weissman, Paul
Winchevsky, Morris
Wisotsky, Isadore
Yanofsky, Saul
Zametkin, Adella
Zametkin, Michael
Zaritsky, Max
Zausner, Philip
Zhitlowsky, Chaim
Zimmerman, Charles
Zolatoroff, H.
Zuckerman, Max
Zwerlin, Abraham

Notes

Chapter 1

1. Arthur Liebman, *Jews and the Left* (New York: John Wiley and Sons, 1979), pp. 1–60; Melvin Dubofsky, "Success and Failure of Socialism in New York City, 1900–1918: A Case Study," *Labor History*, 9:3 (Fall 1968), 370–371; Charles Leinenweber, "The Class and Ethnic Basis of New York City Socialism, 1904–1915," *Labor History*, 22:1 (Winter 1981), 31–56.

2. J. C. Rich, "Sixty Years of the Jewish Daily Forward," *New Leader* 40 (June 3, 1957), 1–38.

3. Daniel Bell, "The Background and Development of Marxian Socialism in the United States," in *Socialism and American Life*, Vol. 1, ed. Donald Drew Egbert and Stow Persons (Princeton: Princeton University Press, 1952), pp. 213–405, and especially 309–318.

4. Wesley and Beverly Allensmith, "Religious Affiliation and Politico-Economic Attitude: A Study of Eight Major U.S. Religious Groups," *Public Opinion Quarterly*, 12:3 (Fall 1948), 378–389; Werner Cohn, "Politics of American Jews," in *The Jews*, Marshall Sklare, ed. (New York: Free Press, 1958), pp. 614–626; Louis Ruchames, "Jewish Radicalism in the United States," in *Ghetto and Beyond*, Peter Rose, ed. (New York: Random House, 1969), pp. 228–252; Irving Howe, *World of Our Fathers* (New York: Harcourt Brace Jovanovitch, 1976); Robert Brym, *The Jewish Intelligentsia and Russian Marxism* (New York: Schocken Books, 1978); Arthur Liebman, *Jews and the Left;* Percy S. Cohen, *Jewish Radicals and Radical Jews* (London Academic Press, 1980); Stanley Rothman and S. Robert Lichter, *Roots of Radicalism: Jews, Christians and the New Left* (New York: Oxford University Press, 1982).

5. Some bristlemakers in Russia were described as half worker and half Yeshiva student. These proved highly susceptible to the labor movement. In 1890 there were bristlemaker strikes in Vilna and several other cities. Ezra Mendelsohn, *Class Struggle in the Pale* (Cambridge: Cambridge University Press, 1970), pp. 72–73.

6. Interview, Pearl Halpern, Amerikaner-Yiddishe Geshichte Bel Pe, YIVO, November 11, 1965, pp. 1–2.

7. In a generally useful book, Arthur Liebman makes the following questionable assertion: ". . . there is little evidence to support the hypothesis that Judaism predisposes its adherents (or former adherents) toward a socialist political identification or support for socialism." *Jews and the Left*, p. 11. This study comes to a very different conclusion.

8. Morris Winchevsky, "Reminiscences," reprinted in *Jewish Currents*, 32:8 (September 1978), 30–32.

9. Lucy Dawidowicz, "From Past to Past," in *Jewish Presence* (New York: Holt, Rinehart and Winston, 1977), pp. 105–115; C. B. Sherman, "Nationalism, Secularism and Religion in the Jewish Labor Movement," *Voices from the*

Yiddish, ed., Irving Howe and Eliezer Greenberg (New York: Schocken Books, 1975), p. 222; Oscar Handlin, *Adventure in Freedom: Three Hundred Years of Jewish Life in America* (New York: McGraw Hill, 1954), p. 217; Will Herberg, "Socialism, Zionism and Messianic Passion," *Midstream,* 2 (Summer 1956), 65–74; Moses Rischin, "The Jewish Labor Movement in America: A Social Interpretation," *Labor History,* 4:3 (Fall 1963), 227–247; Aileen Kraditor, *The Radical Persuasion: 1890–1917* (Baton Rouge: Louisiana State University Press, 1980).

10. Everett Stonequist, *The Marginal Man* (New York: Scribners, 1937); Milton Goldberg, "A Qualification of the Marginal Man Theory," *American Sociological Review,* 6 (1941), 52–58; Arnold Green, "A Reexamination of the Marginal Man Concept," *Social Forces,* 26 (1947), 167–171; Aaron Antonovsky, "Toward a Refinement of the Marginal Man Concept," *Social Forces,* 35 (1956), 57–62; William Kornhauser, *The Politics of Mass Society* (Glencoe, Illinois; Free Press, 1959); Neil Smelser, *Theory of Collective Behavior* (New York: Free Press of Glencoe, 1963). George Theodorson and Achilles Theodorson, *Modern Dictionary of Sociology* (New York: Thomas Y. Crowell, 1969), p. 242; T. F. Hoult, *Dictionary of Modern Sociology* (Totowa, New Jersey: Littlefield Adams, 1974), p. 192; Henry Pratt Fairchild, *Dictionary of Sociology* (New York: Philosophical Library, 1944), p. 188; Arnold Rose, *Sociology: The Study of Human Relations* (New York: Alfred Knopf, 1956), p. 151.

11. Interview, Pearl Halpern, p. 2. The strike was part of the stunning "Uprising of 20,000," which is referred to herein several times.

12. Isaac Deutscher, "The Non-Jewish Jew," *The Non-Jewish Jew and Other Essays* (London: Oxford University Press, 1968), pp. 25–41; Robert Park, "Human Migration and the Marginal Man," *American Journal of Sociology,* 23 (1928), 881–893; Robert Michels, "Intellectuals," *Encyclopedia of Social Sciences,* Vol. 8 (New York: MacMillan, 1932), pp. 118–126; Thorstein Veblen, "The Intellectual Pre-eminence of Jews in Modern Europe," *The Portable Veblen,* ed., Max Lerner (New York: Viking Press, 1948), 467–479.

13. Georg Simmel, *Conflict and the Web of Group Affiliations,* Trans. by Kurt Wolff and Reinhard Bendix (New York: Free Press, 1964).

14. Interview, Adolph Held, Amerikaner-Yiddishe Geshichte Bel Pe, YIVO, June 6, 1964, pp. 13–14.

15. On the general Jewish immigration, see Samuel Joseph, *Jewish Immigration to the United States from 1881 to 1910* (New York: Columbia University Press, 1914); Liebmann Hersch, "International Migration of the Jews," *International Migrations,* Vol. II, ed. Imre Ferenczi and Walter Willcox (New York: National Bureau of Economic Research, 1931), pp. 471–520; and Irving Howe's analysis of these materials in *World of Our Fathers,* pp. 57–63. Of 76 Jewish immigrant socialists for whom I could find this kind of information, 32 came to the United States with members of their immediate families, 5 with cousins and uncles, and 22 to relatives already in America.

16. Interview, Pearl Halpern, p. 2.

17. Interview, Sam Rubin, Amerikaner-Yiddishe Geshichte Bel Pe, YIVO, June 26, 1965, pp. 1–2.

18. Interview, Julius Gershin, Amerikaner-Yiddishe Geshichte Bel Pe, YIVO, January 27, 1964, p. 1.

19. Unfortunately this information rarely finds its way into the filiopietistic literature on Jewish life in America. This is, however, changing. See, for example Reena Sigman Friedman, " 'Send Me My Husband Who Is in New

York City': Husband Desertion in the American Jewish Immigrant Community, 1900–1926," *Jewish Social Studies*, 44 (Winter 1982), 1–18.

20. Hutchins Hapgood, *Spirit of the Ghetto* (New York: Schocken Books, 1966), p. 32.

21. Some of this, including the phenomenon of so-called self-hate, is dealt with in chapters 4 and 5. That many labor radicals continued to identify as Jews does not by itself allow us to say that Jewish culture was a major contributing factor to the emergence of their radicalism. But it is just as true that by itself, explicit rejection of Jewishness by some other radicals does not allow us to assume that their Jewishness played no important role in shaping their radicalism.

22. Emma Goldman, *Living My Life*, Vol. 1 (New York: Alfred Knopf, 1931), p. 3. Emphasis mine.

23. Richard Drinnon, *Rebel in Paradise* (New York: Harper and Row, 1976), p. 19.

24. Ibid. pp. 3–29.

25. The issues of *Mother Earth* that were edited by Goldman, series 1, Vol. 1–12, March 1906 to August 1917, are conveniently reprinted in *Mother Earth* (New York: Greenwood Reprint Corp., 1968).

26. Fannia Cohn to Evelyn Preston, April 10, 1922, Fannia Cohn Papers, New York Public Library, Manuscript Division.

27. This theoretical position is meticulously delineated in Anthony Oberschall, *Social Conflict and Social Movements* (Englewood Cliffs, New Jersey: Prentice Hall, 1973), and is credibly applied to major historical instances in Charles Tilly et al., *The Rebellious Century, 1830–1930* (Cambridge: Harvard University Press, 1975); Barrington Moore, Jr., *Social Origins of Dictatorship and Democracy* (Boston: Beacon Press, 1966), and in several essays in Clifford Geertz, ed., *Old Societies and New States* (Glencoe, Illinois: Free Press, 1963).

28. That this interpretive framework may be applicable to the various experiences of other immigrant groups is made plausible by several distinguished works. See John Bodnar, *Immigration and Industrialization: Ethnicity in an American Mill Town, 1870–1940* (Pittsburgh: University of Pittsburgh Press, 1977); Victor Greene, *The Slavic Community on Strike* (South Bend, Indiana: Notre Dame University Press, 1968), Josef J. Barton, *Peasants and Strangers: Italians, Rumanians, and Slovaks in an American City 1890–1950* (Cambridge, Mass: Harvard University Press, 1975); Virginia Yans-McLaughlin, "Patterns of Work and Family Organizations: Buffalo's Italians," *Journal of Interdisciplinary History*, 2 (1971), 305–311; Corinne Azen Krause, "Urbanization Without Breakdown: Italian, Jewish and Slavic Immigrant Women in Pittsburgh, 1900–1945," *Journal of Urban History*, 4:3 (May 1978), 291–306. A particularly relevant piece is Michael Passi, "Fishermen on Strike: Finnish Workers and Community Power in Astoria, Oregon, 1880–1900," in *The Finnish Experience in the Western Great Lakes Region: New Perspectives*, ed., Michael Karni et al. (Turku, Finland: Vammala, 1975), pp. 89–103.

Chapter 2

1. Arthur Ruppin, *The Jews in The Modern World*, (London: MacMillan, 1934), p. 23; Liebmann Hersch, "International Migration of the Jews," in *International Migrations*, eds. Imre Ferenczi and Walter Willcox (New York: National Bureau of Economic Research, 1931), Vol. 2, pp. 479–481.

2. Abraham Menes, "The Jewish Socialist Movement in Russia and Po-

land," *Jewish People: Past and Present,* 2 (1948), 355–369; Henry J. Tobias, "The Jews in Tsarist Russia: The Political Education of a Minority," in *Minorities and Politics,* eds. Henry Tobias and Charles Woodhouse (Albuquerque: University of New Mexico Press, 1969), pp. 19–38; Robert Wistrich, *Revolutionary Jews from Marx to Trotsky* (New York: Harper and Row, 1976); Robert Brym, *The Jewish Intelligentsia and Russian Marxism* (New York: Schocken, 1978); Jonathan Frankel, *Prophecy and Politics: Socialism, Nationalism and the Russian Jews, 1862–1917* (Cambridge: Cambridge University Press, 1981).

3. Maurice Samuel, *The World of Sholem Aleichem* (New York: Alfred Knopf, 1962), pp. 26–27.

4. R. J. Zwi Werblowsky, "Messianism in Jewish History," *Jewish Society Through the Ages,* ed. H. H. Ben-Sasson and S. Ettinger (New York: Schocken Books, 1971) pp. 32–38.

5. Yehezkel Kaufmann, "Israel in Canaan," *Great Ages and Ideas of the Jewish People,* ed. L. W. Schwarz (New York: Modern Library, 1956), 38–53; Gershom Scholem, *The Messianic Idea in Judaism* (New York: Schocken Books, 1971), p. 1.

6. Will Herberg, "Socialism, Zionism and Messianic Passion," *Midstream* 2 (Summer 1956), 65.

7. Robert D. Reynolds, "The Millionaire Socialists: J. G. Phelps Stokes and His Circle of Friends" (Ph.D. dissertation, University of South Carolina, 1974), p. 97; Rose Cohen, *Out of the Shadow* (New York: G. H. Doran, 1918), p. 13.

8. Fannia Cohn to A. Plotkin, August 6, 1959, Fannia Cohn Papers, New York Public Library.

9. Matthew Josephson, *Sidney Hillman: Statesman of American Labor* (Garden City, New York: Doubleday, 1952), p. 24.

10. Baruch Charney Vladeck, "Autobiography," Vladeck Papers, Tamiment Library, New York University, Collection 37, reel 20, pp. 3–4.

11. Kenneth Kann, *Joe Rapoport: Life of a Jewish Radical* (Philadelphia: Temple University Press, 1981), p. 19.

12. Ibid., p. 18.

13. Joshua Rothenberg, "Demythologizing the Shtetl," *Midstream,* 27 (March 1981), 25–31; Arthur A. Goren, *New York Jews and the Quest for Community: The Kehillah Experiment, 1908–1922* (New York: Columbia University Press, 1970), pp. 1–12.

14. Ezra Mendelsohn, *Class Struggle in the Pale* (Cambridge: Cambridge University Press, 1970), p. 27.

15. Rose Schneiderman, *All for One* (New York: Paul S. Erikson, 1967), p. 12.

16. Elias Tcherikower, *The Early Jewish Labor Movement in the United States,* trans. A. Antonovsky (New York: YIVO, 1961), p. 8.

17. Menes, "The Jewish Socialist Movement," p. 356.

18. Interview, Flora Weiss, Amerikaner-Yiddishe Geshichte Bel Pe, YIVO, June 15, 1964, p. 2.

19. Michael Stanislawski, *Tsar Nicholas I and the Jews: The Transformation of Jewish Society in Russia, 1825–1855* (Philadelphia: Jewish Publication Society of America, 1983), pp. xii–xiii. 28–48.

20. Salo Baron, *The Russian Jews Under Tsars and Soviets* (New York: MacMillan, 1964), pp. 81–84; Martin Gilbert, *Jewish History Atlas* (New York: Collier, 1969), p. 67; Stanislawski, *Tsar Nicholas I and the Jews,* pp. 170–182.

21. Baron, *Russian Jews,* pp. 113–114.

22. Simon Kuznets, "Immigration of Russian Jews," *Perspectives in American History,* 9 (1975), 35–124.

23. Rothenberg, "Demythologizing the Shtetl," pp. 27–30.

24. Tcherikower, *Early Jewish Labor Movement,* p. 17.

25. Mendelsohn, *Class Struggle,* pp. 14–15.

26. Erza Mendelsohn, "The Russian Jewish Labor Movement," *YIVO Annual,* 14 (1969), 90.

27. Mendelsohn, *Class Struggle,* p. 8; Mendelsohn "The Russian Jewish Labor Movement," p. 94.

28. See for example the work of E. P. Thompson for England, William Sewell and Joan Wallach Scott for France, Robert Brym for Russia, and Herbert Gutman for the United States.

29. Kuznets, "Immigration," p. 73. In 1897, at least 37.9 percent of Jews gainfully employed in the Russian Empire were proletarians. Of the Jewish immigrants in this study who were radicalized in Europe, only 30 percent were proletarians.

30. Interview, Morris Shatan, Amerikaner-Yiddishe Geshichte Bel Pe, YIVO, August 20, 1968, part 1, pp. 1–8.

31. Ibid., part 2, pp. 1-5.

32. See note 28.

33. Interview, Paul Novick, Howe Collection, YIVO, March 29, 1968, p. 3.

34. Interview, Abraham Lieb Goldman, Amerikaner-Yiddishe Geshichte Bel Pe, YIVO, January 24, 1964, p. 3.

35. Stanislawski, *Tsar Nicholas I and the Jews,* p. xiii.

36. Ibid., pp. 17, 42–67.

37. Ibid., p. 67; Louis Greenberg, *The Jews in Russia,* Vol 1 (New Haven: Yale University Press, 1944), p. 83; Ezra Mendelsohn, "The Russian Roots of the American Jewish Labor Movement," *YIVO Annual* 16 (1976), p. 171.

38. Charlotte Baum, Paula Hyman and Sonya Michel, *The Jewish Woman in America* (New York: Dial Press, 1976), p. 71.

39. Allan Wildman, *The Making of a Workers' Revolution: Russian Social Democracy, 1891–1903* (Chicago: University of Chicago Press, 1967), p. 60; Leonard Shapiro, "The Role of the Jews in the Russian Revolutionary Movement," *Slavonic and Eastern European Review* 40:84 (Dec. 1961), 148; Brym, *Jewish Intelligentsia,* pp. 2–3.

40. Abraham Cahan, *Bleter fun mein leben,* I (New York: Forward Association, 1926), pp. 393, 404.

41. Quoted in Frankel, *Prophecy and Politics,* p. 33.

42. Ibid., p. 41. Emphasis mine.

43. Ibid., p. 46.

44. Gregory Weinstein, *Reminiscences of an Interesting Decade* (New York: International Press, 1928), pp. 8–9.

45. Cahan, *Bleter,* I, p. 500.

46. Antisemitism meant that a Russian Jew, even with a university degree, could scarcely look forward to employment in Russian academic, professional, or bureaucratic circles. Only in a radically changed society would this be possible. Robert Brym, in *Jewish Intelligentsia and Russian Marxism,* makes this argument for the Russian "intelligentsia" generally, pointing to the revolutionary potential inherent in the situation of education outrunning opportunities created by economic modernization.

47. Moshe Mishkinski, "Regional Factors in the Formation of the Jewish

Labor Movement in Czarist Russia," *YIVO Annual,* 14 (1969), 46.

48. Mendelsohn, *Class Struggle,* pp. 27–40; Menes, "Jewish Socialist Movement" p. 365.

49. Interview, Julius Gershin, Amerikaner-Yiddishe Geshichte Bel Pe, YIVO, January 27, 1964, pp. 5–6.

50. Personal Interview, Jacob Levenson, October 14, 1981.

51. Mendelsohn, *Class Struggle,* pp. 88–89; Menes, "Jewish Socialist Movement," pp. 366–367.

52. Jacob Bross, "The Beginning of the Jewish Labor Movement in Galicia," *YIVO Annual,* 5 (1950), 64.

53. Ibid., p. 65.

54. Andrei S. Markovits, *Response,* 11:2 (Fall 1977), 85.

55. Frankel, *Prophecy and Politics,* pp. 256–257.

56. Lucy Dawidowicz, *The Golden Tradition: Jewish Life and Thought in Eastern Europe* (Boston: Beacon Press, 1967), p. 423.

57. Mendelsohn, *Class Struggle,* pp. 109–110.

58. Rose Pesotta, *Days of Our Lives* (Boston: Excelsior Publishers, 1958), p. 93.

59. Personal Interview, Lucy Sperber, November 25, 1981.

60. Harry Haskel, *A Leader of the Garment Workers: The Biography of Isidore Nagler* (New York: ILGWU, 1950), pp. 15–24.

61. Personal Interview, Florence Levenson, October 14, 1981.

62. Interview, Louis Painkin, Irving Howe Collection, YIVO, April 17, 1968, p. 2.

63. Hillel Rogoff, *An East Side Epic: The Life and Work of Meyer London* (New York: Vanguard Press, 1930), p. 8; Pesotta, *Days,* p. 93.

64. David Dubinsky and A. H. Raskin, *David Dubinsky: A Life with Labor* (New York: Simon and Schuster, 1977), p. 35.

65. Benjamin Stollberg, *A Tailor's Progress* (New York: Doubleday, 1944), p. 161.

66. Ibid.

67. Elie Wiesel, *The Testament* (New York: Summit Books, 1981), pp. 96–97.

68. Interview, I. E. Rontch, Oral History of the American Left, Tamiment Institute, New York University, April 14, 1980.

69. Ruth Landes and Mark Zbrowski, "Hypotheses Concerning the Eastern European Jewish Family," *Psychiatry,* 13 (1950), 447–464; Stanley Rothman and S. Robert Lichter, *Roots of Radicalism: Jews, Christians and the New Left* (New York: Oxford University Press, 1982).

70. Rothman and Lichter, *Roots of Radicalism;* Milton Himmelfarb, "Negroes, Jews and Muzhiks," *Commentary* (October 1966), 83–86; Percy Cohen, *Jewish Radicals and Radical Jews* (London: Academic Press, 1980). For a recent powerful fictional depiction of these relationships see Jay Neugeboren, *The Stolen Jew* (New York: Pinnacle Books, 1981).

71. Frankel, *Prophecy and Politics,* p. 90.

72. Sergei Ingerman Papers, Tamiment Institute.

73. Irving Howe, *World of Our Fathers* (New York: Harcourt Brace Jovanovich, 1976), p. 117; Samuel Joseph, *Jewish Immigration to the United States from 1881 to 1910* (New York: Columbia University Press, 1914), p. 119.

74. Interview, Minnie Rivkin, Oral History of the American Left, Tamiment Institute, 1980.

75. Personal Interview, Jack Sperber, November 25, 1981.

Chapter 3

1. Newman's dates are difficult to pin down, but by using the information in four different interviews and matching that with her allusions to particular events, it appears that she was born in 1890, arrived in America in 1901, and went to work that same year.

2. Morris Schappes, "Jewish Mass Immigration from Europe, 1881–1914," *Jewish Life*, 8:10 (November 1954), 20–21.

3. Joan Morrison and Charlotte F. Zabusky, *American Mosaic: The Immigrant Experience in the Words of Those Who Lived It* (New York: Dutton, 1980), p. 9; Interview, Pauline Newman, Amerikaner-Yiddishe Geshichte Bel Pe, YIVO, January 19, 1965, p. 2.

4. Pauline Newman, Talk, March 1975, Cornell University, in Barbara M. Wertheimer, *We Were There: The Story of Working Women in America* (New York: Pantheon Press, 1977), pp. 294–295.

5. Allen Forman, "Some Adopted Americans," *The American Magazine*, 9 (November, 1888), 51–52, cited in Moses Rischin, *The Promised City: New York's Jews, 1870–1914* (New York: Corinth Books, 1964), pp. 82–83.

6. Interview, Abraham Sherer, Amerikaner-Yiddishe Geshichte Bel Pe, YIVO, November 25, 1965, p. 3.

7. Interview, Charles Zimmerman, Amerikaner-Yiddishe Geshichte Bel Pe, YIVO, November 11, 1964, p. 3; and Personal Interview, May 17, 1982.

8. Bella Dvorin, Letter to author, March 8, 1982.

9. Interview, Pauline Newman, Columbia Oral History Collection, June 15, 1965, p. 3.

10. Pauline Newman, Talk, in Wertheimer, *We Were There*, pp. 294–295.

11. Interview, Louis Nelson, Amerikaner-Yiddishe Geshichte Bel Pe, YIVO, October 5, 1965, p. 2.

12. Judith Greenfield, "The Role of the Jews in the Development of the Clothing Industry," *YIVO Annual*, 2–3 (1947–48), 203–204.

13. Table compiled from figures in Liebmann Hersch, "International Migration of the Jews," in Imre Ferenczi and Walter Willcox, eds., *International Migrations* (New York: National Bureau of Economic Research, 1931), Vol. II, pp. 498–503; Samuel Joseph, *Jewish Immigration to the United States from 1881 to 1910* (New York: Columbia University Press, 1914), pp. 186–191; Elias Tcherikower, *The Early Jewish Labor Movement in the United States*, trans. A. Antonovsky (New York: YIVO, 1961), p. 357.

14. Interview, Pauline Newman, Amerikaner-Yiddishe Geshichte Bel Pe, YIVO, January 19, 1965, p. 3; Morrison and Zabusky, *American Mosaic*, p. 10.

15. Tcherikower, *Early Jewish Labor Movement in the United States*, pp. 168–169; John Laslett, *Labor and the Left* (New York: Basic Books, 1970), p. 102; Melvyn Dubofsky, *When Workers Organize* (Amherst: University of Massachusetts Press, 1968), p. 8; Alice Kessler-Harris, "The Lower Class as a Factor in Reform: New York, The Jews and the 1890s" (Ph.D. Dissertation, Rutgers, 1968), p. 179.

16. See note 15; and Nathan Goldberg, *Occupational Patterns of American Jewry* (New York: JTSP University Press, 1947), p. 21.

17. Louis Waldman, *Labor Lawyer* (New York: E. P. Dutton, 1944), p. 28.

18. Personal Interview, Charles Zimmerman, May 17, 1982.

19. Morrison and Zabusky, *American Mosaic*, p. 10; Interview, Isidore

Schoenholtz, Amerikaner-Yiddishe Geshichte Bel Pe, YIVO, April 16, 1964, pp. 1–2.

20. Interview, Abraham Hershkowitz, Amerikaner-Yiddishe Geshichte Bel Pe, YIVO, May 26, 1965, pp. 2–3.

21. Morris R. Cohen, *A Dreamer's Journey* (Boston: Beacon Press, 1949), p. 21.

22. Quoted in Nora Levin, *While Messiah Tarried: Jewish Socialist Movements, 1871–1917* (New York: Schocken, 1977), p. 129.

23. Interview, Louis Nelson, Amerikaner-Yiddishe Geshichte Bel Pe, YIVO, October 5, 1965, p. 1.

24. Leon Stein, *The Triangle Fire* (Philadelphia: J. B. Lippincott and Co., 1962).

25. Sydelle Kramer and Jenny Masur, eds., *Jewish Grandmothers* (Boston: Beacon Press, 1976), p. 95.

26. Interview, Schoenholtz, p. 3.

27. Waldman, *Labor Lawyer*, pp. 24–25.

28. Philip Zausner, *Unvarnished: The Autobiography of a Union Leader* (New York: Brotherhood Publishers, 1941), pp. 31–32.

29. Interview, Haskel Gittelson, Amerikaner-Yiddishe Geshichte Bel Pe, YIVO, January 10, 1964, p. 3.

30. Rose Cohen, *Out of the Shadow* (New York: G. H. Doran, 1918), p. 104.

31. Isadore Wisotsky, Unpublished "Autobiography," YIVO, p. 21.

32. Ari Lloyd Fridkis, "Desertions in the American Jewish Immigrant Family: The Work of the National Desertion Bureau in Cooperation with the Industrial Removal Office," *American Jewish History*, 71:2 (December 1981), 285–299; Isaac Metzker, ed. *A Bintel Brief* (New York: Ballantine Books, 1971); Marvin Bressler, "Selected Family Patterns in W. I. Thomas' Unfinished Study of the *Bintl Brief*," *American Sociological Review*, 17 (October 1952), 567–569 and the novels and stories of Mary Antin, Yente Serdatzky, Daniel Fuchs, and Abraham Cahan. For those who read Yiddish, the YIVO "autobiographies" collection is a mine of information.

33. Irving Howe, *World of Our Fathers* (New York: Harcourt Brace Jovanovich, 1976), p. 123.

34. Elizabeth Hasanovitz, *One of Them* (Boston: Houghton, Mifflin, 1918), pp. 33–34.

35. Quoted in Tcherikower, *Early Jewish Labor Movement*, p. 115.

36. Rose Schneiderman, *All For One* (New York: Paul S. Erikson, 1967), p. 42.

37. Marcus Ravage, *An American in the Making: The Life Story of an Immigrant* (New York: Harper, 1917), p. 144.

38. Morris Hillquit, *Loose Leaves from a Busy Life* (New York: Da Capo Press, 1971), p. 9.

39. Personal Interview, Dora Solomon, February 17, 1982.

40. Interview, Hyman Rogoff, Amerikaner-Yiddishe Geshichte Bel Pe, YIVO, November 17, 1963, pp. 2–4.

41. Louis Wirth, *The Ghetto* (Chicago: University of Chicago Press, 1928), pp. 222–223.

42. Arthur Goren, *New York Jews and the Quest for Community: The Kehillah Experiment, 1908–1922* (New York: Columbia University Press, 1970), pp. 20–21.

43. Isadore Wisotsky, Unpublished "Autobiography," pp. 10–14.

44. Interview, Abraham Belson, Amerikaner-Yiddishe Geshichte Bel Pe, YIVO, December 7, 1963, pp. 6–7.

45. Interview, Bernard Fenster, Amerikaner-Yiddishe Geshichte Bel-Pe, YIVO, December 6, 1963, p. 5.

46. Moses Rischin, *The Promised City*, p. 56; Charlotte Baum, Paula Hyman, and Sonya Michel, *The Jewish Woman in America* (New York: Dial Press, 1976), p. 99.

47. Melech Epstein, "Pages from My Stormy Life," *American Jewish Archives*, 14 (1962), 133.

48. "It is significant . . . that a whole host of *other institutions* with which Jewish unions are often historically allied *were already in existence* in the first years . . . *before* the Jewish *unions gathered strength* and became permanent bodies." Daniel Bell, "Jewish Labor History," *American Jewish Historical Quarterly*, 46, 3 (March 1957), 258. Emphasis mine.

It is also important to look at the experiences of other groups in this regard. Italians, for example, with a far more fragmented communal infrastructure, did not choose militant unionism or socialism. The Finns, however, were attracted to socialism and were far more easily radicalized and mobilized *after* other cultural and social institutions were transplanted or created here.

49. Stephen Whitfield, "The Radical Persuasion in American Jewish History," *Judaism*, 32:2 (Spring 1983), 136–152; Greenfield, "The Role of the Jews," p. 204; Alice Kessler-Harris, "Organizing the Unorganizable: Three Jewish Women and Their Union," *Labor History*, 17:1 (Winter 1976), 5–23; State of New York, *Bulletin of the Bureau of Labor Statistics*, Vol. 1, 2 (Albany: J. B. Lyons, 1901); State of New York, *Bulletin of the Department of Labor*, 19 vols. (Albany: J. B. Lyons, 1901–1917).

50. Eli Katz, "Bovshover, Kobrin, Libin and Pinski," *Jewish Currents*, 25:10 (November 1972), 7.

51. Arthur Liebman, *Jews and the Left* (New York: John Wiley and Sons, 1979), p. 142.

Chapter 4

1. Quoted in Melech Epstein, *Jewish Labor in the U.S.A.*, Vol. 1 (New York: KTAV, 1950), pp. 22–23.

2. Ronald Sanders, *Downtown Jews: Portraits of an Immigrant Generation* (New York: Harper and Row, 1969), p. 51; Abraham Cahan, *Bleter fun mein leben*, II (New York: Forward Association, 1926–1931), pp. 104–105.

3. Cahan, *Bleter*, p. 105.

4. Quoted in Ezra Mendelsohn, "Russian Roots of the American Jewish Labor Movement," *YIVO Annual*, 16 (1976), 173.

5. Morris Hillquit, *Loose Leaves from a Busy Life* (New York: Da Capo Press, 1971), pp. 2–6.

6. Irving Howe, *World of Our Fathers* (New York: Harcourt Brace Jovanovich, 1976), p. 106.

7. Elias Tcherikower, *The Early Jewish Labor Movement in the United States*, trans. A. Antonovsky (New York: YIVO, 1961), p. 257.

8. Ezra Mendelsohn, "Russian Roots," pp. 168–169.

9. Interview, Morris Feinstone, David J. Saposs Papers, Box 22, Folder 2, State Historical Society of Wisconsin, March 4, 1919.

10. *Reports of the United States Industrial Commission,* Vol. 15 (Washington: House of Representatives, 57th Congress, First Session, 1901), pp. 325, 327. Emphasis mine.

11. The process was repeated in Philadelphia in 1891 and in Chicago in 1896. The socialist nature of the Federation in New York was made clear in its declaration of principles:

> With the concentration of capital in the hands of a few, the meaning of so-called political freedom remains void and empty. There can be no peace between capital and labor within the present social order, for the simple reason that capital depends upon interest, rent and profits which are unjustly wrested from the workers.

Quoted in Tcherikower, *Early Jewish Labor Movement,* p. 327. For a full discussion of the origins of the United Hebrew Trades see Morris Schappes, "The Political Origins of the United Hebrew Trades, 1888," *Journal of Ethnic Studies,* 5:1 (Spring 1977), 13–44.

12. Quoted in Israel Knox and Irving Howe, *The Jewish Labor Movement in America: Two Views* (New York: Jewish Labor Committee, Workmen's Circle 1958), p. 152.

13. Isaac M. Rubinow, "Economic and Industrial Condition: New York," in C. S. Bernheimer, ed., *The Russian Jew in the United States* (Philadelphia: J. C. Winston, 1905), pp. 104–121.

14. Rose Cohen, *Out of the Shadow* (New York: G. H. Doran, 1918), p. 212.

15. Interview, Louis Glass, Amerikaner-Yiddishe Geshichte Bel Pe, YIVO, November 4, 1963, p. 9.

16. Interview, Marsha Farbman, Amerikaner-Yiddishe Geshichte Bel Pe, YIVO, December 17, 1963, pp. 8–9.

17. Jonathan Frankel, *Prophecy and Politics: Socialism, Nationalism and the Russian Jews, 1862–1917* (Cambridge: Cambridge University Press, 1981), pp. 118–119.

18. Hubert Perrier, "The Socialists and the Working Class in New York: 1890–1896," *Labor History,* 22:4 (Fall 1981), 501.

19. Charles Leinenweber, "Socialists in the Streets: New York City Socialist Party in Working-Class Neighborhoods, 1908–1918" (Unpublished paper, Department of Sociology, SUNY, New Paltz), 25.

20. Charles Leinenweber, "The Class and Ethnic Basis of New York City Socialism, 1904–1915," *Labor History,* 22:1 (Winter 1981), 43.

21. Ray Stannard Baker, "The Spiritual Unrest: The Disintegration of the Jews," *Leslie's Monthly,* 68 (1909), 602.

22. Commons's views on Jews extended to other southern and eastern European groups, including the Slavs. Recently, Victor Greene concluded that "far from weakening labor organization the Polish, Lithuanian, Slovak and Ukranian mineworkers, their families, and their communities supported labor protest . . . enthusiastically . . . and were essential to the establishment of unionism permanently in the coal-fields." One of the important things making this possible was that the "Slav hardly arrived alone, lost, uprooted, disoriented . . . [R]elatives and friends in the already developing immigrant community brought him here . . . greeted him . . . and got him a job." *The Slavic Community on Strike* (South Bend, Indiana: Notre Dame University Press, 1968), pp. xv, 210–211.

23. Interview, Isidore Schoenholtz, Amerikaner-Yiddishe Geshichte Bel Pe, YIVO, May 16, 1964, p. 4.

24. Alice Kessler-Harris, "The Lower Class as a Factor in Reform: New York, the Jews and the 1890s" (Ph.D. dissertation, Rutgers University, 1968), p. 179.

25. The Yiddish version of this song appears in Ruth Rubin, *Voices of the People: The Story of Yiddish Folksong* (New York: McGraw-Hill Book Company, 1973), pp. 286–287. The translation is my own.

26. Paula Scheier, "Clara Lemlich Shavelson: 50 Years in Labor's Front Line," in *The American Jewish Woman: A Documentary History*, ed. J. Marcus (New York: KTAV, 1981), pp. 574–575.

27. Charlotte Baum, Paula Hyman, and Sonya Michel, *The Jewish Woman in America* (New York: Dial Press, 1976), pp. 140–144; Mary Jo Buhle, *Women and American Socialism, 1870–1920* (Urbana: University of Illinois Press, 1981), p. 192. Lemlich's speech is variously quoted in the newspapers of the day and variously translated in the secondary literature. What appears here is a composite.

28. Clara Lemlich Shavelson, "Remembering the Waistmakers' General Strike, 1909," *Jewish Currents*, 36:10 (November 1982), 10.

29. Louis Levine, *The Women's Garment Workers* (New York: Huebsch, Inc., 1924), pp. 144–167; Baum et al., *The Jewish Woman in America*, p. 140–144; Buhle, *Women and American Socialism, 1870–1920*, pp. 175–226; Melvyn Dubofsky, *When Workers Organize* (Amherst: University of Massachusetts Press, 1968), pp. 58–60.

30. Abraham Rosenberg, *Di klokmacher un zeyere yunyons* (New York: Cloak Operators Union, Local 1, 1920), p. 208.

31. Louis Waldman, *Labor Lawyer* (New York: E. P. Dutton, 1944), pp. 33–34.

32. Ibid., p. 39.

33. David Dubinsky and A. H. Raskin, *David Dubinsky: A Life with Labor* (New York: Simon and Schuster, 1977), p. 40.

34. Fannia Cohn to E. G. Lindeman, February 7, 1933, and Fannia Cohn to Emma [?], May 8, 1953, Fannia Cohn Papers, New York Public Library.

35. Rose Schneiderman, *All For One* (New York: Paul S. Erikson, 1967), p. 101.

36. Louis Ruchames, "Jewish Radicalism in the United States," in *The Ghetto and Beyond*, ed. Peter I. Rose (New York: Random House, 1969), p. 237.

37. Melvyn Dubofsky, "Success and Failure of Socialism in New York City, 1910–1918," *Labor History*, 9:3 (Fall 1968), 370–371.

38. Ira Kipnis, *The American Socialist Movement, 1897–1912* (New York: Monthly Review Press, 1952), p. 345; James Weinstein, "The Socialist Party: Its Roots and Strengths, 1912–1919," *Studies on the Left*, 1 (Winter 1960), 5–27.

39. Zosa Szajkowsky, "The Jews and New York City's Mayoralty Election of 1917," *Jewish Social Studies*, 32:4 (1970), 286–306.

40. Daniel Bell, *Marxian Socialism in the United States* (Princeton, N.J.: Princeton University Press, 1967), p. 79; Morris Hillquit, *History of Socialism in the United States* (New York: Funk and Wagnalls, 1903), p. 290; James Weinstein, *Decline of American Socialism, 1912–1925* (New York: Vintage Books, 1969), pp. 158–159, 172.

41. Theodore Draper, *Roots of American Communism* (New York: Viking Press, 1957), pp. 33–35.

42. Richard W. Fox, "The Paradox of Progressive Socialism: The Case of Morris Hillquit, 1901–1914," *American Quarterly,* 26:1 (March 1974), 127–140.

43. Interview, Adolph Held, Columbia University Oral History Collection, 1967, p. 4.

44. John Higham, *Strangers in the Land: Patterns of American Nativism, 1860–1925* (New York: Atheneum, 1966), pp. 35–106, 158–194; Robert Wiebe, *The Search for Order: 1877–1920* (New York: Hill and Wang, 1967), pp. 38–106.

45. Wiebe, *Search for Order,* pp. 111–195; John Buenker, *Urban Liberalism and Progressive Reform* (New York: Charles Scribner's Sons, 1973), pp. 1–117, 198–239.

46. Irwin Yellowitz, *Labor and the Progressive Movement in New York State, 1897–1916* (Ithaca: Cornell University Press, 1965), pp. 49–99; Melvyn Dubofsky, *When Workers Organize,* p. 24; Alice Kessler-Harris, "The Lower Class as a Factor in Reform: New York, the Jews and the 1890s," pp. 231–234.

47. See note 46.

48. Alice Kessler-Harris, "The Lower Class."

49. Tcherikower, *Early Jewish Labor Movement in the United States,* pp. 272–273.

50. Moses Rischin, *The Promised City: New York's Jews, 1870–1914* (New York: Corinth Books, 1964), p. 157.

51. Bernard Weinstein, *Di yidishe yunyons in Amerika* (New York: United Hebrew Trades, 1929), pp. 491–493.

52. Ibid., pp. 269–270.

53. Sanders, *Downtown Jews,* pp. 86–87.

54. "Autobiography," #45, YIVO, p. 61.

55. Tcherikower, *Early Jewish Labor Movement,* p. 257.

56. Leon Kobrin, *Meine fuftsik yor in Amerika* (Buenos Aires: Society for Yiddish Secular Schools, 1955), pp. 246–247.

57. Everett V. Stonequist, *The Marginal Man* (New York: Scribners, 1937), p. 174; Anthony Oberschall, *Social Conflict and Social Movements* (Englewood Cliffs, N.J.: Prentice-Hall, 1973), pp. 118–135; Clifford Geertz, ed. *Old Societies and New States* (Glencoe, Ill.: Free Press, 1963).

58. Bernard Bloom, "Yiddish-Speaking Socialists in America, 1892–1905," *American Jewish Archives,* 12:1 (April 1960), 60.

59. Arthur Goren, *The New York Jews and the Quest for Community* (New York: Columbia University Press, 1970), p. 195.

60. Harry Golden in *A Bintel Brief,* ed. Isaac Metzker (New York: Ballantine Books, 1971), p. 70.

61. Kenneth Kann, *Joe Rapoport: Life of a Jewish Radical* (Philadelphia: Temple University Press, 1981), p. xi.

62. Interview, Flora Weiss, Amerikaner-Yiddishe Geshichte Bel Pe, YIVO, June 15, 1964, p. 11; Joseph Schlossberg in Charles Zaretz, *Amalgamated Clothing Workers of America: A Study in Progressive Trades-Unionism* (New York: Ancon Publishing Co., 1934), p. 94.

63. Elizabeth Hasanovitz, *One of Them* (Boston: Houghton Mifflin, 1918), pp. 326–327.

64. Irving Howe, *World of Our Fathers,* pp. 292–294.

65. Moses Rischin, "The Jewish Labor Movement in America: A Social

Interpretation," *Labor History*, 4:3 (Fall 1963), 235.

66. Lucy Lang, *Tomorrow is Beautiful* (New York: MacMillan Co., 1948), p. 292.

67. Robert M. Crunden, *Ministers of Reform: The Progressives' Achievement in American Civilization, 1889–1920* (New York: Basic Books, 1982), pp. 3–89.

68. Frederick C. Howe, *The Confessions of a Reformer* (New York: Charles Scribner's Sons, 1925), pp. 16–17.

69. C. Wright Mills, *White Collar* (New York: Oxford University Press, 1951), p. 325.

70. Interview, Morris Feinstone, March 4, 1919.

71. Interview, Abraham Belson, Amerikaner-Yiddishe Geshichte Bel Pe, YIVO, December 7, 1963, pp. 2–5.

72. Hasanovitz, *One of Them*, p. 31.

73. Interview, Flora Weiss, Amerikaner-Yiddishe Geshichte Bel Pe, YIVO, June 15, 1964, p. 11. Emphasis mine.

74. Cited in Isaac Metzker, ed. *A Bintel Brief* (New York: Ballantine Books, 1971), p. 13.

75. Goren, *The New York Jews and the Quest for Community*, pp. 198–200. Jewish socialists also got hopelessly entangled in the American Jewish Congress movement between 1914 and 1918. Unable to decide whether to denounce or join the Congress, which included Zionists and capitalists, socialists made several ill-timed changes of course. These included a temporary "alliance" with the bourgeois element, that socialists made out of a profound dread of Zionist domination of the Jewish community. Additional radical reversals between 1915 and 1918 left socialists divided and in general disarray by the end of World War I. Jonathan Frankel, "The Jewish Socialists and the American Jewish Congress Movement," *YIVO Annual*, 16 (1976), 202–341; and *Prophecy and Politics*, pp. 509–547.

76. Interview, Louis Painkin, Irving Howe Collection, YIVO, April 17, 1968, p. 3.

77. Personal interview, Jacob Levenson, October 14, 1981.

78. Dubofsky, *When Workers Organize*, pp. 126–151.

79. Ibid.; Charles Leinenweber, "*World of Our Fathers* as Socialist History" (Unpublished paper, Department of Sociology, SUNY, New Paltz), p. 7.

80. Wiebe, *Search for Order*, pp. 111–132, 145–155; Goren, *Quest for Community*, p. 17.

81. Interview, Joseph Schlossberg, Columbia University Oral History Collection, June 2, 1965, p. 2.

82. New York *Call*, September 12, 1908.

83. Arthur Gorenstein, "A Portrait of Ethnic Politics: The Socialists and the 1908 and 1910 Congressional Elections on the East Side," *Publication of the American Jewish Historical Society*, 50 (1960), 202–238.

84. New York *Call*, November 9, 1914.

85. Hillel Rogoff, *An East Side Epic: The Life and Work by Meyer London* (New York: Vanguard Press, 1930), p. 69.

86. New York *Times*, November 2, 1917.

87. New York *Call*, November 4, 1917.

88. Will Herberg, "The American Jewish Labor Movement," *American Jewish Year Book*, 80 (1952), 25.

89. Ibid., p. 26; Howe, *World of Our Fathers*, p. 327. Emphasis mine.

Chapter 5

1. Interview, Max Deutschman, Amerikaner-Yiddishe Geshichte Bel Pe, YIVO, February 3, 1964, pp. 2–3.

2. Interview, Pauline Newman, Amerikaner-Yiddishe Geshichte Bel Pe, YIVO, January 19, 1965, p. 13.

3. Interview, Joseph Schlossberg, Columbia University Oral History Collection, June 2, 1965, p. 4.

4. Quoted in Charles Zaretz, *Amalgamated Clothing Workers of America: A Study in Progressive Trades-Unionism* (New York: Ancon Publishing Co., 1934),p. 94.

5. Interview, Abe Hershkowitz, Amerikaner-Yiddishe Geshichte Bel Pe, YIVO, May 26, 1965, p. 4.

6. Interview, Oscar Feuer, Amerikaner-Yiddishe Geshichte Bel Pe, YIVO, November 11, 1963, p. 2.

7. Marie Ganz, *Rebels Into Anarchy and Out* (New York: Dodd and Mead, 1920), pp. 112–127.

8. Gary Endelman, "Solidarity Forever: Rose Schneiderman and the Women's Trade Union League" (Ph.D. dissertation, University of Delaware, 1978), p. 21.

9. Personal Interview, Jacob Levenson, New York, October 14, 1981.

10. Interview, Abraham Sherer, Amerikaner-Yiddishe Geshichte Bel Pe, YIVO, November 25, 1965, p. 5.

11. Interview, Pauline Newman, YIVO, p. 14.

12. Interview, Pauline Newman, Columbia University Oral History Collection, June 15, 1965, pp. 6–7.

13. Rose Cohen, *Out of the Shadow* (New York: G. H. Doran, 1918), p. 127.

14. Jacob Panken, unpublished "Autobiographical Notes," Panken Papers, Tamiment Institute, Collection #46, Box 3, p. 2.

15. Louis Waldman, *Labor Lawyer* (New York: Dutton and Co., 1944), pp. 28–29.

16. Interview, Bernard Fenster, Amerikaner-Yiddishe Geshichte Bel Pe, YIVO, December 6, 1963, p. 2.

17. Interview, Joseph Gutterman, Amerikaner-Yiddishe Geshichte Bel Pe, YIVO, December 10, 1963, p. 6; Rose Schneiderman, *All for One* (New York: Paul S. Erikson, 1967), p. viii.

18. Sydelle Kramer and Jenny Masur, eds. *Jewish Grandmothers* (Boston: Beacon Press, 1976), p. 101.

19. Interview, Feigl Shapiro, Amerikaner-Yiddishe Geshichte Bel Pe, YIVO, August 6, 1964, p. 3.

20. Personal Interview, Jack Sperber, New York, November 25, 1981.

21. Fannia Cohn to Evelyn Preston, May 3, 1923, Fannia Cohn Papers, New York Public Library.

22. Fannia Cohn to Evelyn Preston, April 10, 1922, Fannia Cohn Papers, New York Public Library.

23. Abraham Cahan to Spivackofsky, 1883–1884, in Melech Epstein, *Jewish Labor in the U.S.A.* (New York: KTAV, 1950), Vol. I, p. 140.

24. Quoted in Jonathan Frankel, *Prophecy and Politics: Socialism, Nationalism and the Russian Jews, 1862–1917* (Cambridge: Cambridge University Press, 1981), p. 132.

25. Melech Epstein, *Profiles of Eleven* (Detroit: Wayne State University Press, 1965), p. 106.

26. Ronald Sanders, *Downtown Jews: Portraits of an Immigrant Generation* (New York: Harper and Row, 1969), pp. 276–286.

27. Leonard Dinnerstein, *The Leo Frank Case* (New York: Columbia University Press, 1968). The Georgia State Senate resolved, in the face of evidence corroborating the innocence of Leo Frank, to conduct an investigation into the case with the possibility of granting a posthumous pardon. The Georgia State Board of Pardon and Parole in December 1983 refused to grant the pardon.

28. Sanders, *Downtown Jews*, p. 366.

29. Abraham Cahan, *The Rise of David Levinsky* (New York: Harper and Brothers, 1960), p. 530.

30. Robert Wistrich, *Revolutionary Jews from Marx to Trotsky* (New York: Harper and Row, 1976). Even with these men and women, however, the imputation of self-hatred as a precondition for radicalism is based on not much more than inference. It is good to remember that Victor Adler, for example, converted to Protestantism in 1878 and only afterwards became a socialist—no earlier than the mid-1880s. One could argue that only after Adler dealt directly with his alleged self-hatred, through baptism, did he achieve the stability to commit himself to radical politics.

31. *Di tsukunft*, July 1912, p. 450, in Isaiah Trunk, "The Cultural Dimension of the Jewish Labor Movement," *YIVO Annual*, 16 (1976), 343.

32. Morris Winchevsky, *Gezamelte verk*, ed. Kalmen Marmor (New York: Freiheit, 1927), Vol. 9, p. 156.

33. Morris Winchevsky, "Reminiscences," reprinted in *Jewish Currents* 32:8 (September 1978), pp. 30–32.

34. Quoted in Irwin Yellowitz, "Morris Hillquit, American Socialism and Jewish Concerns," *American Jewish History*, 68:2 (December 1978), 164.

35. Ibid.

36. Wistrich, *Revolutionary Jews*, p. 8. Wistrich does recognize that coherent, proletarianized Jewish groups in Eastern Europe produced movements and organizations aimed at synthesizing Marxism and Jewish culture. Unfortunately, his analysis of a handful of radical Jewish intellectuals, possibly exceptional even in that categorization, has been borrowed by others to help "explain" the whole of Jewish radicalism.

37. Quoted in Avraham Yarmolinsky, *Road to Revolution: A Century of Russian Radicalism* (New York: MacMillan, 1959), p. 310.

38. Quoted in Epstein, *Profiles of Eleven*, p. 308.

39. Morris Raphael Cohen, *A Dreamer's Journey* (Boston: Beacon Press, 1949), p. 98.

40. Kenneth Kann, *Joe Rapoport: Life of a Jewish Radical* (Philadelphia: Temple University Press, 1981), pp. 10, xi.

41. Morris Winchevsky, *Gezamelte verk*, ed. K. Marmor (New York: Freiheit, 1927), Vol. 7, pp. 30–32.

42. Richard Drinnon, *Rebel in Paradise* (New York: Harper and Row, 1976), p. 29.

43. Emma Goldman, *Living My Life* (New York: Knopf, 1931), Vol. I, p. 370.

44. I have borrowed some of the terminology used by Aaron Antonovsky

in his analysis of second generation Jews. "Toward a Refinement of the Marginal Man Concept," *Social Forces*, 35 (1956), pp. 57–62.

45. Georg Simmel, *Conflict and the Web of Group Affiliations*, trans. Kurt H. Wolff and Reinhard Bendix (New York: Free Press, 1964), p. 142.

46. Samuel Gompers, *Seventy Years of Life and Labor* (New York: E. P. Dutton, 1925), Vol. I, pp. 378, 383.

47. Morris R. Cohen, *Dreamer's Journey*, p. 95.

48. Moses Kligsberg, "Jewish Immigrants in Business," in *The Jewish Experience in America*, ed. Abraham J. Karp (New York: KTAV, 1969), Vol. 5, pp. 254–260. *Tachlis* did not mean mere wealth-getting. In fact, learning and spiritual contentment were higher long-term goals for centuries. Even in the modern period, and among those immigrants for whom an economic *tachlis* was central, restraining factors of a social-moral character came into play. Kligsberg, p. 283.

49. Elizabeth Hasanovitz, *One of Them* (Boston: Houghton Mifflin, 1918), p. 33.

50. Cahan to Spivackofsky, in Epstein, *Jewish Labor*, Vol. I, p. 140.

51. David Dubinsky and A. H. Raskin, *David Dubinsky: A Life With Labor* (New York: Simon and Schuster, 1977), p. 48.

52. Ibid., p. 54.

53. Interview, Pauline Newman, Amerikaner-Yiddishe Geshichte Bel Pe, YIVO, February 2, 1965, p. 33.

54. Interview, Bernard Fenster, Amerikaner-Yiddishe Geshichte Bel Pe, YIVO, December 6, 1963, p. 2.

55. Hubert Perrier, "The Socialists and the Working Class in New York: 1890–1896," *Labor History*, 22:4 (Fall 1981), 503.

56. Interview, Adolph Held, Columbia University Oral History Collection, 1967, p. 4.

Chapter 6

1. Charlotte Baum, "What Made Yetta Work? The Economic Role of Eastern European Jewish Women in the Family," *Response*, 18 (Summer 1973), pp. 32–38.

2. See Chapter 2, pp. 42–43.

3. Emma Goldman, *Living My Life* (New York: Knopf, 1931), vol. I, p. 12.

4. Sydelle Kramer and Jenny Masur, eds. *Jewish Grandmothers* (Boston: Beacon Press, 1976), p. 8.

5. Fannia Cohn to A. Plotkin, August 6, 1959, Fannia Cohn Papers, New York Public Library.

6. Rose Schneiderman, *All For One* (New York: Paul S. Erikson, 1967), p. 14.

7. Personal Interview, Lucy Sperber, New York, November 25, 1981.

8. Ruth Landes and Mark Zbrowski, "Hypotheses Concerning the Eastern European Jewish Family," *Psychiatry*, 13 (1950), pp. 447–464.

9. On raising daughters who are likely to assert independence see Rita Mae Kelly and Mary Boutilier, *The Making of Political Women* (Chicago: Nelson Hall, 1978) p. 23 and Herbert Hyman, *Political Socialization* (Glencoe, Ill: Free Press, 1959), pp. 84–86.

10. Harriet Davis-Kram, "Jewish Women in Russian Revolutionary Movements" (M.A. Thesis, Hunter College, CUNY, 1974), p. 17.

11. Kramer and Masur, *Jewish Grandmothers*, p. 8.

12. Rose Pesotta, *Bread Upon the Waters* (New York: Dodd, Mead and Co., 1944), pp. 9, 6; *Days of Our Lives* (Boston: Excelsior Publishers, 1958), p. 219.

13. The mass of young Jewish immigrant women, socialist or not, appears to have been oriented toward evening school. Between 1910 and 1913 Jewish girls made up the second largest proportion of students in public night schools, See Mary Van Kleeck, *Working Girls in Evening Schools* (New York: Survey Associates, 1914), pp. 22–23; Robert Woods and Albert Kennedy, eds. *Young Working Girls* (Boston: Houghton Mifflin, 1913), p. 11.

14. Kramer and Masur, *Jewish Grandmothers*, p. 95.

15. Interview, Flora Weiss, Amerikaner-Yiddishe Geshichte Bel Pe, YIVO, June 15, 1964, pp. 7–8.

16. Ibid., p. 4.

17. Marie Ganz, *Rebels Into Anarchy and Out* (New York: Dodd and Mead, 1920), p. 89.

18. Kramer and Masur, *Jewish Grandmothers*, p. 11.

19. Charlotte Baum, et al., *The Jewish Woman in America* (New York: Dial Press, 1976), p. 135.

20. Rose Cohen, *Out of the Shadow* (New York: G. H. Doran, 1918), p. 74.

21. Ruth Rubin, *Voices of a People: The Story of Yiddish Folksong* (New York: McGraw Hill Book Co., 1973), p. 290. The translation is my own.

22. Kramer and Masur, *Jewish Grandmothers*, p. 13.

23. Thomas Kessner and Betty Boyd Caroli, "New Immigrant Women at Work: Italians and Jews in New York City, 1880–1905," *Journal of Ethnic Studies*, 5:4 (1978), 25.

24. Susan E. Kennedy, *If All We Did Was to Weep at Home* (Bloomington: Indiana University Press, 1979), pp. 64–66.

25. William Z. Ripley, "Race Factors in Labor Unions," *Atlantic Monthly*, 93 (1904), 300.

26. U.S. Department of Labor, Bureau of Labor Statistics, Bulletin No. 175, *Summary of the Report on the Condition of Women and Child Wage Earners in the United States* (Washington: Government Printing Office, 1916), pp. 86–87.

27. Schneiderman, *All For One*, p. 50.

28. Nancy Dye, "Creating a Feminist Alliance: Sisterhood and Class Conflict in the New York WTUL," *Feminist Studies*, 2:2 (1975), 27.

29. Hutchins Hapgood, *The Spirit of the Ghetto* (New York: Schocken Books, 1966), p. 77.

30. Interview, Hyman Rogoff, Amerikaner-Yiddishe Geshichte Bel Pe, YIVO, November 17, 1963, p. 2.

31. Isabel London, unpublished typescript, "Meyer London: An Appreciation," n.p., n.d., Meyer London Papers, Box 1, Tamiment Institute. Emphasis mine.

32. Sally M. Miller, "From Sweatshop Worker to Labor Leader: Theresa Malkiel, A Case Study," *American Jewish History*, 68:2 (December 1978), 203; Mary Jo Buhle, *Women and American Socialism, 1870–1920* (Urbana: University of Illinois Press, 1981), pp. 177–178.

33. Theresa Malkiel, *The Diary of a Shirtwaist Striker* (New York: Cooperative Press, 1910), p. 13.

34. Interview, Minnie Rivkin, Oral History of the American Left, Tamiment Institute, 1980.

35. Kramer and Masur, *Jewish Grandmothers*, p. 13.

36. Schneiderman, *All For One*, pp. 110, 111.

37. Pauline Newman to Rose Schneiderman, November 7, 1911, Rose Schneiderman Papers, A94, Tamiment Institute.

38. Theresa Wolfson, *The Woman Worker and the Trade Unions* (New York: International Publishers, 1926), pp. 141–142.

39. Ibid., p. 163; Alice Kessler-Harris, *Out To Work: A History of Wage-Earning Women in the United States* (New York: Oxford University Press, 1982), pp. 159–160; Milton Cantor and Bruce Laurie, *Class, Sex and the Woman Worker* (Westport, Connecticut: Greenwood Press, 1977), p. 11.

40. Fannia Cohn to Selig Perlman, December 26, 1951, Fannia Cohn Papers, New York Public Library.

41. Fannia Cohn to Theresa Wolfson, May 15, 1922; Fannia Cohn to Evelyn Preston, September 8, 1922, Fannia Cohn Papers, New York Public Library.

42. Interview, Feigl Shapiro, Amerikaner-Yiddishe Geshichte Bel Pe, YIVO, August 6, 1964, p. 7.

43. Alice Kessler-Harris, "Organizing the Unorganizable: Three Jewish Women and Their Union," *Labor History*, 17:1 (Winter 1976), 17.

44. Interview, Minnie Rivkin, Oral History of the American Left, Tamiment Institute, 1980.

45. Interview, Flora Weiss, Amerikaner-Yiddishe Geshichte Bel Pe, YIVO, June 15, 1964, p. 5.

46. Ibid., p. 8.

47. Quoted in Mary Van Kleeck, *Artificial Flower Makers* (New York: Russell Sage Foundation, 1913), p. 34.

48. Interview, "Anonymous," Charles Leinenweber, Staten Island, 1974.

49. Van Kleeck, *Working Girls*, p. 24.

50. Pauline Newman to Rose Schneiderman, September 20, 1910, Rose Schneiderman Papers, Box A94, Tamiment Institute.

51. Rose Pesotta to David Dubinsky, February 6, 1933, Rose Pesotta Papers, New York Public Library.

52. Buhle, *Women and American Socialism;* Sally M. Miller, "Other Socialists: Native Born and Immigrant Women in the Socialist Party, 1901–1917," *Labor History*, 24:1 (Winter 1983), 84–102.

53. Dye, "Creating the Feminist Alliance," pp. 24–38; Kessler-Harris, "Organizing the Unorganizable," p. 13.

54. Max Fruchter to Rose Schneiderman, March 5, 1911, Rose Schneiderman Papers, Box A94, Tamiment Institute.

55. Pauline Newman to Rose Schneiderman, March 5, 1912, Rose Schneiderman Papers, Box A94, Tamiment Institute.

56. Buhle, *Women and American Socialism*, p. 226.

57. Quoted in Rudolf Glanz, *The Jewish Woman in America* (New York: KTAV, 1976), p. 153.

58. Fannia Cohn to Selig Perlman, December 26, 1951. Fannia Cohn Papers, New York Public Library.

59. Fannia Cohn to Evelyn Preston, September 29, 1922, Fannia Cohn Papers, New York Public Library.

60. Fannia Cohn, "Aims of Workers' Education," n.d., p. 2, Fannia Cohn Papers, Box 6, New York Public Library.

61. Elizabeth Hasanovitz, *One of Them*, p. 8.

62. Quoted in Buhle, *Women and American Socialism,* p. 176.
63. Buhle, *Women and American Socialism,* p. 300.

Chapter 7

1. Isadore Wisotsky, unpublished "Autobiography," YIVO, n.d., p. 3.
2. Wisotsky, "Autobiography," p. 1; Interview, Isadore Wisotsky, Howe Collection, YIVO, 1968, p. 2.
3. Wisotsky, "Autobiography," p. 36.
4. Ibid., p. 3.
5. Interview, Isadore Wisotsky, Amerikaner-Yiddishe Geshichte Bel Pe, YIVO, October 6, 1963, p. 3.
6. Interview, Wisotsky, Howe, p. 2.
7. Interview, Amerikaner-Yiddishe Geshichte Bel Pe, p. 2.
8. Wisotsky, "Autobiography," p. 8.
9. Ibid.
10. Ibid., pp. 2–3; Interview, Amerikaner-Yiddishe Geshichte Bel Pe, p. 1.
11. Wisotsky, "Autobiography," p. 8.
12. Ibid., pp. 6–8.
13. Ibid., p. 13.
14. Interview, Amerikaner-Yiddishe Geshichte Bel Pe, p. 2.
15. Wisotsky, "Autobiography," p. 14; Interview, Amerikaner-Yiddishe Geshichte Bel Pe, p. 3.
16. Wisotsky, "Autobiography," pp. 14, 15.
17. Ibid., p. 27.
18. Ibid., p. 18.
19. Ibid., p. 22.
20. Ibid., pp. 42–45.
21. Rose Pesotta, *Days of Our Lives* (Boston: Excelsior Publishers, 1958), p. 105.
22. Ibid., p. 121.
23. Ibid., p. 93.
24. Ibid., p. 70.
25. Ibid., p. 71.
26. Ibid., p. 177.
27. Ibid., p. 214.
28. Ibid., p. 217.
29. Ibid., p. 219.
30. Ibid., p. 221.
31. Ibid., p. 248.
32. Rose Pesotta, "Typescript," Rose Pesotta Papers, New York Public Library.
33. Diary, Rose Pesotta Papers, November 3, 1931, New York Public Library.
34. Diary, Rose Pesotta Papers, September 20, 1932, New York Public Library.
35. Rose Pesotta to David Dubinsky, September 30, 1933, Rose Pesotta Papers, New York Public Library.
36. Pesotta, *Bread Upon the Waters* (New York: Dodd Mead and Co., 1944), p. 101.
37. Diary, Rose Pesotta Papers, July 22, 1934, NYPL.

38. Rose Pesotta, "Typescript," Rose Pesotta Papers, May 27, 1937, NYPL, p. 6.

39. Diary, Rose Pesotta Papers, November 20, 1936, NYPL.

40. Personal Interview, Charles Zimmerman, New York City, May 17, 1982.

41. Interview, Charles Zimmerman, Howe Collection, YIVO, 1968, pp. 2–3.

42. Personal Interview, Charles Zimmerman, May 17, 1982. Interview, Charles Zimmerman, Amerikaner-Yiddishe Geshichte Bel Pe, YIVO, November 11, 1964, p. 1.

43. Personal Interview, Charles Zimmerman, May 17, 1982.

44. Ibid.

45. Ibid.

46. Interview, Charles Zimmerman, Amerikaner-Yiddishe Geshichte Bel Pe, YIVO, p. 5.

47. Ibid., p. 6.

48. Ibid.; Personal Interview, Charles Zimmerman, May 17, 1982.

49. Interview, Charles Zimmerman, Amerikaner-Yiddishe Geshichte Bel Pe, YIVO, pp. 10–11.

50. Personal Interview, Charles Zimmerman, May 17, 1982; Interview, Charles Zimmerman, Amerikaner-Yiddishe Geshichte Bel Pe, YIVO, p. 8.

51. Personal Interview, Charles Zimmerman, May 17, 1982.

52. Interview, Charles Zimmerman, Amerikaner-Yiddishe Geshichte Bel Pe, YIVO, p. 10.

53. Ibid., p. 9.

54. Personal Interview, Charles Zimmerman, May 17, 1982.

55. Interview, Charles Zimmerman, Amerikaner-Yiddishe Geshichte Bel Pe, YIVO, p. 41. Irving Howe and Lewis Coser, *The American Communist Party* (Boston: Beacon Press, 1957), pp. 245–272; Harvey Klehr, *Communist Cadre: The Social Background of the American Communist Party Elite* (Stanford, Cal.: Hoover Institution Press, 1978), pp. 49, 92, 96.

56. Personal Interview, Clara Weissman, Woodridge, New York, April 3, 1982. All information for this biography is drawn from the interview.

57. Bernard Chasanow, *Tag un yorn: funem leben fun a yidishen arbeiter* (New York: Bernard Chasanow, 1956), p. 12.

58. Ibid., pp. 12–13.

59. Ibid., p. 13.

60. Ibid.

61. Ibid., p. 14.

62. Ibid., p. 16.

63. Ibid., p. 21.

64. Interview, Bernard Chasanow, Oral History of the American Left, Tamiment Institute, May 31, 1978.

65. Interview, I. E. Rontch, Oral History of the American Left, Tamiment Institute, April 14, 1980.

66. Ibid.

67. Ibid.

68. Ibid.

Chapter 8

1. Who among the Jewish radicals joined the Communist Party and who stayed in, or dropped out, and at which "crisis" presents a fascinating and

perplexing set of questions. It would take at least another book-length study to deal with this. My impression is, after looking carefully at the biographical materials on the men and women in this analysis, that it will not be possible to draw a coherent social profile of predictability. For the social origins of Communist Party leaders, see Harvey Klehr, *Communist Cadre: The Social Background of the American Communist Party Elite* (Stanford, Cal.: Hoover Institution Press, 1978).

2. Fannia Cohn to Evelyn Preston, May 22, 1922, Fannia Cohn Papers, New York Public Library.

3. Quoted in Rudolf Glanz, *The Jewish Woman in America,* Vol. I (New York: KTAV, 1976), p. 3.

4. Marvin Bressler, "Selected Family Patterns in W. I. Thomas' Unfinished Study of the *Bintl Brief,*" *American Sociological Review,* 17 (October 1952), 569.

5. A. Cohen, *Everyman's Talmud* (New York: Schocken Books, 1975), pp. 364–370.

6. Daniel Elazar, "American Political Theory and the Political Notions of American Jews: Convergences and Contradictions," in *The Ghetto and Beyond,* ed., Peter I. Rose (New York: Random House, 1969), pp. 203–227; R. J. Zwi Werblowsky, "Messianism in Jewish History," in *Jewish Society Through the Ages,* eds., H. H. Ben-Sasson and S. Ettinger (New York: Schocken Books, 1971), pp. 30–45.

7. Will Herberg, "Socialism, Zionism and Messianic Passion," *Midstream,* 2 (Summer, 1956), 67.

8. See for example Thomas Kessner, *The Golden Door: Italian and Jewish Immigrant Mobility in New York City, 1880–1915* (New York: Oxford University Press, 1977); Eli Ginzburg, "Jews in the American Economy: The Dynamics of Opportunity," in Gladys Rosen, ed., *Jewish Life in America* (New York: KTAV, 1978), pp. 109–119.

9. Interview, Abraham Hershkowitz, Amerikaner-Yiddishe Geshichte Bel Pe, YIVO, May 26, 1965, part 5, p. 1.

10. Interview, Feigl Shapiro, Amerikaner-Yiddishe Geshichte Bel Pe, YIVO, August 6, 1964, p. 31.

11. Interview, Pauline Newman, Columbia University Oral History Collection, June 15, 1965, p. 9.

12. Morris Hillquit, *Loose Leaves from a Busy Life* (New York: Da Capo Press, 1971) p. 332.

13. Joan Morrison and Charlotte Fox Zabusky, *American Mosaic: The Immigrant Experience in the Words of Those Who Lived It* (New York: E. P. Dutton, 1980), p. 14.

14. Kenneth Kann, *Joe Rapoport: Life of a Jewish Radical* (Philadelphia: Temple University Press, 1981), p. 259.

15. Interview, Pauline Newman, Columbia University Oral History Collection, June 15, 1965, p. 9.

Bibliography

The bulk of the research for this study was done at YIVO Institute for Jewish Research in New York City. The archives contain numerous collections of documents, letters, clippings, and autobiographical essays, and an invaluable set of interviews done with labor activists in the 1960s. Most are in Yiddish.

The Tamiment Institute Library at New York University has an extraordinary labor collection, including the papers, letters, notebooks, and typescripts of several important figures in the trade union and socialist movements. It also houses the indispensable Oral History of the American Left, interviews with radicals, done in the 1960s through the 1980s. Most of these are on cassettes and have yet to be transcribed. Some are in Yiddish.

The New York Public Library was most useful for the Fannia Cohn and Rose Pesotta collections, which include innumerable letters, notes, clippings, and, in Pesotta's case, a significant set of journals and diaries. The Columbia University Oral History Collection includes interviews and memoirs of several important socialists of the immigrant generation.

Interviews

Anonymous, Charles Leinenweber, Staten Island, 1974.

Abraham Belson, Amerikaner-Yiddishe Geshichte Bel Pe, YIVO, December 7, 1963.

Theodore Brise, Oral History of the American Left, Tamiment Institute, April 16, 1980.

Fanny Cantor and Herman Cantor, Oral History of the American Left, Tamiment Institute, 1974.

Philip Caplowitz, Oral History of the American Left, Tamiment Institute, November 15, 1980.

Bernard Chasanow, Oral History of the American Left, Tamiment Institute, May 31, 1978.

Hyman Cohen, Author, May 17, 1982.

Samuel Davis, Oral History of the American Left, Tamiment Institute, November 15, 1980.

Max Deutschman, Amerikaner-Yiddishe Geshichte Bel Pe, YIVO, February 3, 1964.

Jack Dubnow, Amerikaner-Yiddishe Geshichte Bel Pe, YIVO, July 22, 1964.

Melech Epstein, Oral History of the American Left, Tamiment Institute, 1974.

Marsha and Moishe Farbman, Amerikaner-Yiddishe Geshichte, Bel Pe, YIVO, December 17, 1963.

Morris Feinstone, David J. Saposs Papers, Box 22, folder 2, State Historical

Society of Wisconsin, March 4, 1919.

Bernard Fenster, Amerikaner-Yiddishe Geshichte Bel Pe, YIVO, December 6, 1963.

Oscar Feuer, Amerikaner-Yiddishe Geshichte Bel Pe, YIVO, November 11, 1963.

Julius Gershin, Amerikaner-Yiddishe Geshichte Bel Pe, YIVO, January 27, 1964.

Haskel Gittelson, Amerikaner-Yiddishe Geshichte Bel Pe, YIVO, January 10, 1964.

Louis Glass, Amerikaner-Yiddishe Geshichte Bel Pe, YIVO, November 4, 1963.

Abraham L. Goldman, Amerikaner-Yiddishe Geshichte Bel Pe, YIVO, January 24, 1964.

Joseph Gutterman, Amerikaner-Yiddishe Geshichte Bel Pe, YIVO, December 10, 1963.

N. Hait, Amerikaner-Yiddishe Geshichte Bel Pe, YIVO, October 27, 1963.

Gershin Halpern, Amerikaner-Yiddishe Geshichte Bel Pe, YIVO, November 11, 1965.

Pearl Halpern, Amerikaner-Yiddishe Geshichte Bel Pe, YIVO, November 11, 1965.

Adolph Held, Amerikaner-YiddisheGeshichte Bel Pe, YIVO, June 6, 1964; Columbia University Oral History Collection, 1967.

Abraham Hershkowitz, Amerikaner-Yiddishe Geshichte Bel Pe, YIVO, May 26, 1965.

Esther Kadar, Amerikaner-Yiddishe Geshichte Bel Pe, YIVO, October 24, 1964.

Charles Krindler, Amerikaner-Yiddishe Geshichte Bel Pe, YIVO, August 2, 1965.

Florence Levenson, Author, October 14, 1981.

Jacob Levenson, Author, October 14, 1981.

Abraham Margolin, Amerikaner-Yiddishe Geshichte Bel Pe, YIVO, January 1, 1967.

Abraham Mendelowitz, Amerikaner-Yiddishe Geshichte Bel Pe, YIVO, November 10, 1964.

Morris Nadelman, Oral History of the American Left, Tamiment Institute, April 8, 1980.

Louis Nelson, Amerikaner-Yiddishe Geshichte Bel Pe, YIVO, October 5, 1965.

Pauline Newman, Amerikaner-Yiddishe Geshichte Bel Pe, YIVO, January 19, 1965; January 26, 1965; February 2, 1965; Columbia University Oral History Collection, June 15, 1965.

Paul Novick, Howe Collection, YIVO, March 29, 1968.

Louis Painkin, Howe Collection, YIVO, April 17, 1968.

Benjamin Rabinowitz, Amerikaner-Yiddishe Geshichte Bel Pe, YIVO, December 23, 1963.

Minnie Rivkin, Oral History of the American Left, Tamiment Institute, 1980.

Hyman Rogoff, Amerikaner-Yiddishe Geshichte Bel Pe, YIVO, November 17, 1963.

I. E. Rontch, Oral History of the American Left, Tamiment Institute, April 14, 1980.

Sam Rubin, Amerikaner-Yiddishe Geshichte Bel Pe, YIVO, June 26, 1965.

Joseph Schlossberg, David Saposs Papers, Box 21, folder 16, State Historical Society of Wisconsin, February 27, 1919; Columbia University Oral History Collection, June 2, 1965.

Hyman Schneid, David Saposs Papers, Box 22, folder 2, State Historical Society of Wisconsin, December 20, 1918.

Isidore Schoenholtz, Amerikaner-Yiddishe Geshichte Bel Pe, YIVO, May 16, 1964.

Mark Schveid, Amerikaner-Yiddishe Geshichte Bel Pe, YIVO, February 25, 1965.

Feigl Shapiro, Amerikaner-Yiddishe Geshichte Bel Pe, YIVO, August 6, 1964.

Morris Shatan, Amerikaner-Yiddishe Geshichte Bel Pe, YIVO, August 20, 1968.

Zelig Sher, Amerikaner-Yiddishe Geshichte Bel Pe, YIVO, October 1, 1965.

Abraham Sherer, Amerikaner-Yiddishe Geshichte Bel Pe, YIVO, November 25, 1965.

Anna Shul, Author, March 3, 1982.

Dora Solomon, Author, February 17, 1982.

Jack Sperber, Author, November 25, 1981.

Lucy Sperber, Author, November 25, 1981.

Flora Weiss, Amerikaner-Yiddishe Geshichte Bel Pe, YIVO, June 15, 1964.

Clara Weissman, Author, April 3, 1982.

Isadore Wisotsky, Amerikaner-Yiddishe Geshichte Bel Pe, YIVO, October 6, 1963; Howe Collection, YIVO, 1968.

Ella Wolf, Amerikaner-Yiddishe Geshichte Bel Pe, YIVO, December 27, 1963.

Philip Zausner, David Saposs Papers, Box 21, folder 16, State Historical Society of Wisconsin, March 13, 1919.

Charles Zimmerman, Amerikaner-Yiddishe Geshichte Bel Pe, YIVO, November 11, 1964; Howe Collection, YIVO, 1968; Oral History of the American Left, Tamiment Institute, 1974: Author, May 17, 1982.

Max Zuckerman, David Saposs Papers, Box 21, folder 16, State Historical Society of Wisconsin, March 3, 1919.

Abe Zwerlin, Amerikaner-Yiddishe Geshichte Bel Pe, YIVO, May 4, 1964; Howe Collection, YIVO, April 12, 1968.

Papers, Memoirs, and Other Archival Materials

Anonymous, "Autobiography," no. 45, YIVO.

Fannia Cohn Papers, New York Public Library.

Bella Dvorin, Letter to author, March 8, 1982.

Oscar Feuer, "Autobiography," no. 318, YIVO.

Morris Hillquit Papers, Tamiment Institute.

Sergie Ingerman Papers, Tamiment Institute.

Meyer London Papers, Tamiment Institute.

Mother Earth. New York: Greenwood Reprint Corp., 1968. See especially series 1, vols 1–12, March 1906 to August 1917, edited by Emma Goldman.

Jacob Panken Papers, Tamiment Institute.

Rose Pesotta Papers, New York Public Library.

Rose Schneiderman Papers, Tamiment Institute.

Socialist Labor Party, Proceedings of the 10th Annual Convention, 1900.

Typescript, Tamiment Institute.
Socialist Party. Local New York Papers and Minute Books, Tamiment Institute.
Socialist Party of America. Proceedings of the Socialist Unity Convention, 1901. Typescript, Tamiment Institute.
Rose Pastor Stokes Papers, Tamiment Institute.
Baruch Charney Vladeck Papers, Tamiment Institute.
Morris Winchevsky, Incomplete Autobiography, YIVO.
Isadore Wisotsky, "Autobiography," no. 288, YIVO.
Max Zaritsky Papers, Tamiment Institute.

Autobiographies and Biographical Studies

Cahan, Abraham. *Bleter fun mein leben.* New York: Forward Association, 1926–1931.
———. *The Rise of David Levinsky.* New York: Harper, 1960.
Chasanow, Bernard. *Tag un yorn: funem leben fun a yidishen arbeiter.* New York: Bernard Chasanow, 1956.
Cohen, Morris R. *A Dreamer's Journey.* Boston: Beacon Press, 1949.
Cohen, Ricki C. M. "Fannia Cohn and the ILGWU." Diss. University of Southern California, 1976.
Cohen, Rose. *Out of the Shadow.* New York: G. H. Doran, 1918.
DeLeon, Solon. *American Labor Who's Who.* New York: Hanford Press, 1925.
Drinnon, Richard. *Rebel in Paradise.* New York: Harper and Row, 1976.
Dubinsky, David and A. H. Raskin. *David Dubinsky: A Life with Labor.* New York: Simon and Schuster, 1977.
Endelman, Gary E. "Solidarity Forever: Rose Schneiderman and the Women's Trade Union League." Diss. University of Delaware, 1978.
Epstein, Melech. "Pages from My Stormy Life." *American Jewish Archives,* 14 (1962): 129–174.
———. *Profiles of Eleven.* Detroit: Wayne State University Press, 1965.
Fink, Gary, ed. *Biographical Dictionary of American Labor Leaders.* Westport, Conn.: Greenwood Press, 1974.
Fliegel, Hyman. *Life and Times of Max Pine.* New York: Privately Published, 1959.
Freeman, Joseph. *An American Testament.* New York: Farrar and Rinehart, 1936.
Ganz, Marie. *Rebels Into Anarchy and Out.* New York: Dodd and Mead, 1920.
Ginzburg, Eli and Hyman Berman. *American Worker in the Twentieth Century: A History through Autobiographies.* New York: Free Press, 1963.
Goldman, Emma. *Living My Life.* 2 Volumes. New York: Knopf, 1931.
Gompers, Samuel. *Seventy Years of Life and Labor.* New York: E. P. Dutton, 1925.
Hasanovitz, Elizabeth. *One of Them.* Boston: Houghton Mifflin, 1918.
Haskel, Harry. *A Leader of the Garment Workers: The Biography of Isidore Nagler.* New York: Amalgamated Ladies Garment Cutter's Union, Local 10, ILGWU, 1950.
Hillquit, Morris. *Loose Leaves from a Busy Life.* New York: Da Capo Press, 1971.
Howe, Frederick C. *The Confessions of a Reformer.* New York: Charles Scribner's Sons, 1925

Inglehart, Babbette. "Daughters of Loneliness: Anzia Yezierska and the Immigrant Woman Writer." *Studies in American Jewish Literature,* 1 (Winter 1975): 1–10.

Josephson, Matthew. *Sidney Hillman: Statesman of American Labor.* Garden City, N.Y.: Doubleday, 1952.

Julianelli, Jane. "Bessie Hillman: Up from the Sweatshop." *Ms.* (May 1973): 16–20.

Kann, Kenneth. *Joe Rapoport: Life of a Jewish Radical.* Philadelphia: Temple University Press, 1981.

Katz, Eli. "Bovshover, Kobrin, Libin and Pinski," *Jewish Currents,* 25:10 (November 1972): 5–9.

Kobrin, Leon. *Meine fuftsik yor in Amerika.* Buenos Aires: Society for Yiddish Secular Schools, 1955.

Kramer, Sydelle and Jenny Masur, eds. *Jewish Grandmothers.* Boston: Beacon Press, 1976.

Lang, Lucy R. *Tomorrow is Beautiful.* New York: MacMillan, 1948.

Lewis, Marx. *Abraham Mendelowitz at the Halfway Mark.* New York: New York Joint Board, Millinery Workers' Union, 1944.

———. *Max Zaritsky at Fifty.* New York: Max Zaritsky Anniversary Committee, 1935.

Lynd, Staughton and Alice, eds. *Rank and File: Personal Histories of Working Class Organizers.* Boston: Beacon Press, 1973.

Malkiel, Theresa. *The Diary of a Shirtwaist Striker.* New York: Cooperative Press, 1910.

Miller, Sally M. "From Sweatshop Worker to Labor Leader: Theresa Malkiel, A Case Study." *American Jewish History,* 68:2 (December 1978): 189–205.

Morrison, Joan and Charlotte Fox Zabusky. *American Mosaic: The Immigrant Experience in the Words of Those Who Lived It.* New York: Dutton, 1980.

Pesotta, Rose. *Bread Upon the Waters.* New York: Dodd, Mead and Co., 1944.

———. *Days of Our Lives.* Boston: Excelsior Publishers, 1958.

Pratt, Norma. *Morris Hillquit.* Westport, Conn.: Greenwood Press, 1978.

Ravage, Marcus. *An American in the Making: The Life Story of an Immigrant.* New York: Harper, 1917.

Reynolds, Robert D. "The Millionaire Socialists: J. G. Phelps Stokes and His Circle of Friends." Diss. University of South Carolina, 1974.

Rogoff, Hillel. *An East Side Epic: The Life and Work of Meyer London.* New York: Vanguard Press, 1930.

Rosenberg, Abraham. *Di klokmakher un zeyere yunyons.* New York: Cloak Operators Union, Local 1, 1920.

Roskolenko, Harry. *The Time That Was Then.* New York: Dial Press, 1971.

Sanders, Ronald. *Downtown Jews: Portraits of an Immigrant Generation.* New York: Harper and Row, 1969.

Scheier, Paula. "Clara Lemlich Shavelson: 50 Years in Labor's Front Line." In *The American Jewish Woman: A Documentary History,* ed. J. Marcus. New York: KTAV, 1981.

Schneiderman, Rose. *All For One.* New York: Paul S. Erikson, 1967.

Shavelson, Clara Lemlich. "Remembering the Waistmakers' General Strike, 1909." *Jewish Currents,* 36:10 (November 1982): 9–11, 15.

Stollberg, Benjamin. *A Tailor's Progress.* New York: Doubleday, 1944.

Waldman, Louis. *Labor Lawyer.* New York: E. P. Dutton, 1944.

Weinstein, Bernard. *Di yidishe yunyons in Amerika.* New York: United Hebrew
     Trades, 1929.
Weinstein, Gregory. *Reminiscences of an Interesting Decade.* New York: Interna-
     tional Press, 1928.
Winchevsky, Morris. *Gezamelte verk,* ed. Kalmen Marmor. New York: Freiheit,
     1927.
————. "Reminiscences." *Jewish Currents,* 32:8 (September 1978): 30–32.
Yorburg, Betty. *Utopia and Reality: A Collective Portrait of American Socialists.*
     New York: Columbia University Press, 1969.
Zausner, Philip. *Unvarnished: The Autobiography of a Union Leader.* New York:
     Brotherhood Publishers, 1941.
Zhitlowsky, Hayim. "The Jewish Factor in My Socialism." In *Voices from the
     Yiddish,* ed. Irving Howe and Eliezer Greenberg. New York: Schocken
     Books, 1975, pp. 126–134.

Theoretical and Comparative Materials

Allensmith, Wesley and Beverly Allensmith. "Religious Affiliation and
     Politico-Economic Attitude: A Study of Eight Major U.S. Religious
     Groups." *Public Opinion Quarterly,* 12:3 (Fall 1948): 378–389.
Antonovsky, Aaron. "Toward a Refinement of the Marginal Man Concept."
     Social Forces, 35 (1956): 57–62.
Barton, Josef J. *Peasants and Strangers: Italians, Rumanians, and Slovaks in an
     American City, 1890–1950.* Cambridge, Mass.: Harvard University Press,
     1975.
Benkin, Richard L. "Social and Cultural Development of Jewish Life in East-
     ern Europe and Specification of American Jewishness." Diss. University of
     Pennsylvania, 1976.
Bodnar, John. *Immigration and Industrialization: Ethnicity in an American Mill
     Town, 1870–1940.* Pittsburgh: University of Pittsburgh Press, 1977.
Deutscher, Isaac. "The Non-Jewish Jew." In *The Non-Jewish Jew and Other
     Essays.* London: Oxford University Press, 1968, pp. 25–41.
Fairchild, Henry Pratt. *Dictionary of Sociology.* New York: Philosophical Li-
     brary, 1944.
Geertz, Clifford, ed. *Old Societies and New States.* Glencoe, Ill.: Free Press, 1963.
Gilbert, Martin. *Jewish History Atlas.* New York: Collier, 1969.
Glazer, Nathan. *Social Bases of American Communism.* New York: Harcourt
     Brace, 1961.
Goldberg, Milton. "A Qualification of the Marginal Man Theory." *American
     Sociological Review,* 6 (1941), 52–58.
Green, Arnold W. "A Reexamination of the Marginal Man Concept." *Social
     Forces,* 26 (1947) 167–171.
Greene, Victor. *The Slavic Community on Strike.* South Bend, Ind.: Notre Dame
     University Press, 1968.
Himmelfarb, Milton. "Negroes, Jews, and Muzhiks." *Commentary* (October
     1966), 83–86.
Hoult, T. F. *Dictionary of Modern Sociology.* Totowa, N.J.: Littlefield Adams,
     1974.
Hyman, Herbert. *Political Socialization.* Glencoe, Ill.: Free Press, 1959.
Karni, Michael G. et al. *The Finnish Experience in the Western Great Lakes Region:
     New Perspectives.* Turku, Finland: Vammala, 1975.

————. *For the Common Good: Finnish Immigrants and the Radical Response to Industrial America.* Superior, Wisc.: Tyomies Society, 1977.

Kelly, Rita Mae and Mary Boutilier. *The Making of Political Women.* Chicago: Nelson Hall, 1978.

Kornhauser, William. *The Politics of Mass Society.* Glencoe, Ill.: Free Press, 1959.

Kraditor, Aileen. *The Radical Persuasion: 1890–1917.* Baton Rouge: Louisiana State University Press, 1980.

Krause, Corinne Azen. "Urbanization Without Breakdown: Italian, Jewish and Slavic Immigrant Women in Pittsburgh, 1900–1945." *Journal of Urban History,* 4:3 (May 1978), 291–306.

Landes, Ruth and Mark Zbrowski. "Hypotheses Concerning the Eastern European Jewish Family." *Psychiatry,* 13 (1950): 447–464.

Lederhendler, Eli M. "Jewish Immigration to America and Revisionist Historiography: A Decade of New Perspectives." *YIVO Annual,* 18 (1983): 391–410.

Lewin, Kurt. "Self-Hatred Among Jews." *Contemporary Jewish Record,* 4 (1941): 219–232.

Michels, Robert. "Intellectuals." *Encyclopedia of Social Sciences,* Vol. 8. New York: MacMillan, 1932.

Mills, C. Wright. *White Collar.* New York: Oxford University Press, 1951.

Moore, Barrington, Jr. *Social Origins of Dictatorship and Democracy.* Boston: Beacon Press, 1966.

Niebuhr, H. Richard. *Social Sources of Denominationalism.* New York: Holt, 1929.

Oberschall, Anthony. *Social Conflict and Social Movements.* Englewood Cliffs, N.J.: Prentice-Hall, 1973.

Park, Robert. "Human Migration and the Marginal Man." *American Journal of Sociology,* 23 (1928): 881–893.

Rodgers, Daniel. "Tradition, Modernity and the American Industrial Worker." *Journal of Interdisciplinary History,* 7:4 (Spring 1977): 655–681.

Rose, Arnold. *Sociology: The Study of Human Relations.* New York: Alfred Knopf, 1956.

Rosenblum, Gerald. *Immigrant Workers: Their Impact on American Labor Radicalism.* New York: Basic Books, 1973.

Rothman, Stanley and S. Robert Lichter. *Roots of Radicalism: Jews, Christians and the New Left.* New York: Oxford University Press, 1982.

Sewell, William. "Social Change and the Rise of Working Class Politics in Nineteenth Century Marseille." *Past and Present,* 65 (1974): 75–109.

Simmel, Georg. *Conflict and the Web of Group Affiliations.* Trans. by Kurt H. Wolff and Reinhard Bendix. New York: Free Press, 1964.

Slater, Philip. *Footholds: Understanding the Shifting Sexual and Family Tensions in Our Culture.* New York: E. P. Dutton, 1977.

Smelser, Neil. *Theory of Collective Behavior.* New York: Free Press of Glencoe, 1963.

Sorokin, Pitirim. "Leaders of Labor and Radical Movements." *American Journal of Sociology,* 33 (November 1927): 382–411.

Stonequist, Everett V. *The Marginal Man.* New York: Scribners, 1937.

Theodorson, George and Achilles Theodorson. *Modern Dictionary of Sociology.* New York: Thomas Y. Crowell, 1969.

Thompson, E. P. "Time, Work, Discipline, and Industrial Capitalism." *Past and Present*, 38 (1967): 56–97.

Tilly, Charles et al. *The Rebellious Century, 1830–1930.* Cambridge, Mass.: Harvard University Press, 1975.

Veblen, Thorstein. "The Intellectual Pre-eminence of Jews in Modern Europe." *The Portable Veblen,* ed. Max Lerner. New York: Viking Press, 1948, pp. 467–479.

Whitfield, Stephen J. "The Radical Persuasion in American Jewish History." *Judaism,* 32:2 (Spring 1983): 136–152.

Yans-McLaughlin, Virginia. "A Flexible Tradition: Immigrant Families Confront A New Work Experience." *Journal of Social History,* 7:4 (Summer 1974): 429–445.

———. "Patterns of Work and Family Organizations: Buffalo's Italians." *Journal of Interdisciplinary History,* 2 (1971): 305–311.

Government Documents

Edwards, Alba M. "Comparative Occupation Statistics for the United States, 1870–1940." *Sixteenth Census of the United States.* Washington: Government Printing Office, 1943.

Rubinow, I. M. "Economic Conditions of the Jews in Russia." *Bulletin of the Bureau of Labor.* No. 72 (September 1907): 487–583. Washington: Government Printing Office, 1907.

State of New York. *Bulletin of the Bureau of Labor Statistics.* 2 Vols. Albany: J. B. Lyons, State Printer, 1901.

———. *Bulletin of the Department of Labor.* 19 Vols. Albany: J. B. Lyons, State Printer, 1901–1917.

United States Bureau of the Census. *Thirteenth Census of the United States Taken in the Year 1910.* Washington: Government Printing Office, 1913.

United States Department of Labor, Bureau of Labor Statistics. Bulletin No. 175. *Summary of the Report on the Condition of Woman and Child Wage-Earners in the United States.* Washington: Government Printing Office, 1916.

United States House of Representatives: 57th Congress, First Session. House Doc. No. 184. "Immigration and Education." Washington: Government Printing Office, 1901.

———. *Reports of the United States Industrial Commission.* Vol. 15. Washington: Government Printing Office, 1901.

United States Senate: 61st Congress, 2nd Session. Senate Document No. 747. *Abstracts of Reports of the Immigration Commission on Immigrants in the United States.* Washington: Government Printing Office, 1911–1912.

———. Senate Document No. 645. 19 Volumes. *Report on Conditions of Woman and Child Wage-Earners in the United States.* Washington: Government Printing Office, 1910.

Secondary Sources

Abramovitch, Raphael. "Jewish Socialism in Russia and Poland, 1897–1919." *Jewish People: Past and Present,* 2 (1948): 367–398.

Baker, Ray Stannard. "The Spiritual Unrest: The Disintegration of the Jews." *Leslie's Monthly,* 68 (1909): 590–603.

Baron, Salo. *The Russian Jew under Tsars and Soviets.* New York: MacMillan, 1964.

Baum, Charlotte. "What Made Yetta Work? The Economic Role of Eastern European Jewish Women in the Family." *Response,* 18 (Summer 1973): 32–38.

Baum, Charlotte et al. *The Jewish Woman in America.* New York: Dial Press, 1976.

Bell, Daniel. "Jewish Labor History." *American Jewish Historical Quarterly,* 46:3 (March 1957): 257–260.

———. *Marxian Socialism in the United States.* Princeton, N.J.: Princeton University Press, 1967.

———. "The Background and Development of Marxian Socialism in the United States." In *Socialism and American Life,* Vol. 1, ed. Donald Drew Egbert and Stow Persons. Princeton, N.J.: Princeton University Press, 1952, pp. 213–405.

Bernheimer, Charles S. *The Russian Jew in the United States.* Philadelphia: J. C. Winston, 1905.

Bloom, Bernard H. "Yiddish-Speaking Socialists in America, 1892–1905." *American Jewish Archives,* 12:1 (April 1960): 34–68.

Bressler, Marvin. "Selected Family Patterns in W. I. Thomas' Unfinished Study of the *Bintl Brief.*" *American Sociological Review,* 17 (October 1952): 563–571.

Bross, Jacob. "The Beginning of the Jewish Labor Movement in Galicia." *YIVO Annual* 5 (1950): 55–84.

Brower, David. "Student Political Attitudes and Social Origins: The Technological Institute of St. Petersburg." *Journal of Social History,* 6:2 (Winter 1972–3): 202–213.

———. "Fathers, Sons and Grandfathers: Social Origins of Radical Intellectuals in Nineteenth Century Russia." *Journal of Social History,* 2:4 (Summer 1969): 333–356.

Brym, Robert. *The Jewish Intelligentsia and Russian Marxism.* New York: Schocken Books, 1978.

Buenker, John D. *Urban Liberalism and Progressive Reform.* New York: Charles Scribner's Sons, 1973.

Buhle, Mary Jo. *Women and American Socialism, 1870–1920.* Urbana: University of Illinois Press, 1981.

Buhle, Paul. "Jews and American Communism: The Cultural Question." *Radical History Review,* 23 (Spring 1980): 9–33.

Cahnman, Werner S. "Role and Significance of the Jewish Artisan Class." *Jewish Journal of Sociology,* 7 (1965): 207–220.

Cantor, Milton. *The Divided Left: American Radicalism, 1900–1975.* New York: Hill and Wang, 1978.

Cantor, Milton and Bruce Laurie. *Class, Sex and the Woman Worker.* Westport, Conn.: Greenwood Press, 1977.

Cohen, Percy. *Jewish Radicals and Radical Jews.* London: Academic Press, 1980.

Cohn, Werner. "Politics of American Jews." In *The Jews,* ed. Marshall Sklare. New York: Free Press, 1958, pp. 614–626.

Crunden, Robert M. *Ministers of Reform: The Progressives' Achievement in American Civilization, 1889–1920.* New York: Basic Books, 1982.

Davis-Kram, Harriet. "Jewish Women in Russian Revolutionary Movements." M.A. Thesis, Hunter College CUNY, 1974.

Dawidowicz, Lucy. "From Past to Past." *Jewish Presence.* New York: Holt, Rinehart and Winston, 1977, pp. 105–115.

———. *The Golden Tradition: Jewish Life and Thought in Eastern Europe.* Boston: Beacon Press, 1967.

Dinnerstein, Leonard. *The Leo Frank Case.* New York: Columbia University Press, 1968.

Draper, Theodore. *Roots of American Communism.* New York: Viking, 1957.

Dubofsky, Melvyn. *When Workers Organize.* Amherst: University of Massachusetts Press, 1968.

———. "Success and Failure of Socialism in New York City, 1900–1918: A Case Study." *Labor History,* 9:3 (Fall 1968): 361–375.

Dye, Nancy. "Creating a Feminist Alliance: Sisterhood and Class Conflict in the New York WTUL." *Feminist Studies,* 2:2 (1975): 24–38.

Elazar, Daniel J. "American Political Theory and the Political Notions of American Jews: Convergences and Contradictions." In *The Ghetto and Beyond: Essays on Jewish Life in America,* ed. Peter I. Rose. New York: Random House, 1969.

Epstein, Melech. *Jewish Labor in the U.S.A.,* 2 vols. New York: KTAV, 1950, 1953.

Feuer, Lewis. "The Legend of the Socialist East Side." *Midstream,* 24:2 (February 1978): 23–35.

Foner, Philip. *The Fur and Leather Workers' Union.* Newark: Norden Press, 1950.

Fox, Richard W. "The Paradox of Progressive Socialism: The Case of Morris Hillquit, 1901–1914." *American Quarterly,* 26:1 (March 1974): 127–140.

Frankel, Jonathan. *Prophecy and Politics: Socialism, Nationalism and the Russian Jews, 1862–1917.* Cambridge: Cambridge University Press, 1981.

———. "The Jewish Socialists and the American Jewish Congress Movement." *YIVO Annual* 16 (1976): 202–341.

Fridkis, Ari Lloyd. "Desertion in the American Jewish Immigrant Family: The Work of the National Desertion Bureau in Cooperation with the Industrial Removal Office." *American Jewish History,* 71:2 (December 1981): 285–299.

Friedman, Philip. "Political and Social Movements and Organizations." *Jewish People: Past and Present,* 4 (1955): 142–176.

Friedman, Reena Sigman. " 'Send Me My Husband Who Is in New York City': Husband Desertion in the American Jewish Immigrant Community, 1900–1926," *Jewish Social Studies,* 44 (Winter 1982), 1–18.

Fuchs, Lawrence. *The Political Behavior of American Jews.* Glencoe, Ill.: Free Press, 1956.

Ginzburg, Eli. "Jews in the American Economy: The Dynamics of Opportunity." In *Jewish Life in America,* ed. Gladys Rosen. New York: KTAV, 1978, pp. 109–119.

Glanz, Rudolf. *The Jewish Woman in America.* 2 Vols. New York: KTAV, 1976.

Goldberg, Nathan. *Occupational Patterns of American Jewry.* New York: JTSP University Press, 1947.

Goldhagen, J. "The Ethnic Consciousness of Early Russian Jewish Socialists." *Judaism,* 23 (1974): 479–496.

Goren, Arthur. *New York Jews and the Quest for Community: The Kehillah Experiment, 1908–1922.* New York: Columbia University Press, 1970.

Gorenstein, Arthur. "A Portrait of Ethnic Politics: The Socialists and the 1908 and 1910 Congressional Elections on the East Side." *Publications of the American Jewish Historical Society,* 50 (1960): 202–238.

Greenberg, Louis. *The Jews in Russia.* Vol. 1. New Haven: Yale University Press, 1944.

Greenfield, Judith. "The Role of the Jews in the Development of the Clothing Industry." *YIVO Annual* 2–3 (1947–1948): 180–204.

Handlin, Oscar. *Adventure in Freedom: Three Hundred Years of Jewish Life in America.* New York: McGraw Hill, 1954.

———. *The Uprooted.* Boston: Little, Brown and Co., 1951.

Hapgood, Hutchins. *The Spirit of the Ghetto.* New York: Schocken Books, 1966.

Hardman, J. B. S. "Jewish Workers in the American Labor Movement." *YIVO Annual* 7 (1952): 229–254.

———. "The Jewish Labor Movement in the U.S.: Jewish and Non-Jewish Influences." *American Jewish Historical Quarterly,* 52 (December 1962): 98–132.

Helfgott, Ray B. "Trade Unionism Among the Jewish Garment Workers of Britain and the United States." *Labor History,* 2:2 (Spring 1961): 202–214.

Herberg, Will. "The American Jewish Labor Movement." *American Jewish Year Book,* 80 (1952): 3–74.

———. "Socialism, Zionism and Messianic Passion." *Midstream,* 2 (Summer 1956): 65–74.

Hersch, Liebmann. "International Migration of the Jews." In *International Migrations,* eds. Imre Ferenczi and Walter Willcox. New York: National Bureau of Economic Research, 1931, Vol. 2, pp. 471–520.

Herscher, Uri D., ed. "The East European Immigrant Jew in America, 1881–1981." *American Jewish Archives,* 33 (April 1981): 1–140.

Higham, John. *Strangers in the Land: Patterns of American Nativism, 1860–1925.* New York: Atheneum, 1966.

Hillman, Bessie. "Gifted Women in the Trade Unions." In *American Women: The Changing Image,* ed. Beverly Cassara. Boston: Beacon Press, 1961.

Hillquit, Morris. *History of Socialism in the United States.* New York: Funk and Wagnalls, 1903.

Hourwich, Isaac. *Immigration and Labor.* New York: G. P. Putnam's Sons, 1912.

Howe, Irving. *The World of Our Fathers.* New York: Harcourt Brace Jovanovich, 1976.

Howe, Irving and Lewis Coser. *The American Communist Party.* Boston: Beacon Press, 1957.

Joseph, Samuel. *Jewish Immigration to the United States from 1881 to 1910.* New York: Columbia University Press, 1914.

Katz, Jacob. *Out of the Ghetto: The Social Background of Jewish Emancipation, 1770–1870.* Cambridge, Mass.: Harvard University Press, 1973.

Kaufmann, Yehezkel. "Israel in Canaan." In *Great Ages and Ideas of the Jewish People,* ed. L. W. Schwarz. New York: Modern Library, 1956, pp. 30–56.

Kennedy, Susan Estabrook. *If All We Did Was to Weep at Home.* Bloomington: Indiana University Press, 1979.

Kessler-Harris, Alice. "Organizing the Unorganizable: Three Jewish Women and Their Union." *Labor History,* 17:1 (Winter 1976): 5–23.

———. *Out to Work: A History of Wage-Earning Women in the United States.* New York: Oxford University Press, 1982.

———. "The Lower Class as a Factor in Reform: New York, the Jews and the 1890s." Diss. Rutgers University, 1968.

Kessner, Thomas. *The Golden Door: Italian and Jewish Immigrant Mobility in New York City, 1880–1915.* New York: Oxford University Press, 1977.

Kessner, Thomas and Betty Boyd Caroli. "New Immigrant Women at Work: Italians and Jews in New York City, 1880–1905." *Journal of Ethnic Studies,* 5:4 (1978): 19–31.

Kiel, Mark. "The Jewish Narodnik." *Judaism,* 19:3 (Summer 1970): 295–310.

Kipnis, Ira. *The American Socialist Movement, 1897–1912.* New York: Monthly Review Press, 1952.

Klehr, Harvey. *Communist Cadre: The Social Background of the American Communist Party Elite.* Stanford, Cal.: Hoover Institution Press, 1978.

Kligsberg, Moses. "Jewish Immigrants in Business: A Sociological Study," In *The Jewish Experience in America,* ed. Abraham Karp. New York: KTAV, 1969, Vol. 5, 249–284.

Knox, Israel and Irving Howe. *The Jewish Labor Movement in America: Two Views.* New York: Jewish Labor Committee, Workmen's Circle, 1958.

Kuznets, Simon. "Immigration of Russian Jews." *Perspectives in American History,* 9 (1975): 35–124.

Lagemann, Ellen C. *A Generation of Women: Education in the Lives of Progressive Reformers.* Cambridge, Mass.: Harvard University Press, 1979.

Laslett, John. *Labor and the Left.* New York: Basic Books, 1970.

Leinenweber, Charles. "The Class and Ethnic Basis of New York City Socialism, 1904–1915." *Labor History,* 22:1 (Winter 1981): 31–56.

———. "Socialists in the Streets: New York City Socialist Party in Working-Class Neighborhoods, 1908–1918." Unpublished paper, Department of Sociology, SUNY, New Paltz.

———. "*World of Our Fathers* as Socialist History." Unpublished paper, Department of Sociology, SUNY, New Paltz.

Levin, Nora. *While Messiah Tarried: Jewish Socialist Movements, 1871–1917.* New York: Schocken Books, 1977.

Levine, Louis. *The Women's Garment Workers.* New York: Huebsch, Inc., 1924.

Liebman, Arthur. *Jews and the Left.* New York: John Wiley and Sons, 1979.

Lurie, H. L. "Jewish Communal Life in the United States." *Jewish People: Past and Present,* 4 (1955): 187–242.

Manning, Caroline. *The Immigrant Woman and Her Job.* Washington, D.C.: Government Printing Office, 1930.

Marcus, Jacob R. *The American Jewish Woman: A Documentary History.* New York: KTAV, 1981.

Mendelsohn, Ezra. *Class Struggle in the Pale.* Cambridge: Cambridge University Press, 1970.

———. "The Russian Jewish Labor Movement." *YIVO Annual* 14 (1969): 87–98.

———. "The Russian Roots of the American Jewish Labor Movement." *YIVO Annual* 16 (1976): 150–177.

Menes, Abraham. "The East Side and the Jewish Labor Movement." In *Voices from the Yiddish,* eds. Eliezer Greenberg and Irving Howe. New York: Schocken Books, 1975, pp. 202–218.

———. "The Jewish Labor Movement." *Jewish People: Past and Present,* 4 (1955): 334–390.

———. "The Jewish Socialist Movement in Russia and Poland." *Jewish People: Past and Present,* 2 (1948): 355–369.

Mergen, Bernard. "'Another Great Prize': The Jewish Labor Movement in the Context of American Labor History." *YIVO Annual* 16 (1976): 394–423.

Metzker, Isaac, ed. *A Bintel Brief.* New York: Ballantine Books, 1971.

Miller, Sally M. "Other Socialists: Native Born and Immigrant Women in the Socialist Party of America, 1901–1917." *Labor History,* 24:1 (Winter 1983): 84–102.

Mishkinski, Moshe. "Regional Factors in the Formation of the Jewish Labor Movement in Czarist Russia." *YIVO Annual* 14 (1969): 27–53.

———. "The Jewish Labor Movement and European Socialism." In *Jewish Society through the Ages,* eds. H. H. Ben-Sasson and S. Ettinger. New York: Schocken Books, 1971, pp. 284–296.

Montgomery, David. "New Unionism and the Transformation of Workers' Consciousness in America, 1909–1922." In *Workers' Control in America.* Cambridge: Cambridge University Press, 1979.

Neidle, Cecyle S. *America's Immigrant Women.* Boston: Twayne, 1975.

Neugeboren, Jay. *The Stolen Jew.* New York: Pinnacle Books, 1981.

Perrier, Hubert. "The Socialists and the Working Class in New York: 1890–1896." *Labor History,* 22:4 (Fall 1981): 485–511.

Pipes, Richard. *Social Democracy and the St. Petersburg Labor Movement, 1885–1897.* Cambridge, Mass.: Harvard University Press, 1963.

Pratt, Norma F. "Culture and Radical Politics: Yiddish Women Writers, 1890–1940." *American Jewish History,* 70 (1980): 68–90.

Quint, Howard. *The Forging of American Socialism.* Indianapolis: Bobbs-Merrill, 1953.

Rich, J. C. "Jewish Labor Movement in the United States." *Jewish People: Past and Present,* 2 (1948): 399–430.

———. "Sixty Years of the Jewish Daily Forward." *New Leader,* 40 (June 3, 1957): 1–38.

Riis, Jacob. *How the Other Half Lives.* New York: Charles Scribner's Sons, 1900.

Rischin, Moses. "The Jewish Labor Movement in America: A Social Interpretation." *Labor History,* 4:3 (Fall 1963): 227–247.

———. *The Promised City: New York's Jews, 1870–1914.* New York: Corinth Books, 1964.

Ripley, William Z. "Race Factors in Labor Unions," *Atlantic Monthly,* 93 (1905): 300.

Robinson, Donald. *Spotlight on a Union: The Story of the United Hatters, Cap and Millinery Workers' Union.* New York: Dial Press, 1948.

Rogoff, Abraham. *Formative Years in the Jewish Labor Movement in the United States, 1890–1900.* New York: n.p., 1945.

Rontch, I. E., ed. *Di yidishe landsmanshaftn fun New York.* New York: Y. L. Peretz Shrieber Farein, 1938.

Rosenberg, Jan. "Jewish Women in U.S. History." *Jewish Currents,* 37:3 (March 1983): 10–15.

Rothenberg, Joshua. "Demythologizing the Shtetl." *Midstream,* 27 (March 1981): 25–31.

Rubin, Ruth. *Voices of a People: The Story of Yiddish Folksong.* New York: McGraw Hill Book Co., 1973.

Rubinow, Isaac M. "Economic and Industrial Condition: New York." In *The Russian Jew in the United States,* ed. C. S. Bernheimer. Philadelphia: J. C. Winston, 1905, pp. 104–121.

Ruchames, Louis. "Jewish Radicalism in the United States." In *The Ghetto and Beyond,* ed. Peter I. Rose. New York: Random House, 1969.

Ruppin, Arthur. *The Jews of the Modern World.* London: MacMillan, 1934.

Samuel, Maurice. *The World of Sholem Aleichem.* New York: Alfred Knopf, 1962.

Saposs, David. *Left-Wing Unionism.* New York: International Publishers, 1926.

Schappes, Morris. "Jewish Mass Immigration from Europe, 1881–1914." *Jewish Life,* 8:10 (November 1954): 20–21.

————. "The Political Origins of the United Hebrew Trades, 1888." *Journal of Ethnic Studies,* 5:1 (Spring 1977): 13–44.

Schlossberg, Joseph. *The Rise of the Clothing Workers.* New York: Amalgamated Clothing Workers of America, 1921.

Scholem, Gershom. *The Messianic Idea in Judaism.* New York: Schocken Books, 1971.

Seidman, Joel. *The Needle Trades.* New York: Farrar and Rinehart, Inc., 1942.

Seller, Maxine S. *Immigrant Women.* Philadelphia: Temple University Press, 1981.

Shannon, David. *The Socialist Party in America.* Chicago: Quadrangle Books, 1955.

Shapiro, Leonard. "The Role of the Jews in the Russian Revolutionary Movement." *Slavonic and Eastern European Review,* 40:84 (December 1961): 148–167.

Sherman, C. B. "Nationalism, Secularism and Religion in the Jewish Labor Movement." In *Voices from the Yiddish,* eds. Irving Howe and Eliezer Greenberg. New York: Schocken Books, 1975, pp. 219–233.

Stanislawski, Michael. *Tsar Nicholas I and the Jews: The Transformation of Jewish Society in Russia, 1825–1855.* Philadelphia: Jewish Publication Society of America, 1983.

Stein, Leon. *The Triangle Fire.* Philadelphia: J. B. Lippincott Co., 1962.

Szajkowski, Zosa. "The Jews and New York City's Mayoralty Election of 1917." *Jewish Social Studies,* 32:4 (1970): 286–306.

Tcherikower, Elias. *The Early Jewish Labor Movement in the United States.* Translated by A. Antonovsky. New York: YIVO, 1961.

Tobias, Henry J. "The Jews in Tsarist Russia: The Political Education of a Minority." In *Minorities and Politics,* eds. H. J. Tobias and Charles Woodhouse. Albuquerque: University of New Mexico Press, 1969.

Trunk, Isaiah. "The Cultural Dimension of the Jewish Labor Movement." *YIVO Annual* 16 (1976): 342–393.

Van Kleeck, Mary. *Artificial Flower Makers.* New York: The Russell Sage Foundation, 1913.

————. *Working Girls in Evening Schools.* New York: Survey Associates, 1914.

Van Vorst, Mrs. John and Marie. *The Woman Who Toils.* New York: Doubleday, 1903.

Weiler, N. Sue. "Walkout: The Chicago Men's Garment Workers' Strike, 1910–1911." *Chicago History* 8 (Winter 1979–80): 238–249.

Weinryb, Bernard. "The Adaptation of Jewish Labor Groups to American Life." *Jewish Social Studies,* 8 (October 1946): 219–244.

Weinstein, James. *Decline of American Socialism, 1912–1925.* New York: Vintage Books, 1969.

————. "The Socialist Party: Its Roots and Strengths, 1912–1919." *Studies on the Left,* 1 (Winter 1960): 5–27.

Werblowsky, R. J. Zwi. "Messianism in Jewish History." In *Jewish Society*

Through the Ages, eds. H. H. Ben-Sasson and S. Ettinger. New York: Schocken Books, 1971, pp. 30–45.

Wertheimer, Barbara. *We Were There: The Story of Working Women in America.* New York: Pantheon Press, 1977.

Wiebe, Robert H. *The Search for Order: 1877–1920.* New York: Hill and Wang, 1967.

Wiesel, Elie. *The Testament.* New York; Summit Books, 1981.

Wildman, Allan. *The Making of a Workers' Revolution: Russian Social Democracy, 1891–1903.* Chicago: University of Chicago Press, 1967.

Wirth, Louis. *The Ghetto.* Chicago: University of Chicago Press, 1928.

Wistrich, Robert S. *Revolutionary Jews from Marx to Trotsky.* New York: Harper and Row, 1976.

Wolfson, Theresa. *The Woman Worker and the Trade Unions.* New York: International Publishers, 1926.

Woodhouse, Charles and H. J. Tobias. "Primordial Ties and the Political Process in Pre-Revolutionary Russia: The Case of the Jewish Bund." *Comparative Studies in Society and History,* 8 (1965–6): 331–360.

Woods, Robert and Albert Kennedy, eds. *Young Working Girls.* Boston: Houghton Mifflin, 1913.

Yarmolinsky, Avraham. *Road to Revolution: A Century of Russian Radicalism.* New York: MacMillan, 1959.

Yellowitz, Irwin. "Jewish Immigrants and the American Labor Movement, 1900–1920." *American Jewish History,* 71:2 (December 1981): 188–217.

———. *Labor and the Progressive Movement in New York State, 1897–1916.* Ithaca: Cornell University Press, 1965.

———. "Morris Hillquit, American Socialism and Jewish Concerns." *American Jewish History,* 68:2 (December 1978): 163–188.

Zaretz, Charles. *Amalgamated Clothing Workers of America: A Study in Progressive Trades-Unionism.* New York: Ancon Publishing Co., 1934.